South Asian Women
in the Diaspora

South Asian Women in the Diaspora

Edited by
Nirmal Puwar and Parvati Raghuram

Oxford • New York

First published in 2003 by
Berg
Editorial offices:
1st Floor, Angel Court, 81 St Clements St, Oxford OX4 1AW, UK
838 Broadway, Third Floor, New York, NY 10003–4812, USA

Berg is the imprint of Oxford International Publishers Ltd.

Library of Congress Cataloging-in-Publication Data

A catalogue record for this book is available from the Library of Congress.

British Library Cataloguing-in-Publication Data

A catalogue record for this book is available from the British Library.

ISBN   1 85973 696 3 (Cloth)
       1 85973 602 5 (Paper)

Typeset by JS Typesetting Ltd, Wellingborough, Northants.
Printed in the United Kingdom by Biddles Ltd, Guildford and King's Lynn.

Contents

Contents

Acknowledgements

The intellectual energy for this project initially came out of a seminar 'Theoretical Considerations on Gender and the South Asian Diaspora', held in Leicester University in 1999. We would like to thank all those who came for this and subsequent seminars, and most particularly those whose contributions have been included for their forbearance during the writing of this book.

We would especially like to thank Olwyn Ince for her editorial assistance and the geography division of The Nottingham Trent University for making this possible. Thanks too to an anonymous reviewer whose thorough comments were useful in alerting us to how this volume may be read and to Kathryn Earle and Samantha Jackson at Berg for their patience. The supportive environment at University College Northampton, provided especially by Nick Sage's ability to manage a workable teaching/research timetable for Nirmal Puwar and Professor Helen Rainbird's limitless encouragement also needs to be mentioned.

Notes on Contributors

Fauzia Ahmad is a Researcher at the University of Bristol, Department of Sociology. She has previously worked as a Lecturer at Brunel University and with FAIR (Forum Against Islamophobia and Racism). Her current research interests include representations of British Muslims, particularly Muslim women as professionals. Her doctoral research focuses on British South Asian Muslim women in higher education and employment. She has published in *Gender and Education* and *Social Work in Europe*.

Nandi Bhatia is Associate Professor of English at the University of Western Ontario. Her publications, which have appeared in journals such as *Modern Drama, Theatre Journal,* and *Centennial Review* and in other edited collections, deal with issues pertaining to colonialism, imperialism, and nationalism in literature, film and theatre. Her book, *Acts of Authority/Acts of Resistance: Theatre and Politics in Colonial and Postcolonial India* is forthcoming from the University of Michigan Press.

Rani Kawale is a P D working on questions of sexuality and space. The place of emotions in the interaction with sexuality is an area that she is currently developing.

Bakirathi Mani is Assistant Professor in the Department of English Literature at Swarthmore College. Her ongoing interdisciplinary research focuses on the production of racialized citizenship and gendered national subjectivity in literary, cinematic, and performative narratives of South Asian immigration to the United States. She is a contributor to *Contours of the Heart: South Asians Map North America* (Asian American Writers Workshop, 1996), and publishes in *Trikone* and *SAMAR magazines*.

Nayanika Mookherjee submitted her Ph.D. thesis entitled '"A Lot of History": Sexual Violence, Public Memory and the Bangladesh Liberation War of 1971' to SOAS, UK. At present she is a Post-doctoral fellow of the

Society for South Asian Studies, British Academy in the School of African and Asian Studies (AFRAS), Department of Social Anthropology, body, embodiment and trauma, sexual violence, and the state and nationalism, regionally in South Asia and trans-regionally in diasporic communities. She has published articles on South Asian masculinities, contestations of 'Bengali' diasporic identity, and sartorial problems during fieldwork in edited collections and journals.

Mala Pandurang is the Head of the Department of English, Dr B.M.N. College of Home Science, Matunga, Mumbai, India. She is also visiting faculty at the Postgraduate English Departments of the University of Mumbai and the SNDT Women's University. She is a Fellow of the Alexander von Humboldt Foundation, Bonn, and is currently working on a project theorizing the Indian Diasporic Experience. Her publications include *Post-Colonial African Fiction. The Crisis of Consciousness* (1997), *Articulating Gender* (co-edited) (2000) and *Vikram Seth. Multiple Locations: Multiple Affiliations* (2001).

Tej Purewal is a Lecturer in Development Studies/Sociology at the University of Manchester, UK. Her research interests include the political economy of development, social inequality and social change, particularly in Punjab and South Asia, and the socio-cultural context of gender and population. She is the author of *Living on the Margins: Social Access to Shelter in Urban South Asia* (Ashgate, 2000) and *Teach Yourself Panjabi* (Hodder & Stoughton, 1999). She has also written on the impacts of the partition in South Asia as well as on son preference and reproductive technologies.

Nirmal Puwar is a Lecturer/Senior Research Fellow in Sociology at University College Northampton. Her research interests are concerned with the interaction of questions of space and bodies with those of 'race', gender and class. She has published in the journals *Feminist Review* and *Sociology*. With Nandi Bhatia she is editing a special issue of the journal *Fashion Theory* on Orientalism. Her book *Space Invaders: race, gender and bodies out of place* (Berg) is forthcoming.

Parvati Raghuram is a Lecturer in the Department of International Studies at The Nottingham Trent University. Her doctoral research focused on gender and domestic work in India. Her current research interests and topics on which she has published include gender and skilled migration, ethnic minority entrepreneurship and research methodologies. She is co-author of *Gender and International Migration in Europe* (Routledge, 2000) and of *Practices of Cultural Research* (Sage, forthcoming).

Hasmita Ramji is currently an ESRC Postdoctoral Research Fellow in the Department of Sociology, City University, UK. Her research interests include gender, education and employment, 'race' and identity, especially amongst ethnic minorities in the West. She is currently writing articles from her recently completed Ph.D. and is also formulating new projects to develop and enhance her previous research on the impact of education and employment on British Asian women's identity formations.

Shaminder Takhar is Senior Lecturer at South Bank University, London. Her teaching and research interests include gender, 'race' and cultural studies. She has carried out research for her doctoral thesis on South Asian women in London.

Samina Zahir is currently doing a Ph.D. examining syncretic cultural identities and methods of representation within cultural production. She also works as a freelance arts consultant, with a particular interest in community participatory arts projects, and the use of art as a tool for personal development, creative expression and social inclusion.

(Dis)locating South Asian Women in the Academy

Nirmal Puwar and *Parvati Raghuram*

> Spaces of agency exist for black people, wherein we can both interrogate the gaze of the Other but also look back, and at one another, naming what we see (hooks 1991: 199).

This collection looks back at the ways in which the figure of the South Asian woman has been seen and seeks new ways of looking 'at one another' without having to resort to the simplicity of good and bad images. It names the complexity of what it sees from a space that is alert to the objectifying tendencies of so much knowledge on the Other, while recognizing that it is neither pure nor totally separated from its viewing position. We begin in this introduction by situating the chapters that make up this volume, within histories of academic knowledge.

The Arrival of Difference within Academia

Two types of change in relation to the teaching of and research into 'race' and ethnicity are fairly evident from a quick overview of the academy today in comparison to that of twenty years ago. First, bodies of thought have been widened and new perspectives and terminologies have challenged essentialist and pathologizing thinking. Most institutions have at the very least introduced optional modules on 'race' and ethnicity, and a few have even placed this field of study within the compulsory aspects of their curriculum. Research agendas have also been stretched to accommodate questions of 'race' and ethnicity. While it is still no doubt *de rigeur* for these issues to be ignored in the conduct of day-to-day scholarship, nevertheless funding is now available for scholars who do want to grant consideration to questions of race in their research. And in fact, in line with the rise of new specialisms constituted in journals, curricula and conference themes, the umbrella terms 'race' and ethnicity have now mutated into a plethora of research sub-fields, such as diaspora, transnational communities, migration, whiteness and social exclusion. Each of these is in turn embedded in the study of specific ethnicities and regions, such as South Asia, the Caribbean and the Pacific Rim.

In the USA, where there are more scholars and institutes involved with the topic, the whole area of South Asian studies is much more established than in the UK. There is also a historical difference in the disciplinary location of these studies. In the USA much of it is based in Area Studies. In the UK, while there is a strong tradition of South Asian Studies, firmly established in elite institutions like the School of Oriental and African Studies and Cambridge University, there is at the same time a great deal of thought being generated out of more general work on 'race', which has a much wider scope than Area Studies. So while we are witnessing the emergence of South Asian studies in the UK, through specialist conferences, journals and research projects in a fashion that bears some resemblance to institutional developments in the USA, much of the scholarship maintains strong links and conversations with other scholars working on 'race' generally, even if their focus is on the African diaspora rather than the South Asian diaspora. The differences in classed migratory histories between the USA and the UK also means that there are more South Asians in the United States with the cultural and class capital that enables them firstly to enter higher education as students and then to become members of the academy. This difference is exacerbated by the privileging of the South Asian migrant experience in the UK by researchers in the USA, many of whom travel to the UK to do fieldwork. Interestingly, this travelling for research and objectification through research is less likely to occur in the opposite direction.[1]

The second significant change that has taken place alongside the widening of bodies of thought on 'race' and ethnicity in academia is a diversification in the actual bodies that study, research and teach in the humanities and social sciences. The number of students from 'black'[2] and ethnic minority backgrounds has increased, especially within metropolitan cities, where they represent a substantial proportion of the student population. Alongside the increasing presence of 'home-grown' black students in the academy there has also been an increase in the number of students from Third World countries in Western academic institutions. One impact of globalization has been a growth in recognition of the importance of being at the 'core' of global knowledge production at the same time as recruiting abroad has become a major strategy for many universities that are struggling for students in the UK. Thus bodies within the academy have been diversified by a 'black British' presence, but also by an overseas contingent from the 'Third World'.

The whiteness of academia is also interrupted now and then by the existence of lecturers of colour. In the UK both lecturers and the students are concentrated in the less prestigious and less financially lucrative sector of higher education, namely the 'new universities'. A racialized hierarchy can also be observed across the scale, with a tiny number of professors at the top of the scale and an ever-increasing number of people from the racialized ethnic minority group at the bottom, especially in the category of temporary researchers. Gender further complicates the ways in which 'race' impacts upon employment opportunities within academia. 'Black' women are once again, rather depressingly, more likely to be found on the lower rungs of higher education institutions (Modood and Fenton 1999), with a notable presence of South Asian women as researchers.

Impure Bodies in the Academy

By noting the structural marginality of South Asian women in academia, we are not intending rather predictably to utilize the race-gender-class mantra in simplistic terms to invest women of colour with a moral and political superiority that positions them as victims or innocent subjects. The claim of unfettered marginality risks masking the particular and indeed different power relations South Asian women in the academy are themselves inscribed within. There are after all no 'non-contaminated' (Rajan 1993: 8), 'insulated' pure spaces that are altogether outside what we criticize (Grosz 1995: 62–3).

Furthermore, the geometries of global power relations have never presented us with South Asian women as *an* entity. The figure of the *South Asian woman* could in itself be said to be a contested term in its imperious sweep across nations and communities. Differences of power mean that not only are 'we' referring to a heterogeneous figure, but also to an assortment of women who are more often than not positioned in contra-distinction to each other. By speaking of South Asian women in the diaspora we are not aiming to forge a version of international feminism that has been rightly criticized by Kaplan for seeking a 'transnational fiesta of differences' while mystifying and codifying power relations within these collectivities (1994: 141). The very writing of this text, no doubt, relies on different sets of cultural, symbolic and economic capital (Bourdieu 1992), located within 'the machineries of literacy and education, which are affordable only to a privileged few' (Chow 1993: 119). Trying to be alert to '. . . the difference that separates those who speak and those who are spoken of/for' (Chow 1993: 114), we are not in the business of setting up our own authorial subject 'as the implicit referent' (Mohanty 1988: 64) for all South Asian women.

This collection originally took its shape in Britain, but has been augmented through contributions from scholars situated in North America and India. Amongst the twelve contributors the migratory histories are diverse, with some being of the first generation of migrants and others of the second. Differences of class also inform the web of diasporic connections that are bought to bear upon the debates within the chapters; some have migrated as scholars and others are the daughters of working-class parents. What is common to the authors and to the themes they address, however, is a sense that they are all implicated in the figure of the South Asian woman as found in academic discourses. They have all used their space within the academy to write a new language through which the complex subjectivities of diasporic South Asian women may be grasped.

The growth of bodies of colour within the academy has no doubt played a decisive role in widening current frameworks of thought. The publication of *The Empire Strikes Back* (CCCS 1982), for instance, was incredibly significant for unsettling long established dicta and for moving the terrain on to new agendas. While this text was predominantly (but not exclusively) generated by 'black' scholars, the development of a wider body of thought is not necessarily linked to the presence of 'black' bodies. 'Black' scholars are perfectly capable of reproducing paradigms that are problematically located in the long routes of wisdom for questions of 'race' and ethnicity (Mohanty 1988: 62), just as white intellectuals are able to innovate the terms of debate. The mediated nature of experience teaches us that there is 'no necessary or essential correspondence' of anything with anything in terms of a mimetic link between background and politics (Hall 1990). The racialized position of the author thus has no direct bearing upon the political position of the text. There are however reasons why the embodied features of an author cannot altogether be disregarded, even though these reasons cannot be *a priori* determined. Grosz (1995) states '. . .there are ways in which the sexuality and corporeality of the subject leave their traces or marks on the texts produced, just as we in turn must recognize that the processes of textual production also leave their trace or residue on the body of the writer (and readers)' (p. 21). How and indeed what kind of traces are borne is of course specific to context.

Natives in the Academy

In an essay that discusses the dynamics involved in the recruitment of a Chinese scholar from mainland China in her faculty in a Northern American University, Rey Chow offers an observant analysis of how academics respond to the presence within the academy of members of racialized ethnic minorities who have for centuries been objects of study. She notes that for scholars who have invested whole lifetimes in constructing ideal types of these different 'others' and their communities, the entry of these 'ethnic' others can be disturbing, because they may well find that the frameworks they developed to make sense of these people no longer seem to fit. Thus as 'ethnics' enter the academy as something other than pure specimens, what 'confronts the Western scholar is the discomforting fact that the natives are no longer staying in their frames' (Chow 1993: 28). The different institutional histories of how particular natives have been 'known' across different parts of the West and within specific disciplines require close attention. There is, for instance, more of a trend to recruit 'indigenous' scholars to teach subjects such as Indian or Chinese studies in the United States than there is in the United Kingdom; differing colonial histories have much to do with these institutional directions.

At the present moment the entry of South Asian women, who are either home-grown within the West or from the Indian subcontinent, into different locales in Western academia has resulted in a degree of disorientation among those who have studied them in factories, picket lines, youth clubs, women's refuges or development projects. They find that what they have in front of them are entities that are not quite as they had 'imagined'. In lecture halls, canteens and staff meetings scholars find that while these 'specimens' can incite an unhealthy level of 'fascination' in times of global multiculturalism, they can also disappoint those who thought they 'knew' them even before they actually met them. The complicated mix of personalities and traits found in South Asian women can cause great disturbance for academics, and this trauma can continue long after they have become versed in post-colonial theory, which is well versed in the ins and out of impure and nomadic life.

What remains particularly problematic for many of the scholars who are schooled in the attributes of South Asian women is the claim that experience matters. Accusations of essentialism, with images of 'black power' and Malcolm X in the not too distant background, are accompanied by a sense of suspicion for those who seek recognition for racialized embodied existence. While I believe that experience is not 'a guarantor of some essential authenticity', at the same time we support Brah's assertion that 'there is a qualitative difference when this changing fiction we call "I" or "Me" is directly subjected within specific discursive practices. This experience matters' (Brah 1996: 9). As some South Asian women acquire the cultural capital to engage intellectually with the texts and debates in which they have been theorized and described, what we are finding the need for is serious scrutiny of the 'frames' in which they are received. This collection has emerged from South Asian women located within the academy, who have sought to make sense of their own lives, as well as those of their mothers, sisters and grandmothers, and found the current frameworks patronizing and/or unwieldy for discussing the pressures, joys, structures and negotiations they want to develop a language for. With the condescending attitudes found in texts also articulated in the coffee rooms and staff meetings of academia, the need to pose some challenges has become all the more pressing. Calls for a 'change in the narrative' (Bhattacharya 1998: 36) have indeed been made by a long and evolving tradition of women of colour in the academy.

Institutional Streamlining

The institutional streamlining of disciplines has made it difficult for students to gain a complex understanding of the locations and subjectivities of South Asian women. The life of this book started in a workshop that was organized on 'Theoretical Considerations of Gender and the South Asian Diaspora' (Leicester University, 1999). This event was widely advertised through electronic and print networks; most of these were initially academic, but they soon spread into other types of organizations. It was also only open to those who defined themselves as 'South Asian Women'; and there were specific reasons for this. Although within feminist circles writings by and on South Asian women are becoming fairly prolific, in academic forums South Asian women find that much of their energy is still being taken up by (1) insisting that 'race' and difference need to be considered, and (2) on explaining 'what it is like to be a South Asian woman'. Between providing testimony and clamouring for the recognition of 'race' very little space remains within these forums for the concerns of South Asian women. Converseley in the growing area of South Asian studies, while 'race' is automatically taken account of, gender has to be asserted. Rather like the area of subaltern studies where gender issues are treated as a bit of a 'red herring' (Spivak 1988: 218). This workshop was an attempt to get away from familiar scenarios where we are always explaining or battling but never quite arriving at the point of looking at the figure of the South Asian woman in-depth. The call for papers stressed that the discussions had to have a theoretical focus, and could not be purely empirical. An institutional history also lay behind this decision.

In a discussion of the whiteness of art spaces Sarat Maharaj speaks of a trend towards 'multicultural managerialism', based on an 'administrative logic for regulating and managing cultural difference' (1999: 7). Within this logic 'black' artists are pigeon-holed and straitjacketed. They are expected for instance to bring ethnic vibrancy and colour to the field. Steven McQueen (McQueen and Mercer 2001), winner of the Turner Prize in 2000, in a discussion with Kobena Mercer recollected that as an art student at Goldsmiths College (London University) he was expected to produce cultural artefacts associated with Africa, such as masks, but not expected to have much authority on more mainstream theoretical issues in the area of art. Eddie Chambers notes:

> On a general level, Black artists, as metaphoric round pegs, constantly find themselves bludgeoned and stereotyped into metaphoric square pigeon-holes. In other words, nothing that Black artists can say or do has so far managed to convince critics and curators to accept them as artists in their own right – not necessarily bound by considerations of race and nationality (1999: 93).

A similar trend can be observed in academia. Here it is also apparent that 'the flat ironing force of this emergent multiculturalism managerialism' (Maharaj 1999: 7) can limit the fields in which 'black' academics are seen to have the authority for specialism. In projects on racialized minorities managed by senior white academics the appointment of South Asian women as researchers can be confined to providing social documentation of ethnic minorities. Once the 'data' and stories are collected much of the theorizing is then left to the more senior staff. And even if 'black' academics are granted the authority to question the received wisdom in paradigms and models, the theoretical authority will so often be confined to considerations of 'race' and ethnicity. Hence, 'black' academics may be granted the authority of being specialists of ethnic and racial identities, businesses, class relations or migratory patterns, but not in more general areas such as globalization, capitalism, class or migration. Thus we see how whiteness can enjoy a position of privilege by ex-nominating race from white bodies whilst racially marking 'others'. It is this process that enables racially non-marked bodies to masquerade as the universal humanist thinkers, doers, artists, politicians, academics and administrators (Araeen 1994).

The pigeon-holing and straitjacketing of racialized minorities can lead to a further layer of sub-sectioning for women who want to work in gender with the 'race' question. Those who introduce women and gender issues into the theoretical studies of globalization or identities, for instance, risk being confined to having authority within yet another sub-sub-category. The placement of various postcolonial feminists within the landscape of academic expertise reveals how these processes are at work in the day-to-day practices involved in the granting of authority. Taking a critical look at the terms in which one is able to speak within the academy, Spivak has noted the existence of a kind of 'benevolent imperialism' that enables her to speak as an Indian woman today. She notes that 'A hundred years ago it was impossible for me to speak, for the precise reason that makes it only too possible for me to speak in certain circles now' (cited in Landry and MacLean 1995: 194). Thus we have to always be alert to whose agenda we are serving when space is made available for 'black slots' (Chambers 1999: 27).

The restricted grounds from which women of colour within the academy are enabled to speak can become especially apparent when they go outside the remit of 'benevolent multiculturalism' and write about mainstream subjects that occupy a central place in the academic hierarchy of knowledge. This more generalized form of speaking becomes especially problematic if the idioms one uses are a touch unconventional. Those people who engage in the 'legitimate' styles of disciplines are more likely to be embraced as "'one of us". . . "who can speak our language"' (Chambers 1999: 26). Spivak situates the highly publicized critique of her book *A Critique of Post-Colonial Reason* (1999) by Terry Eagleton as being directed from a position that is uncomfortable with the fact that the texts she engages with 'are not confined to Third World women and yet I don't write like Habermas in drag' (Spivak 2001: 21). Explaining the situation further she notes that her presence in the academy is troubling because:

... I am a woman and as it happens a woman of colour who does not remain confined to the modes of discourse that she is allowed to engage in – speaking about women and speaking about Third World women and speaking about our victimage. That's fine. If a person such as me de-anthropologises herself and reads the great texts of European tradition in a way that does not resemble the general rational expectations way of reading then she is punished (2001: 22).

The push firstly to be more than an anthropological specimen of South Asian women and secondly, to open up existing rather unwieldy modes of engagement, highlights the 'guarded' and 'repressive' tolerance in the desire for difference that carries in the unspoken small print of assimilation – a 'drive for sameness' (Maharaj 1999: 6). Through these processes the kind of questions that are asked as well as the voices that are amenable to being heard within the regular channels of academia can become severely restricted.

Production of Knowledge

Rules of the academic genre contain and constrain the performances of South Asian academics. The white bodies who have become figures of authority through their studies of black bodies have defined and delimited what constitutes an appropriate study, and have produced the rules of the game. Theoretical moulds in which they have their own vested interest. The 'production' and 'consumption' of South Asian women within academic discourses have occurred within a limited set of discourses. As a result, South Asian women students who want a more complex understanding of what they see as the simultaneous enactment of racism and patriarchies within their lives are only offered limited theoretical and methodological tools. Moreover, these tools have often been fashioned by the supervisors who are recruiting and supervising these students by being positioned as repositories of 'expert' knowledge, through having obtained grants and supervised other projects. As Linda Smith (1999) argues, these student experiences are then forced into 'a cultural orientation, a set of values, a different conceptualisation of such things as time, space and subjectivity, different and competing theories of knowledge, highly specialised forms of language, and structures of power' (1999:42). What is seriously lacking is then an in-depth engagement with the subjecthoods and locales of South Asian women, leaving students with a set of limited genres and subjectivities with which to start out on their essays, dissertations and doctoral studies.

Similarly, research programme outlines already contain within them the basis on which new research may be done. In outlining the key areas of interest, the programmes often write out projects that have different starting-points. Panels who then decide how and where to spend research monies have thus already laid out the rules of the game.

More recently, these boundaries of knowledge production have been 'loosened' through contradictory pressures to recognize alternative discourses, to acknowledge alternative locations and to validate knowledge from other places. This 'loosening' has involved calls to 'internationalize' the disciplines, and has resulted in the inclusion of people from a greater variety of Third World countries in seminar series and the inclusion of black bodies on research assessment panels. However, these versions of the international, the countries from which people are included, the persons who become 'accepted' in Western academic discourse are those who speak the dominant discursive language, who have learned the rules of the ruling genre. Thus when an Indian scholar is asked to present a paper at a premier research centre and then criticized for using Western theorists to make sense of Indian material, one must ask whether she would have been invited to the centre if she had not framed her analysis within these familiar theoretical frameworks. As Passaro rightly asks, do our methods of knowing give us room to do anything more than 'recreate what we already assume, and . . . re-inscribe the politics of the status quo?' (1997: 151).

The dominance of particular paradigms, of certain ways of knowing is at least partially based in the Western academy's privileging of written texts, of knowledge that has been scripted, so that such knowledges become scriptural. The authority that for long has been ascribed to written knowledge along with the professionalization of knowledge has meant that the texts of the professionals have become scriptures.[3] Scriptural knowledges form the basis for identifying the research question within the hypothetico-deductive model for research, a model that has been widely critiqued by feminists. This model, although disparaged by academics, still provides the framework within which our questions are asked. We identify our questions through a re-vision of current knowledges, of current texts. Our hypotheses or research questions thus emanate from existing knowledge as extensions or problematics framed as disagreements with or augmentations of earlier knowledge. Although this taking account of others in the field is crucial to the dialogic project of creating knowledge, do these accounts then constrain and limit our own ways of making sense? Academic codes still demand that academic research output is framed first within a critique of the literature, an identification of the gaps and then of the contribution of the project, an inherently deductive approach to knowledge. Critical researchers have extensively critiqued the assumptions made by the hypothetico-deductive method, (i.e. hypothesis testing and falsification); but most written scholarly work is still reported within a deductive framework. Academic structures can lead to a paradigmatic straitjacketing; and unless we challenge the power of the scriptures in defining what we can know, our research will remain unrepresentative of all that we want to research.

Feminists have for long espoused the need to recognize the subjectivity of knowledge, arguing that experiential knowledge should form the basis for scriptural knowledges, recognizing that experiences form a most important foundation for constructing what is written. However, even feminists have found it hard to shift experiential knowledge to centre-stage. They have found it difficult to frame their analysis through an experiential lens, to begin their research with the location of that experience. This is even more marked among black people. Drawing on experience to argue a point can lead to charges of 'having a chip on the shoulder' or of unscientific practice. Toril Moi however offers a useful reminder about the importance of experience in constructions of knowledge, arguing that the body encompasses both the objective and subjective aspects of experience. The bodies of South Asian women are then 'a historical sedimentation of our way of living in the world, and of the world's way of living with us' (Moi 1999: 68).

Together, the dominance of scriptural knowledge and the continuing imperative of the hypothetico-deductive framework have limited what we know and how we know it. How many of us define our topic from what are the most faddish questions being addressed in recent journal articles? Some of us may focus on those aspects of the topic that are most relevant to our experience; but how many of us make these linkages explicit and actively use this linkage as a basis for wanting these questions answered? To what extent do we consciously allow, as well as acknowledge, the coalition between experience, inference and text in constructing our research question? What sources of knowledge do we use most when framing our research question? To what extent does scriptural knowledge form the basis for our research questions? These are questions that we all need to ask ourselves if we are to construct more meaningful narratives through our academic research. Despite this critique we also acknowledge that our own knowledge systems do not exist outside of us. Our academic practices are also produced within and infused with the particularities of this knowledge system. And we bear its consequences.

While we undeniably write with an academic signature for this book, at the same time we are hoping to utilize the resources available for opening up a space for ideas that have been suppressed or neglected in academia in discussions pertaining to that broad category, South Asian women. All too often we have had to 'tone down' our claims so that we don't offend other 'palates' and 'tastes' (Chambers 1999: 31). Herein lies a mixture of narratives that do not offer a view from the 'fields', from 'behind the scenes' or 'the back of beyond': just a series of conversations that have had some difficulty in seeing the light of day.

Framing This Volume

Within this volume we have tried to initiate critical dialogues with current paradigms, with existing scriptures, with dominant frames, but also to move beyond these critiques. While the project of critiquing such discourses is well under way, we argue that there has been little space for constructing or expressing alternative narratives that allow for the complexity of South Asian women's subjectivities or localities, without the entrapments of completeness or closure. The chapters presented here thus aim to unsettle contemporary academic accounts, to shift the terms of the debate and to initiate new dialogues. At the same time, we have what Sunej Gunew in a conversation with Spivak terms a 'phobia' for the business of 'speaking "in the name of"' (cited in Landry and MacLean 1995: 198): this volume does not profess to represent all South Asian women. Thus readers seeking an encyclopaedic account of South Asian women in the diaspora will not find it in the pages of this book. Specific textual and institutional spaces mark the formation of this collection.

The chapters in this volume have been divided into three sections. The first aims to interrogate current maps of academic practice and to provide new maps that challenge the orientalizing narratives of earlier discussions. Nirmal Puwar's chapter provides an overview of how South Asian women have been seen (and not heard) within the academy, how they have been 'placed' within melodramatic constructions and postures in the academy. Pointing to the objectifying affects of scholarship on women of colour found in a range of theoretical genres, she calls for an investigation of how the subject positions, hopes and desires of academics themselves are wound up in the subjectivities they assign to others. Fauzia Ahmad addresses the pressing issue of religious identity and South Asian women's subjectivities. She provides a resounding critique of the ways in which Muslim women have been represented in contemporary media, academic and other official discourses. She suggests, like other authors in this volume, that the traditional–modern binary within which South Asian women are caught is limiting in so many ways, and does not offer a place for those whose existence disrupts the binary. As Ahmad suggests, the urgency of the task of trying to understand and critique the increasing saliency of religion as a trope in both Western and South Asian geopolitics cannot be underestimated. The complex ways in which gender interpolates with religion in the construction of heroic tales of Western imperialism must be interrogated. Parvati Raghuram's chapter utilizes the example of a fashion retailing business established by a South Asian woman to interrogate the role of South Asian women in the multiple tales of production and consumption, each of which limits the agency of women in some ways. She examines the ways in which such women are positioned (or not) in the intersecting debates in gender and development, ethnic minority enterprise literature, and the consumption literature. Significantly, she also highlights the ways in which women from different parts of the diaspora are implicated in different ways in the production and consumption of clothing, but also in the operation of power across the globe. Mala Pandurang, on the other hand, provides us with a view from the other side, on the terms of engagement of Indian women located in the subcontinent in discourses of the diaspora. This contribution reminds us of the continuities between colonial discourses, which are often seen to delimit contemporary postcolonial narratives, and the postcolonial realities of the subcontinent and the ways in which links to that 'other space' are used to construct 'South Asian women' as an entity.

The next section offers alternative accounts of South Asian women's embodiment, challenging current ways of thinking racialized and gendered bodies. Nandi Bhatia's chapter offers us an account of how South Asian women are textually produced as objects of desire, but crucially counterposes this account with that of the object herself, who provides an alternative chronicle of this desire. The time-frame within which these events occurred is the 1920s and 1930s, towards the end of direct British colonial rule in South Asia, while the riposte by Maitreyi Devi is more recent. The 'long view' offered by Bhatia highlights the protracted histories of the limited discourses of desire within which South Asian women are placed, but also the fact that the alternative subjectivities that other chapters in this volume suggest are not new. Crucially she looks at the interchanges wrapped up in narratives of romantic transgressions in the colonial zone. Bakirathi Mani offers a contemporary account of how clothing practices are a performative enactment of desire and difference, which requires continuous repetition for the similar and yet different utterances of diasporic bodies. Dress occurs not only under the duress of gendered and racially ethnicized norms, but also through the active engagement and re-engagement of performing bodies, which offer openings for 'new' formations even while they repeat familiar tropes. Navtej Purewal illustrates the ways in which patriarchal social formations are mediated by technological innovations, in this case, the possibilities for female feticide offered by the industry of ultrasound scanning. Purewal's own research highlights the ambiguities of South Asian women's subjectivities and the ways in which women's bodies are both contested and also implicated in sex selection. Nayanika Mookerjee's chapter focuses on a moment of crisis, where there is a fracturing of geopolitical entities, a division between countries, and therefore questions the homogeneity of 'South Asia'. Her analysis brings to light the ways in which middle-class aesthetics place the female body within nationalist constructions and reduce the complex subjectivities of the bodies that suffered through the partition of East and West Pakistan.

The final set of chapters aim to highlight South Asian women's agency and to challenge the image of passivity that has so often been ascribed to them. Rani Kawale's chapter problematizes the heterosexual norm within contemporary discourses on South Asian women. She discusses the social dynamics involved in the power of whiteness within lesbian, gay and bisexual spaces. The need for and joy of alternative spaces for South Asian women is also outlined, showing how *Kiss* and *Club Kali* are a welcome escape from the whiteness of other spaces, that are enormously reassuring. The commonsensical notion that alternative sexualities cannot be realized within South Asian spaces and have to be taken elsewhere to safe 'white' lesbian, gay and bisexual places is seriously disrupted by the simultaneous creation of both new ethnicities and new sexualities. Samina Zahir provides an account of one attempt to engender community participation in an arts project and to create a dialogue amongst South Asian women. She suggests the political possibilities of art, art that allows a different sense of aesthetics. By highlighting the pleasures of new forms of art she suggests that these pleasures also have political implications as they foster an alternative set of relations between different sets of institutions. Shaminder Takhar examines South Asian women's participation in a variety of statutory and voluntary agencies and tries to understand how these women make sense of their location within patriarchal and racialized social formations. This focus on a institutional political participation complements the analysis in other chapters in this section, where a broader version of the political is brought into play. Finally, Hasmita Ramji examines London's up-and-coming middle-class South Asian women's terms of engagement with patriarchy, the ways in which gender and race are reconfigured through the acquisition of middle-class status and wealth. The women in her study also thus disrupt the tradition–modernity dichotomy found in models of patriarchy.

Notes

1. At a recent conference launch of a new journal on 'South Asian Popular Culture' (to be published by Routledge), held at the University of Portsmouth (4–5 April 2002) organized by South Asian scholars in the UK, an overwhelming majority of the speakers were from the USA, as are the members of the editorial board.
2. The use of the term 'black' here refers to those people who are associated with the African and South Asian Diasporas. There has been a productive and contentious discussion of the use of the category 'black' as opposed to ethnic groupings in Britain that ethnicize without paying adequate attention to questions of overlapping and cross-cutting power differentials (Hall 1989; Brah 1992; Housee and Sharma 1999; Mercer 1994).
3. This authority is however not static or permanent, but shifts. For instance, the knowledge of some has greater authority than the texts of others.

References

Araeen, R. (1994), *Making Myself Visible*, London: Kala Press.

Bhattacharya, G. (1998), *Tales of Dark Skinned Women*, London: UCL Press.

Bourdieu, P. (1992), *Language and Symbolic Power: The Economy of Linguistic Exchanges*, Cambridge: Polity.

Brah, A. (1992), 'Difference, Diversity and Differentiation', in J. Donald and A. Rattansi (eds), *Race, Culture and Difference*, London: Open University: Sage.

—— (1996), *Cartographies of Diaspora*, London: Routledge.

CCCS (1982), *The Empire Strikes Back: Race and Racism in 70s Britain*, London: Hutchinson.

Chambers, E. (1999), 'Eddie Chambers: Interview with Petrine Archer-Straw', in E. Chambers (ed.), *Annotations* 5, London: International Institute of Visual Arts (INIVA).

Chow, R. (1993), *Writing Diaspora*, Bloomington and Indianapolis: Indiana University Press.

Grosz, E. (1995), *Space, Time and Perversion: Essays on the Politics of Bodies*, London: Routledge

Hall, S. (1989), 'The Local in the Global' in A. King (ed.), *Culture, Globalization and the World System: Contemporary Conditions for the Representation of Identity*, Albany: SUNY Press.

—— (1990), 'Cultural Identity and Diaspora', in J. Rutherford (ed.), *Identity: Community, Culture and Difference*, London: Lawrence and Wishart.

hooks, b. (1991), *Yearning: Race, Gender and Cultural Politics*, London: Turnaround.

Housee, S. and Sharma, S. (1999), '"Too Black Too Strong"? The Making of South Asian Political Identities in Britain', in T. Jordan and A. Lent (eds), *Storming the Millennium*, London: Lawrence and Wishart.

Kaplan, C. (1994), 'The Politics of Location as Transnational Feminist Practice', in I. Grewal and C. Kaplan (eds), *Scattered Hegemonies*, London: University of Minnesota Press.

Landry, D. and MacLean, G. M. (1995), *The Spivak Reader: Selected Works of Gayatri Chakravorty Spivak*, London: Routledge.

Maharaj, S. (1999), 'Black Art's Autrebiography', in E. Chambers (ed.), *Annotations* 5, London: International Institute of Visual Arts (INIVA).

McQueen, S. and Mercer, K. (2001), in conversation at the Institute of Contemporary Arts (ICA), London.

Mercer, K. (1994), *Welcome to the Jungle: New Positions in Black Cultural Studies*, London: Routledge.

Modood, T. and Fenton, S. (1999), *Ethnicity and Employment in Higher Education*, London: Policy Studies Institute.

Mohanty, C. (1988), 'Under Western Eyes: Feminist Scholarship and Colonial Discourses', *Feminist Review* 30: 60–88.

Moi, T. (1999) *What is a Woman?*, Oxford: Oxford University Press.

Passaro, Joanne. 1997. '"You Can't Take the Subway to the Field!"': "Village" Epistemologies in the Global Village,' in Akhil Gupta and James Ferguson (eds), *Anthropological Locations: Boundaries and Grounds of a Field Science*, pp.147–162. Berkeley, CA: University of California Press.

Rajan, S. R. (1993), *Real & Imagined Women: Gender, Culture and Postcolonialism*, London: Routledge.

Smith. L. T. (1999), *Decolonizing Methodologies,* London: Zed Books.

Spivak, G. S. (1988), *In Other Words: Essays in Cultural Politics,* London: Routledge.

—— (1999), *A Critique of Postcolonial Reason,* Cambridge, MA: Harvard University Press.

—— (2001), 'Mapping the Present: Interview with Gayatri Spivak', by M. Yegenoglu and M. Mutman, *New Formations,* 45: 9–23.

Part I
South Asian Women and Paradigmatic (Im)possibilities

–2–

Melodramatic Postures and Constructions
Nirmal Puwar

A structure belonging to modern Western culture can doubtless be seen in its historiography: intelligibility is established through a relation with the other; it moves (or 'progresses') by changing what it makes of its 'other' – the Indian, the past, the people, the mad, the child, the Third World. Through these variants that are all heteronomous – ethnology, history, psychiatry, pedagogy – unfolds a problematic form basing its mastery of expression upon what the other keeps silent, and guaranteeing the interpretative work of a science (a 'human' science) by the frontier that separates it from an area awaiting this work in order to be known (de Certeau 2000: 157).

[There is] . . . a circuit of productivity that draws its capital from others' deprivation while refusing to accept its own presence as endowed . . . they choose to see in others' powerlessness an idealized image of themselves and refuse to hear the dissonance between the content and manner of their speech their own complicity with violence (Chow 1993: 14).

By naming the academic postures and constructions that surround the subaltern female (a highly heterogeneous and fractured entity) as melo-dramatic this chapter looks back at the academy, from the insides of the beast, that is from the privileges of academia, through the eyes of someone who is at least partially inculcated in its language and habitus (Bourdieu 1988). Working through different academic moments, with genres loosely marking them out, the discussion will focus on academic representations of South Asian women, and at the ways in which the subjectivities of academics themselves are related to the subjecthoods we assign to Others. In this sense, this chapter is a call for academics to pause in their scholarly tracks and to think about how their own investments are intimately linked to the very postures and productions they produce.

Looking at the historical scholarship on childhood, a discipline that she is a participant in, Carol Steedman notes 'the split between children and "the child"' (2000: 18) as a figure in academic construction. Locating this split in a transferential relationship, whereby we project our own fantasies of childhood, she asks scholars to 'make plainer to ourselves the arena of romanticism and post-romanticism within which we describe and theorise childhood' with the realization 'that as we watch, talk to, teach and write about children, we desire them, want something from them, which is our own lost childhood' (2000: 24).

The body of the subaltern female – in the image of the hybrid metropolitan youth who dons saris and trainers, the *sati* on the funeral pyre of her husband, the sweatshop worker in the East End of London, the domestic cleaners in the homes, offices and airports of global cities and the 'dextrous' fingers on electronic circuits in free trade zones – is the text upon which a whole array of academic fantasies and anxieties are written. The benevolence of charity, the calling for salvation, the guilt of class and racial privilege, the excitement of exotica as well as metropolitan hybridity, the longing for revolutionary change and the search for ethical love, all hover around the haloes of these objects (subjects?). Melodrama marks the place of this figure in popular, official and academic, including feminist, Western discourses. Looking at the long routes of academic wisdom alone, in relation to the figure of the South Asian woman it is possible to map at least four melodramatic moments, all of which bear traces of each other. A great many of these conceptualizations and compositions sway between the extremes of victimhood and heroinehood, pity and celebration, even though they are located in competing and diverse theoretical orientations.

Mapping is no doubt always an act of power; it determines what is visible and how it is visible. The voyeurism available to a panoramic view of the world can easily delight in the position of being a superior onlooker, situated on the outside of what one is looking at. The mapping in this chapter is not conducted from a lofty position that pokes fun at the dealings of those who are the subjects of its observation (academics). The view from which my observations are offered has its own positionality. Specific histories lie behind the cartography I chart. Located within the structures that I have the power to map, I am both object and subject. Certain observations throughout my academic life have brought me to the particular signature the writing of this chapter carries. Too often South Asian women in the academy as students and scholars feel the force of relations and conceptions that objectify them within reified frameworks, that offer some sense of eschewed recognition while containing vestiges of personal violation (epistemic, symbolic and bodily). I make a strategic intervention in this territory by looking at the some of the effects of the postures and constructions surrounding the academic study of South Asian women. Furthermore, I make a plea for scholars to think about their own investments in the subjects we study and the entities we create. We need to consider our own positionalities in a much more difficult way than what has now become the customary laying out of the 'me' in the usual 'race', class and gender mantra.

Intellectuals are no doubt needed for setting the record straight, in so many respects. Yet at the same time, by raising the plight of the underdogs we can't hide behind the radicalness of our labour. Academics are not outside the power relations that they document. In bearing witness to the ills and joys of the world we also need to be alert to the *subjects* (as in people) to which we give life in the course of our pronouncements. I am not writing off the radical potential of intellectuals to generate powerful critiques that governments and other power brokers would rather do without. I fully sign up to Edward Said's assertion that the role of the intellectual 'has an edge to it, and cannot be played without a sense of being someone whose place it is publicly to raise embarrassing questions, to confront orthodoxy and dogma (rather than produce them)' (Said 1994: 11). The 'insiders, experts, coteries, professionals who make public opinion "conformist" should be criticised by intellectuals' (1994: xiii). Simultaneously we need to be alert to our own academic orthodoxies as these emerge in our midst, as we play the 'big' power wars. Embarrassing questions need to be put to our own 'experts' and 'coteries'. The question this chapter seeks to put on the academic table is, I repeat: How are the subjectivities of academics intimately mingled with the subjecthoods we assign to 'others'? What investments do academics have in the constructions we make and the postures we adopt in this very making? The story of the figure of the South Asian woman in academia has some telling clues for us.

Blazing Fires: The White Man's (and Woman's) Burden

The first time a student of social theory has to meet the figure of a South Asian woman in academic texts is usually through Emile Durkheim's work on suicide. In textbooks and lecture halls the notion of fatalistic suicide is illustrated with reference to the ghostly figure of *sati*, the image of a widow burning on a funeral pyre in India. While flames and memories of barbaric, uncivilized Other Eastern cultures where women are held captive and ruthlessly oppressed are certainly ignited, there is, hardly ever, any discussion of how orientalism marks this specific anthropological gaze, which trollops and gallivants around the world, collecting facts and figures, and undertakes the noble task of comparative social analysis for the sake of discovering universal social rules of behaviour. This of course is the high noon of anthropology. It is the classic moment where distinctions between the West and the Rest give rise to a method of epistemic jurisdiction encased in observations, measurements, categorizations, spectacles and cabinets of curiosity (Said 1978; Hall 1997). The bodies of women from these 'Other' places have occupied a central place in the production of difference, between the barbaric and the civilized, the spiritual and the rational, the passive and the strong. All that is seen to be enticing as well as repulsive and in need of correction from these 'Other' places is projected on to these female figures.

Images of downtrodden sensuous women full of eastern promise who need to be freed from the captivity of backward cultures by Western discourses run riot in the Western imagination (Bhattacharya 1998). Representing the white man's as well as the white woman's burden, women from 'Other' places, including South Asian women, have offered a sense of mission to those who have looked to the East for a career (Said 1978), constituting for them a sense of identity as politicians, social reformers, travellers or indeed academics. The particular and interstitial ways in which this politics of salvation is repeated throughout different contexts is of course specific to both time and space. They can, and indeed often do, sit side by side with a politics of celebration. Political, economic, social and institutional locations are incredibly important for appreciating the local contexts out of which the specific idealization, romanticization, pathologization and celebration of the female subaltern arises.

The language of feminism and the liberation of women was used by colonialists, such as Cromer, to mark the boundary between the liberated West and the barbaric East, and thereby to produce a subject position for white colonial masculinity. The irony is that while the men in the Victorian establishment resisted the feminist cause in the their own countries, they captured the language of feminism and colonialism and '. . . redirected it, in the service of colonialism, toward Other men and the cultures of Other men' (Ahmed 1992: 6). Looking at this from the ghostly figure of the blazing *sati*, so often repeated in Western discourses, Spivak has famously noted that the abolition of *sati* and the series of laws that were enacted on behalf of Indian women by the British were a classic case of 'White men saving brown women from brown men' (Spivak 1988a: 296), making way for what Rajan describes as a 'trope of chivalry', a rite of passage for young white men into amorous masculinity (Rajan 1993: 6). The depiction of women who underwent the practice of *sati* in official accounts as victims or heroines, precluded the possibility of a 'female subjectivity that is shifting, contradictory, inconsistent' (Rajan 1993: 11), but enabled the proliferation of a 'rescue paradigm' (Rajan 1993: 6), which was often tinged by 'voyeuristic pleasure', especially if the *sati* was tragically considered to be young and beautiful (Mani 1992: 400, 1998).

It was not, however, only the knight in shining armour who set about saving women in India and other parts of the colonies under the masquerade of the 'rescue paradigm'; Western women, 'Imperial Ladies', also donned this cloak, albeit with a different affectation, to style, perhaps unconsciously, a subject position for themselves (Burton 1994; Chaudhuri and Strobel 1992). The fashioning of Western women as enlightened agents who took on the mission of relieving the patriarchal plight of women in the colonies was pivotal to the yielding of political rights and agency by Western women. They could use charitable postures to assert themselves as agents against the exclusionary political agendas of white masculinity in the face of conceptions of the liberal political 'individual' that did not include women. The exclusions in the body politic posed by the 'sexual contract' (Pateman 1988) were undercut by a gendered 'racial contract' (Mills 1997). Thus 'in the process of campaigning for women whom they considered to be more badly treated than themselves . . . Western women could achieve a subject position for themselves, often at the expense of indigenous women's subject position and sense of agency' (Mills 1998: 105). Here we see the beginnings of the 'productive' power of limited representations of Indian women for men and women located in the West.

Between Pathology and Pity

The image of the passive downtrodden South Asian woman is replicated in what can be identified as a second moment in which Area Studies meets the metropolis. This is the moment when anthropology comes home and watches people from the ex-colonies in the metropolitan industrial centres, in the form of an ethnography that goes searching for stories. Pitted against a tradition of social research that either (1) ignored the plight of these newly arrived immigrants or (2) documented some aspects of these lives with a view to assimilating these arrivals into the normatively defined British way of life, an 'insider' account, whose influence has unfortunately been long-lasting, emerged. Based on neat managerial categories of ethnic difference, this posture sought to both understand and assist in the so-called cultural splits faced by South Asian women. Verity Khan's (1977) work is a classic case of a study that is itself caught in the 'caught in-between two cultures' paradigm that is so often used to describe the state of South Asian women who are torn between the freedom and liberation of Western values and backward, tradition-bound families. This version of the melodramatic missionary image of women from Other places as victims of archaic patriarchal practices who are desperately in need of help was at the time and has been since reproduced by institutional discourses, including the state, schools (Brah and Minhas 1985) and the media. It is a posture that is particularly prone to rear its ugly head in discussions of highly determined issues, such as *sati*, which became 'a larger-than-life symbol of "Hindu" and "Indian" culture in a way which transcended the actual facts of this limited practice' (Narayan 1997: 65). Arranged marriages and veiling occupy a similar place in postcolonial Britain. This framework also continues to be the principal means by which students are encouraged to make sense of the lives of South Asian women.

Working out of Black feminism in Britain, and influenced by black feminists in the United States, articles in *The Empire Strikes Back* (CCCS 1982), the special issue of *Feminist Review* (1984) and the anthology *Charting the Journey* (Grewal *et al.* 1988) led the way in interrogating the ways in which South Asian women had up until then been made visible in academia. These pioneering black feminist accounts paid particular attention to the imperial nature of Eurocentric feminist perspectives on families, sexuality and political activism. Pathological accounts of Asian families and stereotypes of passive Asian women who need 'help' were called into question. The 'culturalism of anthropological works' (Grewal *et al* 1988: 6) was criticized for taking cultural practices and traditions out of their specific social and historical circumstances and interpreting them, as the practice of *sati* had been in colonial India (Mani 1998), as being timeless, static and uniformly applicable to all Asians. An overemphasis upon the 'ethnic' features of these women's lives meant that the place of structures of racism was overlooked in favour of accounts that sealed Asian families and their cultures in little ethnic social vacuums. At the same time, a similar critique was directed at feminist studies of 'third world' women on an international scale, including the urban centres of the West. In a highly influential article Chandra Mohanty pointed out the 'latent ethnocentrism' within Western feminism, which had a tendency to: (1) produce/represent a monolithic category of the 'average third world woman' and (2) to measure and judge the lives of these Other women through a 'yardstick' which took the lives of middle-class women in the West as the norm, 'as the implicit referent' (1988: 64).

Picking up on an academic genre that was becoming increasingly popular within feminism, as well as working-class histories, as it was seen to allow for the possibility of hearing perspectives and voices that had hitherto been ignored and silenced, black feminists interrogated the use of in-depth qualitative methods as a quick-fix for the racist thinking that percolated through existing epistemic frameworks. The presumed 'goodness' of oral histories that sought to give a voice to black women and to reverse the so-called bad stereotypes and invisibility of black women in feminist frameworks with real and positive images was problematized for engaging in a process of objectification that all too easily disavowed relations of power. Carby asserted: 'In arguing that feminism take account of the lives, herstories and experiences of black women we are not advocating that teams of white feminists should descend upon Brixton, Southall, Bristol or Liverpool to take black women as objects of study in modes of resistance. We don't need that kind of intrusion . . .' (1982: 232).

Texts that sought to 'give voice' to Asian women were, perhaps unwittingly, feeding the historic Western 'need' to feel pain and intense sympathy for this figure. Commenting on Amrit Wilson's *Finding a Voice*, Pratibha Parmar noted that, while this book goes a long way in dispelling the notion that Asian women are 'helpless creatures', it lacks a political and economic framework, which makes it easier for the readers, including academics, social and community workers, to exclaim "'I had to put it down, half way through reading it, because it made me cry'" (1982: 252).

Parmar (1982) stressed the importance of taking account of how patriarchal, imperial, social and political economic factors came together in the lives of these women. She, like other black feminists, asserted that an analysis of the interactions of capitalism, racism and patriarchy as they were experienced by South Asian women needed to take precedence over an obsession with capturing the culture of these ethnic Others in packaged descriptions.

Despite the force of the black feminist arguments, to this day students, especially Asian women who want to study the dynamics of gender in Asian communities, are more often than not asked to start off with descriptions, no doubt for the sake of the curiosity of their tutors, of what it means to be a Muslim or a Sikh, for instance. Thus the search for quick-fix guidebook-version accounts of Other cultures is continually endorsed through academic practices and regimes. And so is the urban anthropological fascination with collecting stories or reading stories by women of colour internationally. This academic practice is, as I shall show later, especially rife in our existing moment. Carby's critique seems to have fallen on deaf ears. While the methods for gaining contact with the Other have changed, the quest to know the Other has not gone away; it's just that the technological tools have shifted.

For now, I will turn to a third moment, a moment that is somewhat pre-empted in Parmar's call for understanding the 'oppression' of South Asian women through attention to racist structures of capitalism and patriarchy. However, as we shall see in the next section, this relatively radical emphasis does not preclude tears, postures of pity, or a politics of salvation. In fact, even in the hard-nosed area of political economy, idealization marks the order of the day. These are some of the dormant effects of this scholarship. They have, however, remained largely underexplored.

Heroic Cogs in Wheels

Much of the feminist analysis that has looked at the economic location of South Asian women has emerged out of series of points of contestation over the place of race and gender within a Marxist analyses of class (Westwood 1984; Phizacklea 1990). The studies have focused on the ailing industries the first generation of South Asian women were concentrated in as workers, especially textiles, and have been incredibly important for giving recognition to the labour of South Asian women. Despite this contribution, to borrow a phrase from Chow, these texts are however riddled with the anguish of undertaking the 'noble' task of returning the hitherto 'defiled' images of South Asian women to their 'sanctified' correct image of workers and fighters. And the problem is that 'defilement and sanctification belong to the same symbolic order', that of idealization (1993: 53–4).

As the daughters of the workers enter the academy as students of the humanities and the social sciences they are finding that while these studies grant recognition to the labour power of their mothers, aunts and sisters, at the same time the framework is eskewed and limited. One of the major problematic effects of these texts is that the subject position of South Asian women is simply and overwhelmingly of producers; they are cogs, albeit important and hitherto ignored cogs, in the capitalist machinery. They are hardly ever recognized as consumers; as impure participants in the circuits of capitalism. Instead they are pitied for their work conditions and idealized for occupying the most oppressed position in the metropolis. They are especially loved when they strike – then they are the heroines who are fighting the system, with saris and banners in tow.

Here we see a different, although little recognized, version of the politics of salvation: the salvation and uplifting of the figure of the downtrodden South Asian sewing machinists bent over their machines, working in sweatshops or as homeworkers. Such constructions enable academics to occupy a subject position that: (1) undertakes the noble task of highlighting the awful plight of the subaltern female in the metropolis of Britain; and (2) hopes to engender social change through this enlightened task, as traces of social philanthropy lie quietly sealed in-between the pages of the research; and (3) by allying themselves with the subalterns in the West these authors create a subject position for themselves, amongst their gender- or race-resistant colleagues, that is seen to be more radical than that of the most radical of Marxists. These academic texts, which are a variant of political economy directions in the area of Development Studies, and more recently of the escalating studies of globalization, can be seen to represent, albeit unconsciously, a version of the economically privileged person's burden in the international capitalist economy. Thus the 'mood of self-congratulation as saviours of marginality' (what Spivak identifies as 1988a: 61) can I argue also reside in constructions ostensibly concerned with the serious issue of capital and labour in a global economy.

The force of the power lines of capitalism in the lives of subaltern women, at assembly lines and as domestics, sex workers and homeworkers, must indeed be underlined. After all, as is pointed out by Spivak, notwithstanding the specificity of Spivak's definition of the subaltern female and the use of the term in a wider sense, 'it is the urban subproletarian female who is the paradigmatic subject of the current configuration of the International Division of Labour' (Spivak 1988b: 218). It is however the ways in which this recognition is granted that is at issue in this chapter. Often it is assumed that one is doing the right thing by adopting analytical frameworks that look at race and gender in the international and globalized economy. This worthy cause is not without its gaps and fantasies. It is, like so many of the other gestures that have gone before it, well-intentioned, it can also project certain anxieties and idealizations on to the figure of the subaltern woman.

In an analysis of feminist texts in the area of development studies (Nelson 1981; Young, Wolkowitz and McCullagh 1981), Aihwa Ong notes that collections which attempt to look at 'women's position in the encounter between global capitalist forces and the everyday life of paid and unpaid work' give more consideration to the mechanisms of capitalism and patriarchy than to the lives of these women. She notes that 'capitalism is delineated as a historically conditioned, polymorphus system; it has more contradictions and personalities than the women and men who are ostensibly the subjects of the volume' (2001: 112).

Working out of a position which had famously criticized the flattening out of complexity in the lives of third world women all around the globe, including the metropoles of the West, Mohanty's contribution to the debates on political economy offers a more nuanced perspective. Women are not simply viewed as innocent workers who are superexploited in the global economy; they are also acknowledged as being contradictory subjects who are themselves implicated as consumers, as well as producers, in the discourses and structures of the globe. Mohanty states:

> The challenges for feminists in this arena are a) understanding Third-World women workers as having objective interests in common as workers (they are thus agents and make choices as workers); and b) recognizing the contradictions and dislocations in women's own consciousness of themselves as workers, and thus of their needs and desires – which sometimes militate against organizing on the basis of their common interests (the results of agency). Thus work has to be done here in analyzing the links between the social location and the historical and current experiences of domination of Third-World women workers on the other. Reviewing the collective struggle of poor, Third-World women workers in relation to the above theorization of common interests provides a map of where our project is at (1997: 24).

The desire for international change through global linkages is the entity that defines what Mohanty refers to as 'our project'. This desire of course is also not beyond the realm of production, in the sense that it too contributes towards the production/representation of third world women. It is however much more alert to noting the heterogeneity of objective locations and the contradictory nature of subjectivities. Whether it manages to escape a romantic association with the 'struggles' of third world women as workers is something that I am not however altogether certain of. Because texts in the mould of Marxist political economy tend to be seen to be much more 'political' and 'radical' than those informed by more culturalist persuasions, the type of subjecthoods and collective subjects they construct can all too often escape scrutiny. Despite Mohanty's adeptness at locating latent trends in feminist analyses, even she manages to overlook the limited representation of subaltern women in the work of scholars who have only been too keen to stress the patriarchal/capitalism/race mantra. Thus we have the cogs and wheels angle being surreptitiously foregrounded at the cost of profundity.

Traditionally debates on production and consumption have at their worst been at loggerheads, or at best, being located in distinct fields, have spoken past each other; with accusations of 'economic determinism', 'identity navel-gazing', 'diehard realism' and 'free-floating subjectivities' flying between them in the exchange of political fire. More recently, interdisciplinary efforts have attempted to re-think questions located in

separate fields together through a recognition of the connection between
(1) commodities in the spheres of production and consumption and (2) the
coexistence of bodies which produce and consume (Du Gay 1997; Kellner
1997; Lash 1997). While this can be grasped as an opportunity to re-think
what it means to be a producer, to view '. . . the native – nowadays often
a synonym for the oppressed, the marginalized, the wronged . . . [as] also
the space of error, illusion, deception and filth' (Chow 1993: 30), there is
still a strong tendency within this new direction of thought, much of which
is still in the making, to imagine the subaltern female producer as an
absolute victim. At a one-day conference on the global fashion industry,
at the Institute of Contemporary Arts, in London (1997), amidst a panel
of journalists and academics, a South Asian woman was, rather like in the
old anthropological sense of an exhibited spectacle, asked to talk about her
life as a textile machinist home-worker. Crocodile tears of pity were once
again rolled out for this occasion by a prominent white feminist in the field
of fashion on the panel, while this woman sat in an alien space, totally out
of keeping with her own habitus, to give testimony; a replay of the readers'
reactions to Asian women 'giving voice' as observed by Parmar? Interestingly, debates on the production and consumption of fashion somehow
seem to congeal problematic postures towards South Asian women
(Nagrath and Puwar 2002).

Celebrations! Peering Otherwise

So much of the analysis of the globalized condition, in a social and
cultural, as well as an economic sense, is seen to reside with what is taken
to be the condition(s) of the subaltern female, the contemporary 'heart of
darkness'. It is amidst growing debates on globalization and its relationship to place-based identities and diasporic existences, that we have the
fourth melodramatic moment. Here we find that the so-called hybrid,
pastiched, negotiated and ambiguous identities of young South Asian
second-generation women are the foci of attention and fascination. The
mixing and matching characterized in the simultaneous donning of saris
and trainers are a somewhat exasperating site for academics, as these
figures are seen to project the archetypal global cultural subject, one that
is beyond borders, in flux and highly syncretic. And even those scholars
who engage in the arduous and sophisticated hoops of dialogic research
seem to rest the final word on the current state of the urban environment
on the analysis of the young, second-generation South Asian woman.
These figures raise unknown levels of excitement in academic ranks,

because their bodies seem to bring the rhizomatic flows of culture and capital to the brink in one carnivalesque affair. Oh what a celebration!

In the last ten years or so we have witnessed a welcome move away from static binary notions towards more complex and nuanced understandings. It is a move that has been particularly fruitful for freeing up the boundedness of groups and cultures for an appreciation of the interconnected, changing and fused nature of identities. Influenced by poststructuralist thinking, the academic conceptual toolbox for understanding life at the margins has become quite expansive. Discourses of hybridity, flows, borderlands, 'becoming minor', the nomadic, ambivalence are all to be found among the motley crew of concepts that are all too often called upon to narrate alterity as well as the path to alterity.

At the same time, there has been, at least in theory, a turning away from the old crude anthropological stance that sought to watch, observe and dissect the Other under the cloak of scientific knowledge. Notions of mimetic realism have been displaced by an acknowledgement of the place of the researcher in the production of the knowledge. Thus the image of the scholar as a Mr Spock figure who is separated from the objects of the world by dint of his cold, rational, transcendental scientific demeanour has been dented, if not altogether replaced, by the recognition that academics are inside their research enterprises (Puwar 2001). That is, who they are affects their whole academic venture. No one can escape, no matter how marginal, progressive, radical, organic and thus morally superior they position themselves as being in relation to their colleagues, their presence within their academically endorsed productions of statistics, philosophical quandaries, 'partial' stories and pictures or improvisational performances. At the same time, the looking-glass of reflexivity has been adopted to gauge the nature of the academic presence, leading some to produce lists along the traditional lines of the race, class, gender sing-song, while others offer in-depth confessional accounts from the field before offering the messy texts of the Other, with a full recognition of the meddling part played by the scholar (Clifford and Marcus 1986; Denzin 1997). Thus we have the troubled and struggling all-knowing epistemic eye.

Although ethnographers will now (a) go to great lengths to make sure their narrations are outside the fixtures of previous taxonomies and as fluid and agile as possible, and (b) attempt to generate and present their research in the most dialogic and ethical terms possible, these mechanisms do not guarantee that the hitherto muted subaltern subjects can speak, in the sense of being heard (Spivak 1988a). Furthermore, what is of particular note is that the desire to look, to see what life is like for those across the tracks or 'down under', has not gone away. Whether this desire is simply curiosity, or a search wrapped up in the politics of salvation, is neither here nor there. It is this desire, curiosity, whatever you want to call it, as well as the effects of it that I want to ponder on. Here it is worth pausing on Patricia Williams's comments in her Reith Lecture (BBC, Radio 4 1997), where she reminds us of the 'racial voyeurism' that propels 'bus loads of tourists [to] flock to black churches on a Sunday morning' in New York and Harlem. Williams sardonically remarks 'It's great theatre, according to the guidebook hit list of hits, all those black people dressed in their quaint finery, singing and swooning and singing some more' (1997: 19). Now, while researchers, unlike the average tourist, will declare sensitivity to the lives they look at (in the streets and clubs of metropoles, distant villages or cultural texts) nevertheless their gaze seeks also to travel, 'look', 'listen' and get a taste. In this sense they are all stomping the same territory, although the ethnographer is now, from time to time, fraught with twitches of reflexivity.

A refuge away from the troubled territory of ethnography is increasingly being sought in public texts (novels, films, art and theatre) by the Other. The quandary of hearing/not hearing, re-presentation and symbolic violence (Bourdieu 1996) is largely sidelined by feasting academic eyes on the Other through already available texts. Academics are using art or novels, for instance, by those who have managed to utilize the means of representation for themselves. This safe position does however I think deserve further interrogation, as it is not without its power lines and institutional conditions of existence – especially as it is a form of academic feeding that has rather problematically become all too familiar in relation to conversations, syllabuses and textbooks on the subaltern female.

Philosophical turns (in short the onset of post-structuralism) and political struggles, in which the efforts of women in colour in the academy to push against the grain of the canon have been absolutely paramount, have all helped to engender an academic environment where the margin, as a text, has come to occupy centre-stage. We have moved from a time when the texts of women of colour were altogether absent or at best, in a spirit of guilt-ridden benevolent multiculturalism, tagged on to a course in the form of a little reading list and one or two lectures, to the following kinds of scenarios: bell hooks notes that 'the courses I teach on black women writers and Third World Literature are overcrowded, with large waiting lists' (1991: 25). Today 'minority discourse' has become 'a hot topic' in the West (Chow 1993: 109). Working from within the black feminist movement in the States, which has fought long and hard battles to acknowledge outside-situated knowledges, specifically those of black women, Ann DuCille (2001), vents her exasperation over the ways in which black women, as texts, sit within the sites of knowledge production as prized commodities. She comments on an 'occult' of 'black woman-hood' whereby black women are now treated as a kind of 'sacred text': 'Why are they so interested in me and people who are like me (meta-phorically speaking)? Why have we – black women – become the sub-jected subjects of so much scholarly investigation, the peasants under the glass of intellectual inquiry in the 1990s?' (2001: 234).

OuCille sums up an academic genre – that haunts all subaltern women, in their heterogeneous locations, as objects of study. A recent conference titled 'Writing Europe 2001: Migrant Cartographies' exemplifies the ways in which the literary texts of women of colour have become common academic currency. Conferences can be great sites for highlighting gest-ures and genres; they are places where not only the content of analyses but the spirit in which the academic enterprise is conducted can come alive. Aside from being a lesson in how the academy is riddled by pecking orders, conferences can show how those scholars whose writings place them at the utmost radical edges of their disciplines, can together, within their own social milieu, generate a mood containing some not-so-radical after-effects. Given the locations of the conference – Amsterdam – known to be one of the most 'cosmopolitan' cities in Europe – and Leiden as well as the subject-matter of the conference, I was most surprised to find that the participants at this conference were predominantly 'white'. I soon tempered my surprise with a quick reminder that this was just a replica of the whiteness of academia back in Britain (cf. Essed 2000), except that in Europe it was much worse and that, somewhat ironically, I needed to bear in mind that Britannia had some of the 'best' race relations throughout Europe.

As I went in and out of numerous sessions over the course of three days my ears became tuned in to a repetition of academic notes that produced a harmonic melody, a mantra that was caught in the rhapsody of the marginal, or at least talk of the marginal, in the most radical idioms. Thankfully, such was the sophistication of this conference that the demons of binary and essentialist speech were abandoned to the monsters of bad social thought in favour of a language that spoke of hybridity, ambival-ence, the minor, the nomad, exile, border, etc. While the concepts them-selves and the history of ideas surrounding them have allowed for new possibilities for thinking about the textuality of racialized immi-grant and postcolonial existence, Coran Kaplan cautions that '. . . despite critiques of humanist categories, poststructuralist methodologies are no less prone to desiring the "other" or exoticizing difference' (1994: 144).

Since the racist murder of the black teenager Steven Lawrence and the publication of the Macpherson Report the expression 'unwitting' has perhaps been over-used for gesturing in the politest way possible: 'I know you have not deliberately caused damage, but that, I am sorry to inform you, has been the unintended consequence.' It is in this spirit that I would like to use the term 'unwitting' to refer to the effect of the academic rapping that prevailed through the repeated use of radical terms in relation to the literature and cultural works of people like Meera Syal, Meena Alexander and Zadie Smith. These works come to function as second-order mediations on the, still, mysterious world of Otherness. Even in the hands of complex analysis, women of colour become objects of know-ledge, a fertile ground for theoretical feasting: spectacles for under-standing the globalized and fractured conditions of the world. The pages of their novels, autobiographies and art works represent highly detailed and complex puzzles for academics to while away whole Sunday after-noons and sabbaticals. The effect of the continuous use of poets, film-makers, writers, and artists from the 'margins' as raw material for theoretical acrobatics can so often be further marginalization. Even those academics who want to write culture otherwise can, as is noted by Cornel West, bring in debates on difference and borders 'in a way that it further marginalizes actual people of difference and otherness'. Once again the 'Other' can be 'made object, appropriated, interpreted, taken over by those in power . . .' (quoted in hooks 1991: 125). Michelle Wallace presents us with a vivid picture of this process when she captures the 'traffic jam' of intellectuals engaged in the analysis of the work of Zora Neale Hurston, who 'like groupies descending on Elvis Presley's estate' are engulfed in 'a mostly ill-mannered stampede to have some memento of the black woman' (Wallace cited in DuCille 2001: 234).

Within the unwitting objectification of women of colour as prized objects of analysis a version of mythification can also prevail, as 'romanti-cizing nomad or guerrilla cultures is a frequent practice in contemporary poststructuralist theories' (Kaplan 1994: 144; Alarcon 1989; Lugone 1990). A romantic attachment to being minor and the hope of becoming minor can undermine the difficulty of existing on the borders. The cultural texts produced by the daughters of second-generation 'immigrants' seem to hold particular fascination. This of course is at a time when fashion has itself, in the world of music, media and clothing, shifted the image of the dirty, smelly, tradition-bound 'Paki' or Arab to the second-generation hip, hybrid, happening, mix-matching, bindhi- denim- and trainer-wearing object of desire, with the 'Asian Babe' being a case in point (Kalra and Hutnyk 1998; Sharma *et al*, 1996; Puwar 2002). At the conference in

Amsterdam it was pointed out to me that if academics want to make an original contribution to their disciplinary fields it is much harder for them to do this by specializing in the traditional canon, such as Shakespeare or Virginia Woolf, for instance. With these literary authors exhausted, the texts of newly discovered authors represent one route to academic recognition. Thus new voyages of discovery and 'virgin' territory can be found in the body of texts produced by women of colour. Once again, the East is a career.

Concluding Remarks

No matter how loving and ethical the search for the 'heart of darkness' is, we need to be alert to the institutional conditions that enable the search, to what are often referred to as the 'conditions of articulation' (Probyn 1993). In a most obvious sense we take the journeys we do, reading novels, describing levels of capitalist exploitation, looking for exile, baggage and travel in the work of articles, taking the work of black female poets to new flights, and writings articles, like this one, that critique the search in the first place, because we can, because we have cultural capital and institutional mechanisms at our disposal, however minimal they may be. This chapter is a call for pushing the politics of location and the research reflexivity that has ensued even further. The ways in which academics obtain a subjecthood for themselves through melodramatic constructions of the female subaltern, in the case of the figure of the South Asian woman, by hemming this figure, no doubt unconsciously, even if she is not left altogether muted, like Spivak's subaltern (1988a: 295), between victimhood, heroic struggle and romantic celebration, need to be interrogated. Now that we have got over replacing bad images with honourable good images (Mercer 1994; Hall 1997), we need not only to think about the limited ways in which subjectivities of Others are constructed, but also to pause and think about the subjecthood academics create for themselves, perhaps unconsciously through their very own creations. In short, we need to ask: What do we think we are doing when we peer into, problematize and recognize the labour and cultural texts of women of colour? And while we can seek ethical responsibility with the subaltern through a one-to-one loving relationship where we systematically unlearn our privileges (Spivak in Landry and MacLean 1995) so that we 'speak to', not 'of' (Minh-ha 1989), we must not escape the probing and uncomfortable question: Why are academics searching for an ethical relationship with the subaltern in the first place? If they hope to transform, save or protect, as many of them do in one guise or another, they must first debunk '. . . the illusion that, through privileged speech, one is helping to save the wretched of the earth' (Chow 1993: 119).

For my own part, I embarked on this journey because, when I, as a student, teacher and researcher, held up the academic images of South Asian women in Britain, to view myself, my sister, sisters-in-law, nieces, mother and neighbours I found that 'we' all almost slipped from view. Glimpses of recognition could be found in the murky waters of representation, but so much of what I saw was eskewed and one-dimensional. What we find is that the figure of the South Asian woman is sandwiched between the voyeurism of the phantastically exotic and a 'rescue paradigm' (Rajan 1993: 6) underlaid by 'salvational motives' (Chow 1993: 3), which are re-played and reformulated in a myriad of contexts, including the 'revolutionary tourism' and 'celebration of testimony' (Spivak 1993: 284) found in feminism.

While my mother and sister-in-laws or sister, for instance, are rather like the Chinese women who troubled Kristeva by their indifference to what she thought and saw (discussed in Chow 1993: 31) I, probably because I partake in the making of academic space, have found that it is absolutely imperative to my own sense of being to engage with the constructions and postures that hover around me. As the 'native' ethnics enter the academy, the academy is somewhat uncomfortably finding that they are no longer staying in the melodramatic 'frames' that they have come to know them over years of scholarly research (Chow 1993: 28). From the position of a 'native' who resides in the academy, with all the cultural, economic and symbolic capital that I embody (Bourdieu 1992), I am hopefully adding to that disruption – without, I hope, slipping into the delusions of 'self-subalternization' (Chow 1993: 6) or speaking about powerlessness from a position of power without an 'espistemological questioning of how it is that I am speaking' (Probyn 1993: 80). Here I am tracking the problematic nature of the academic task of looking for the Other, not only in terms of the frames that have been used, but also with the objectification entailed in the search for. This is the case for even those current re-framings that have gone beyond the limits of the tradition/ modern dichotomy and are now couched in the idioms of contradiction and hybridity. Though the task of resurrection in the face of erasure is compelling, gaps and silences are also constituitive of the defiled images that seek to replace the dichotomous good/bad, heroine/victim, ethnic/ hybrid images. And anyway, while we embark on that process, as many of the following chapters do, there is also a need to make the academy the object of study without reverting to the insatiable academic desire for testimonies, in their current messy and muffled genres.

Acknowledgements

The strategic interventions of Les Back and Richard Johnson were critical to circumventing the disciplinary regimes – that are awakened by any publishing project which rattles established doctrines – without which this Chapter may not have seen the light of day.

References

Ahmed, L. (1992), *Women and Gender in Islam: Historical Roots of a Modern Discourse*, New Haven, CT and London: Yale University Press.

Alarcon, N. (1989), 'Traddutora, Traditora: A Paradigmatic Figure of Chicano Feminism', *Cultural Critique* 13 (Fall): 86–7.

Bhattacharya, G. (1998), *Tales of Dark Skinned Women*, London: UCL Press.

Bourdieu, P. (1988), *Homo Academicus*, Cambridge: Polity.

—— (1992), *Language and Symbolic Power: The Economy of Linguistic Exchanges*, Cambridge: Polity.

—— (1996), 'Understanding', *Theory, Culture and Society*, 13 (2): 17–37.

Brah, A. and Minhas, R. (1985), 'Structural Racism or Cultural Difference: Schooling for Asian Girls', in G. Weiner (ed.), *Just a Bunch of Girls*, Milton Keynes: Open University Press.

Burton, A. (1994), *Burdens of History: British Feminists, Indian Women and Imperial Culture, 1865–1915*, Chapel Hill, NC: University of North Carolina Press.

Carby, H. (1982), 'White Woman Listen! Black Feminism and the Boundaries of Sisterhood', in CCCS *The Empire Strikes Back: Race and Racism in 70s Britain*, London: Hutchinson.

CCCS (1982), *The Empire Strikes Back: Race and Racism in 70s Britain*, London: Hutchinson.

Chaudhuri, N. and Strobel, M. (eds), (1992), *Western Women and Imperialism: Complicity and Resistance*, Bloomington, IN and Indianapolis, IN: Indiana University Press.

Chow, R. (1993), *Writing Diaspora*, Bloomington, IN and Indianapolis, IN: Indiana University Press.

Clifford, J. and Marcus, G. (eds) (1986), *Writing Culture: The Poetics and Politics of Ethnography*, Berkeley, CA: University of California Press.

De Certeau, M. (2000), 'Writings and Histories', in T. Spargo (ed.), *Reading the Past*, Basingstoke: Palgrave.

Denzin, N. (1997), *Interpretative Ethnography: Ethnographic Practices for the 21st Century*, London: Sage.

DuCille, A. (2001), 'The Occult of True Black Womanhood: Critical Demeanor and Black Feminist Studies', in K. Bhavnani (ed.), *Feminism and Race*, Oxford: Oxford University Press.

Du Gay, P. (ed.), (1997), *Production of Cultures/Cultures of Production*, London: Sage Publications and Open University.

Essed, P. (2000), 'Dilemmas in Leadership: Women of Colour in the Academy', *Ethnic and Racial Studies*, 23, (5): 888–904.

Feminist Review (1984), 'Many Voices, One Chant: Black Feminist Perspectives', Feminist Review, 17.

Grewal, S., Kay, J., Landor, L., Lewis, G. and Parmar, P. (1988), *Charting the Journey: Writings by Black and Third World Women*, London: Sheba.

Hall, S. (1997), 'The Spectacle of the "Other"', in S. Hall, *Representation: Cultural Representations and Signifying Practices*, London: Sage and Open University.

hooks, b. (1991), *Yearning: Race, Gender and Cultural Politics*, London: Turnaround.

Kalra, V. and Hutnyk, J. (1998), 'Brimful of Agitation, Authenticity and Appropriation: Madonna's Asian Kool', *Postcolonial Studies*, 1 (3): 339–56.

Kaplan, C. (1994), 'The Politics of Location as Transnational Feminist Practice', in I. Grewal and C. Kaplan (eds), *Scattered Hegemonies*, London: University of Minnesota Press.

Kellner, D. (1997), 'Critical Theory and Cultural Studies: The Missed Articulation', in J. McGuigan (ed.), *Cultural Methodologies*, pp. 12–41, London: Sage.

Khan, V. S. (1977), 'The Pakistanis: Mirpuri Villagers at Home and in Bradford', in J. L. Watson (ed.), Between Two Cultures: Migrants and Minorities in Britain, Oxford: Blackwell

Landry, D. and MacLean, G. M. (1995), *The Spivak Reader: Selected Works of Gayatri Chakravorty Spivak*, London: Routledge.

Lash S. (1997), *The Culture Industries: Biographies of Cultural Products.* Available at HYPERLINK http://www.goldsmiths.ac.uk/cultural-studies/html/cultural.html http://www.goldsmiths.ac.uk/cultural-studies/html/cultural.html

Lugone, M. (1990), 'Playfullness, 'World'-Travelling, and Loving Perception', in G. Anzaldua (ed.), *Haciendo Caras/Making Face, Making Soul*, San Francisco: Aunt Lute.

Mani, L. (1992), 'Cultural Theory, Colonial Texts: Reading Eyewitness Accounts of Widow Burning', in L. Grossberg, C.Nelson and P. Treicher (eds), *Cultural Studies*, London: Routledge.

—— (1998), *Contentious Traditions: The Debate on Colonial Sati in India*, London: University of California Press.

Mercer, K. (1994), 'Reading Racial Fetishism', in K. Mercer (ed.), Welcome to the Jungle, London: Routledge.

Mills, C. (1997), *The Racial Contract*, New York: Ithaca Press.

—— (1998), 'Post-colonial Feminist Theory', in S. Jackson and J. Jones (eds), *Contemporary Feminist Theories*, Edinburgh: Edinburgh University Press.

Minh-ha, T. T. (1989), *Woman, Native, Other: Writing Post Coloniality and Feminism*, Indianapolis, IN: Indiana University Press.

Mohanty, C. (1988), 'Under Western Eyes: Feminist Scholarship and Colonial Discourses', *Feminist Review* 30: 60–88.

—— (1997), 'Women Workers and Capitalist Scripts: Ideologies of Domination, Common Interests, and the Politics of Solidarity', in J. Alexander and C. T. Mohanty, *Feminist Genealogies, Colonial Legacies, Democratic Futures*, New York: Routledge.

Nagrath, S. and Puwar, N. (2002), '"Stitched Up": Towards an Analysis of Production and Consumption', *Feminist Review*, 71: 95–101

Narayan, U. (1997), *Dislocating Cultures: Identities, Traditions and Third World Feminism*, London: Routledge.

Nelson, N. (ed.) (1981), *African Women in the Development Process*, London: Routledge and Kegan Paul.

Ong, A. (2001), 'Colonialism and Modernity: Feminist Re-Presentations of Women in Non-Western Societies', in Bhavnani (ed.), *Feminism and Race*, Oxford: Oxford University Press.

Parmar, P. (1982), 'Gender, Race and Class: Asian Women in Resistance', in CCCS *The Empire Strikes Back: Race and Racism in 70s Britain*, London: Hutchinson.

Pateman, C. (1988), *The Sexual Contract*, Cambridge: Polity.

Phizacklea, A. (1990), *Unpacking the Fashion Industry*, London: Routledge.

Probyn, E. (1993), *Sexing the Self: Gendered Positions in Cultural Studies*, London: Routledge.

Puwar, N. (2001), 'Problematising Seeing, Hearing & Telling: Reflections on the Research Enterprise', in M. Haralambos (ed.), *Developments in Sociology*, Leeds: Causeway Press.

—— (2002), 'Multi-Cultural Fashion . . . Stirrings of Another Sense of Aesthetics and Memory', *Feminist Review*, 71: 63–87

Rajan, S. R. (1993), *Real & Imagined Women: Gender, Culture and Postcolonialism*, London: Routledge.

Said, E. (1978), Orientalism, New York: Pantheon Books.

—— (1994), *Representations of the Intellectual*, New York: Vintage Books.

Sharma, S., Hutnyk, J. and Sharma, A. (eds) (1996), *Dis-Orienting Rhythms*, London: Sage.

Spivak, G. C. (1988a), 'Can the Subaltern Speak?', in C. Nelson and L. Grossberg, (eds), *Marxism and the Interpretation of Culture*, London: Macmillan.

—— (1988b), *In Other Words: Essays in Cultural Politics*, London: Routledge.

—— (1993), *Outside in the Teaching Machine*, London: Routledge.

Steedman, C. (2000), 'The Watercress Seller', in T. Spargo (ed.), *Reading the Past*, Basingstoke: Palgrave.

Westwood, S. (1984), *All Day Every Day*, London: Pluto Press.

Williams, P. J. (1997), *Seeing a Color-Blind Future: The Paradox of Race*, London: Virago Press.

Young, K., Wolkowitz. C. and McCullagh, R. (eds) (1981), *Of Marriage and the Market: Women's Subordination in International Perspectives*, London: CSE Books.

–3–

Still 'In Progress?' – Methodological Dilemmas, Tensions and Contradictions in Theorizing South Asian Muslim Women[1]

Fauzia Ahmad

Introduction

Why Focus on British South Asian Muslim Women?

Located as we are, within various competing gendered, racialized and regulating discourses such as religion, colonialism and imperialism, representations of South Asian Muslim women in Britain in both media and academic discourses appear, for the most part, to be unsurprisingly 'fixed'. Historical and contemporary encounters continue to embody South Asian Muslim women through cultural and religious frameworks as essentialized oppressed figures of victimhood and despair, but also as sexualized and fetishized 'Others'. Neither representation offer the possibility of empowerment through social or political agency. Within a diasporic context, these embodiments are no less prevalent, as popular fiction, media, documentaries, narratives and academic endeavours reproduce these processes of objectification under the guise of social and political frameworks (such as anti-racism and multiculturalism) that also rely and focus on reductive depictions of religion and culture. Here, I attempt to offer some thoughts on representations of South Asian Muslim women in the British context within academic discourses, and consider some questions of subjectivity that have arisen for me as a researcher from 'within', that is, as a Muslim woman researching other Muslim women.

During the development of my research interests, issues of subjectivity, researcher responsibility and the subsequent location these lines of thought occupy within academia have become my personal foci of concern. While writing about Muslim South Asian women from a position of 'outsider' can accrue a certain hegemonic authority (with obvious acknowledgement of the marginalized position this work occupies within academia), writing as an 'insider' presents rather more complex methodological, ethical and political tensions. These tensions become all the more apparent when the research in question suggests that a critical review of previously accepted discourses that have dominated both academic and State representations of South Asian Muslim women is urgently warranted. Before I go on to describe some of these issues and dilemmas, it may be helpful first to consider the historical and social background that underpins the ways in which South Asian Muslim women in Britain have been and continue to be objectified and situated.

Britain's colonial history is reflected in the numbers and origins of the vast majority of the Muslim communities who migrated from the Indian subcontinent in the 1960s and 1970s, as well as in the smaller number who in one way or another followed the empire in the hundred years preceding that period. In the absence of any formal means for estimating the numbers of Muslims in Britain, surveys have relied on accepted, though crude, assumptions that ethnicity may correspond to religion, particularly with reference to Pakistanis and Bangladeshis.[2] Statistical estimates, backed up by surveys such as the 4th PSI Survey (Modood *et al* 1997) and Labour Force Surveys (cited in Lewis 1994) suggest that the Muslim population in Britain numbers between half a million and two million. Of this latter figure, South Asian Muslims are thought to represent around 80 per cent, with the remaining 20 per cent comprising Arabs, Africans and Mediterranean Muslims (Peach, cited in Lewis 1994). It is also of course a figure that is on the increase amongst the young.

Older research monographs on first-generation South Asian migrants concentrated very much on anthropological accounts of kinship systems and Punjabi *biraderi's*, household structures, female-focused concepts of *izzat* (an over-emphasis I believe), arranged marriages, veils, generational conflicts, the phenomena of being 'caught between two cultures', links with the country of origin and structural disadvantage. 'Insularity' was seen to be a defining feature of migrant families then (and some would add that it still is), as the 'myth of return' seemed, at first, a possibility. This prospect appeared increasingly distant as families began to settle, grow and adapt to life in Britain (Khan 1977; Shaw 1988, 1994; Ballard 1994; Brah 1996; Anwar 1998). Migrant women, far from confirming stereotypes of secluded and 'passive Asian women' played key roles in their contributions towards household economies, the reconstruction of cultural traditions, labour movements and emerging political dialogues (Wilson 1978; Khan 1977; Bhachu 1988; Werbner 1988; Brah 1996).

Some of the newer research on British second- and third-generation diasporic subjects – the daughters and grand-daughters of these early pioneers – stresses issues such as 'identity', hybridity, agency and social change, and seeks to situate subjects as diverse and dynamic politicized individuals within both macro- and micro- contexts. Influenced by contemporary post-structuralist and feminist responses, researchers are further encouraged to engage with questions of subjectivity, power dynamics and self-reflection (Knott and Khokher 1993; Lyon 1995; Brah 1996; Basit 1997; Butler 1999; Dwyer 1999). Nevertheless, despite these developments and acknowledgements towards reflexivity, persistent and deterministic themes and structures such as religion, 'arranged marriages' and the *hijab* and veiling remain central points of focus as far as studies on British South Asian Muslim women are concerned, limiting the scope of discourse on British Asian and Muslim families. By also locating fieldwork in areas of high Asian or Muslim concentration, the search for structure that underpins much ethnographic work sometimes inadvertently 'tribalizes' and essentializes Asian and Muslim families, reducing them to simply being 'objects' of social research.[3] This not only influences the media and wider public opinion, but also, as I shall go on to discuss, Asian or Muslim men and women working within academia who may reproduce such discursive formations. Social class, histories, specific regional and family dynamics so on, are differences that can play a role in the ways in which Islamic practices may, or equally, may not, impact on the lives of women. To ignore these in discussions of religion and gender produces reductive categories.

Numerous stories of relevance either to British Muslims in general or South Asian British Muslims in particular have made the headlines in Britain. These have included debates on 'forced marriages'; teenage runaways and honour killings;[4] domestic violence; the state funding of Muslim schools; and the Anti-Terrorism Act (2001), which spotlighted Muslim groups with alleged terrorist connections in Britain. The summer of 2001 saw young British Asian Muslim men feature heavily in the news, first because of their 'over-exuberance' as Pakistani cricket supporters during the 2001 Natwest Cricket series involving Pakistan, England and Australia, and then as 'disaffected youth' after a wave of summer riots spread across socially and economically deprived towns and cities in the north of England.

Here, working-class tensions were exploited by the far-right British National Party (BNP), particularly in Oldham, after Asian youths attacked a white pensioner. Despite the pensioner's insistence that his attack was not racially motivated, the attack was widely reported as a racist incident, a misconception that was not helped by senior police officials highlighting an increase in Asian upon white crime in recent years whilst failing to draw attention to the corresponding increase in white on Asian attacks. The BNP effectively managed to manipulate such tensions, fuelling suspicions that vital regeneration funds were being prioritized towards 'Asian Muslim' areas at the expense of local white populations. This tactic proved successful for the BNP, who secured approximately 12,000 votes in Oldham during the June 2001 election. What marked the BNP campaign as profoundly significant and sinister was their specific targeting of Asian Muslims, ironically inviting people from black, mixed race, Hindu and Sikh backgrounds to join them against 'Muslim racists'.

Compounded by poor socio-economic prospects and institutionalized racism, and provoked by the activities of far-right groups, waves of discontent and frustration spread across to the towns of Burnley and Bradford. Asian youth clashed with local police over what they perceived as double standards on the part of the police in failing to respond to their concerns of attacks by white racists. That summer witnessed some of the worst street riots the UK had seen in recent decades. These incidents brought to light some painful realities for the local communities concerned, and led to the government's commissioning a number of exploratory reports.[5] Firstly, they drew attention to the pernicious and deep-seated racism that was found to be deeply embedded within public and private British sectors; secondly, they stressed that cultural and religious intolerance, particularly since the Rushdie affair, had played a significant part in reinforcing stereotypes that served to ferment and strengthen social divisions; thirdly, they showed an inherent failure on the part of civic, community and religious 'leaders' to be able to 'connect' and understand the concerns of local youth. In short, anti-racist and multicultural policies, as operationalized in these northern towns, had failed. Younger Asian youth, particularly men, were refusing to follow the paths of their parents in 'accepting' subordination, demanding equality and acceptance, not simply 'tolerance'.[6]

British Muslims were already frustrated with the media's insistent usage of sensationalist terminologies such as 'Islamic terrorists' and Muslim 'fundamentalists' when discussing the Middle East, Kashmir, or the Balkans, for example. Sectarian violence in Northern Ireland has been spared from any such religious tarring, with clashes between Catholics and Protestants referred to as clashes between 'loyalists' and 'nationalists'. The terrible subjugation of women in Afghanistan under the Taliban was yet another source of unease, as increasing numbers of smuggled documentaries and reports depicted the extreme constraints and harsh realities of life under the Talibanist brand of Islam. Some Western commentators including feminists have been all too quick in their generalizing of 'Islamic societies' which have been prepared to present and 'accept' Talibanist Islam as 'pure and true' Islam, with little thought or care for the effects their projected stereotypes have on the women they claim to pity.

Then 11th September 2001 happened. The terrorist attacks on the USA placed Islam and Muslims of every hue in the media and political spotlight. Since 11th September the huge media interest in the British Muslim community and their responses to the atrocities against the United States have spawned a number of experts, analysts and surveys to comment on the Muslim world. While some have genuinely sought to understand Muslim discontent and educate against irrational prejudices and stereotypes, others have focused instead on playing upon fears of 'Islamic terrorism', 'fundamentalism', the 'enemy within' and the 'clash of civilizations'.

Although some level of anti-Muslim sentiment was expected, with police units offering protection to religious buildings, the strength of anti-Muslim hostility from all quarters of society was surprising. Muslim organizations across the UK and elsewhere in the Western world began to hear appalling reports of a swift anti-Muslim backlash. Buildings, mosques, homes, and people were physically and verbally attacked, and became the targets of telephone and email threats. Even non-Muslims, such as Sikhs, were targeted for simply looking 'Arabic' or 'Muslim'. Muslim women, especially visible *hijab*-wearing women, were amongst the most vulnerable victims of indiscriminate physical and verbal assaults. A climate of fear was in the making. Ironically, this heightened sense of religious bigotry, not helped by inflammatory media sound-bites that gave disproportionate amounts of air-time to the vocal minority of younger, extremist, pro-Taliban, male-dominated Muslim political groups in the UK, acted to curtail the very freedom of movement the Taliban had been accused of expropriating from women.

Jihad once again entered the British vernacular, but understood only in military, aggressive terms.[7] The moderate Muslim majority openly condemned the actions and splutterings of their more extreme co-religionists, and continued to criticize the press for giving such groups and individuals the oxygen of publicity they craved; but to little avail. Newspapers and politicians, in turn, demanded that British Muslims prove their loyalty to the State, as age-old suspicions about 'militant Islam' resurfaced. Throughout the campaign, President George Bush, with the support of Prime Minister Tony Blair, has insistently issued the ultimatum

'You're either with us or against us', thus effectively rendering dissent (especially from Muslims) from military action an act of treachery.

The views and experiences of Muslim women have only recently been sought and featured, but often only as victims of the anti-Muslim back-lash, or of 'Islam' and the Taliban, or as objects of curiosity. In the past, 'liberal fundamentalist' feminists such as the journalist Polly Toynbee (a self-confessed 'Islamophobe', 1997) and the acerbic and deliberately provocative columnist Julie Burchill (who once described Islam as 'shit' and *burqas* as 'mobile prisons', 2001), have vented in public their disgust at Islam, describing it as backward, inherently oppressive towards women, militant, uncivilized, intolerant and bloodthirsty. Throughout the Afghan crisis, Muslim women, veils and *burqas* (often perceived as one and the same) and the subjugation of women in Afghanistan have featured heavily in an increasing number of accounts *about* Muslim women. Even the British Prime Minister's wife, Cherie Blair, following the lead of George Bush's wife Laura, spoke of the *burqa* as a 'symbol of women's oppression'. She thus managed effectively (though perhaps inadvertently) to distance herself from British Muslim women's groups, as she failed to appreciate the inherently reductionist discourse of '*burqa* on – oppression, *burqa* off – liberation' she stumbled into (Dejevsky 2001).

Some journalists and writers have sought to understand what 'being a modern British Muslim woman' is about – how issues such as institutional discrimination and racism impinge on Muslim women's everyday lives, their relationships with their families, their reactions and views on the crisis outlined above and the resultant call to political activism felt by some (cf. Bunting 2001; Chrisafis 2001). They have also recognized that we too are professional, independent, articulate, powerful and empowered; all qualities that Western women value and share. There is now a genuine interest in Islam, and many Muslim women are emerging as successful, if sometimes reluctant, ambassadors for their faith, challenging stereotypes and, in many cases, being far more successful in promoting positive inter-faith relations than men.

Before 11th September, the 'victimhood' of Muslim women was already embedded in foreign and domestic policies through various measures, from the granting of asylum to women fleeing gender-related persecution, particularly from Muslim countries, to the more publicized measures the government took to tackle the controversial issue of 'forced marriages'. This issue was largely ignored by the government until the Labour MP for Keighley (in the north of England), Mrs Ann Cryer, decided to intervene. A Commission to investigate 'forced marriages' was established that set about consulting with various cultural and religious groups. When she spoke out in the House of Commons against the 'treatment of Asian Muslim women by their families' (House of Commons, 1999), her intervention, though timely, was controversial for a number of reasons. Although efforts were made by the Government to stress that forced marriages were not solely a 'Muslim problem' her comments ensured that British Muslims were once again negatively spotlighted. Ann Cryer herself continued to criticize her local Asian Muslim community when, after the riots of 2001, she accused Asian Muslim families who arranged marriages in Pakistan or Bangladesh of 'importing poverty', and urged the Home Secretary to consider introducing stringent immigration policies to ensure that only English-speaking spouses were given entry to the UK. She went on to further suggest that British Asian Muslim families should 'select partners for their children from the sort of home-grown variety of Muslim Asians' (Evening Standard, 2001).

Without digressing into the details of the work of the Commission, Muslim women's groups such as *An-Nisa* and the *Muslim Women's Helpline*, who were consulted by the Commission, have felt some unease about the ways in which this debate has been handled, for a variety of reasons. Their previous work on this issue had been disregarded until Ann Cryer's intervention created the impression that Muslim women's groups had been ignoring the issue, when they had not. Cryer herself, as a white woman, assumed a Western feminist position of 'protector' of 'silent and suffering' South Asian Muslim women that further contributed to the already sensationalized and homogenized media portrayal of Muslim communities. And while the issue of forced marriage is important and urgent, continuing to feature in Home Office and Foreign and Commonwealth Office agendas, other concerns have been ignored, such as the failure of social policies to recognize the distinct faith needs of minority communities in social welfare and family law (Shah-Kazemi 2001). Grassroots organizations have also been concerned that the government used the forced marriage debate as a means to curb further immigration from the Indian subcontinent into Britain.

When set alongside sociological findings that situate British Muslims of Pakistani and Bangladeshi origin as amongst some of the most socially disadvantaged groups, described as a 'new under-class', Muslim communities are repeatedly framed within a fixed set of competing reductive problematizing discourses. Against this backdrop of media hype, then, to what extent are academic institutions and the resultant discourses reflecting popular mis-conceptualizations and fascinations? How are those of us working from 'within' influenced by such competing discourses and in what ways? What parts do we play in the reproduction of collusion in or reaction to debates? Are we consumers of knowledge or producers of it? Where are the epistemological points of connection and disconnection? How do we know if we are asking the 'right' questions?

Methodological Issues, Dilemmas, Tensions

In my research on British South Asian Muslim women in higher education and professional employment and on the representation and involvement of British Muslim women in social welfare and socio-legal systems, a number of key themes have emerged. These include diversity of expression, experiences, continuity and discontinuity, motivations, mobilizations, agency and shifting subjectivities, all highlighting the importance of contextualizing personal experiences within local historical and socio-political arenas that structure women's lives. They also point towards an urgent need to re-evaluate many prevalent discourses used to influence social policy concerns of minority diasporic women.

In those contested and de-centred spaces where social and psycho-analytic subjectivities reside and oscillate between conscious and unconscious articulations, whilst intersecting with structural forces at critical junctures, our need to acknowledge our own points of 'un-location' becomes increasingly urgent. Issues of representation, history and retrospection, orientation, authenticity, power, and personal and academic responsibility, therefore, become inextricably and fundamentally intertwined when engaging with research and discourses that situate the researcher as potentially, the researched too.

From a research perspective then, a number of overlapping methodological concerns and questions need addressing. I hope to elaborate on some of these below; they are issues that I have continued to struggle with. The following points are not meant to be an exhaustive or complete methodological 'checklist', nor are they entirely 'original'. They do however, illustrate issues that can arise in the relationships between the researcher, the researched and the institutions and frameworks 'Othered' women have to work within.

Definitional Concerns: 'Whose Feminism'?

Western feminism, as a theoretical project, has some serious theoretical shortcomings where non-Western women are concerned. Many of these have been addressed by 'black feminists', who launched a searing critique of the hegemonic and Eurocentric project of Western feminism (cf. Brah

1996; Mirza 1997), accusing Western women of reproducing male-biased regulating and racist discourses that pathologized black women and their families. This backlash proved to be a powerful voice that (alongside the rejection of grand narratives characteristic of post-modernism) has since facilitated debates around difference and diversity, although the juxta-positions between gender and ethnicity are still not always considered.

Primary questions, however, around definitions of 'feminism' are still often lacking from contemporary discourses; the rupture with Western feminist thought by black feminists, while helpful and necessary, is still predominantly located within a secular Western ideological framework – one that when contextualized in terms of gender relations, stresses the attainment of equality between the sexes in both public and private spheres. This concept is significantly different to Islamically rooted notions of gender relations, though these, in practice, are subject to much cultural variation and differing interpretations. Broadly, Islamically rooted notions favour instead a recognition and embracing of sexual difference: hence the model of 'different but equal'.

The Algerian-born sociologist Marnia Lazreg questions the very nature of the Western 'feminist project', criticizing it as 'inherently 'Western gynocentric' (1988: 96) in that it exerts a 'power of interpretation' over 'different' or 'other' women that ultimately gives status and credibility to academic feminists. It is this hegemonic authority, the privileging of one (Western) social standard over another (non-Western) that, she argues, has resulted in the failure of the Western feminist project as an emancipatory venture. She criticizes current notions of 'difference' (based in decon-struction and discourse analysis) as leading to reductionism and essen-tialism that prevent the acknowledgement of other forms or 'modes of being different' (1988: 97), and suggests that the issue of 'intersub-jectivity' and shared experiences is lost when this occurs. This, she believes, is necessary in order to acknowledge the lives of 'Othered' women as meaningful and coherent and not overwhelmingly rooted in negativity/sadness.

Lazreg argues that intersubjectivity within the research process should facilitate attributing agency to 'other' women and respecting their right to express their lives through their own constructs, while recognizing that *their* definitions of certain constructs both exist as their *own* and, at the same time, are subject to different definitions, without needing definition or validation from the Western researcher or feminist.

Categories such as 'Muslim woman' have, as a result of the essential-izing of difference, become 'erased' and abstracted. Katherine Bullock (2002) in a recent and detailed analysis of colonial and feminist interpretations and writings on Muslim women and veils, argues that Western assessments of the veil as inherently oppressive are based on 'liberal' understandings of equality that exclude alternative definitions and serve Western political interests. Lazreg suggests a phenomenological approach to the study of women's lived experiences as a means of diffusing boundaries between categories and promoting an agenda that takes its cues from those it proposes to study, not those with the defining authority. Citing also the use of certain 'leading questions' that are more reflective of Western feminists' attitudes and pre-conceptions towards the 'Oriental object', Lazreg goes on to ask a vital question: 'How then, can an Algerian woman write about women in Algeria when her space has already been defined, her history dissolved, her subjects objectified, her language chosen for her? How can she speak without saying the same things?' (Lazreg 1988: 95).

If Orientalism is one defining framework used to shape discourses on Muslim women, its antithesis is the highly politicized Islamist movement. Like Orientalism, this ideological construct also seeks authority over women's lives and can limit women's own capacities for self-definition. However, unlike Orientalist narratives, Islamist movements (typically dominated by male authority over women) often attract Muslim women seeking empowerment through Islam, rejecting discriminatory practices legitimated (by male interpretations) in the name of religion (S. Khan 1998; Salih 2001). The problem though, with pitting Orientalism against a reactionary framework such as 'Islamism' is that there is little room for women veering at the margins of the Islamist movement – those who identify as Muslim, sometimes strongly so, but believe some Islamist interpretations and practices to be too prescriptive, as in the case, for example, of devout Muslim women who choose not to wear the *hijab*. I'll return to the issue of defining frameworks later.

Ultimately, Lazreg's frustrations are a reflection of the unease she feels at confronting both manifest forms of racist and Islamophobic sentiments and the latent forms that parade under the guise of the secular liberalism enthusiastically advocated by liberal intelligentsias. Despite historical differences, many of these observations also parallel the ways in which South Asian women and South Asian Muslim women are objectified.

The Limits of Black Feminism

Although there are a large number of texts currently available on Muslim women and empowerment struggles, they mostly focus on the situation of women in the Middle East, where the political, social and economic conditions are noticeably different to those in the West (Moghissi 1999). As I discussed in the section above, 'feminism' is not an undisputed category; for some Muslim women, 'female emancipation' is rooted in an ideological religious framework that is inherently and significantly different in its nature and aims from Western feminist projects. This fundamental distinction marks the crucial point of divergence between those who mobilize on the basis of ethnicity, race or gender and those who mobilize on the basis of religion, as many Muslim women's groups both in the UK and elsewhere prefer to do.

Black feminist writings (whilst acknowledging points of convergence and divergence amongst women) have also failed to acknowledge Western feminism's authoritative assault on the lives of Muslim women. Indeed, in many instances, black feminist perspectives, either through remaining largely silent on Orientalist constructions of women or through similar stereotyped perceptions, also collude in denying Muslim women the agency and voice to define their own spaces. On the basis of misinformed texts and sensationalist academic and journalistic writings, both white and black feminists project preconceived attitudes towards Islam and Muslim women that are just as damaging as sexism and racism. Rarely do black and white feminists, when highlighting the oppression of Muslim women in Muslim countries, as in the case of Talibanist Afghanistan, contextualize their articles, point out that the oppression of women is not mandated by the Qur'an, stress the heterogeneity of Muslim cultures and their dynamic nature, or make references to the rights Muslim women are entitled to – rights that women in the West waited centuries for and, in some cases, are still struggling to attain. Religious identities, it seems, are not considered as suitable vehicles for empowerment and debate within Western discourses.

In surveying the development of black women's organizations in the UK, Julia Sudbury appears to interpret Muslim women's mobilizations as an 'unwillingness to choose' between religion and gender (1998: 191). Though some black feminists acknowledge the limitations of an all-encompassing 'black' feminist project that speaks for all minority women, recognizing for instance that the experiences of women who migrated to Britain from South Asia are further differentiated on the basis of religion, culture, language and national origins, they often do not recognize the ways religion or faith can also empower (Muslim) women (Sudbury 2001; Young 2001).[8] An underlying scepticism remains. White Muslim women – including those who have converted to Islam – are also largely ignored in Western feminist thought, and, in some instances, have been described as 'traitors' to their sex (Berrington 1993). Their welfare needs, as women of faith, are not normally considered in social welfare systems that often categorize on the basis of race and ethnicity (Shah-Kazemi, 2001).

Despite the existence of excellent black feminist scholarship and activity, the vast majority (not all) of these writers and activists ignore 'Muslim women' or situate them within pathologized, victim-focused discourses. Even outstanding texts, such as *Black British Feminism* (Mirza 1997), that stress both the importance of political solidarity amongst women in the face of racism and also the fractures that exist within the umbrella term of 'black' (Ang-Lygate 1997), are notably silent on the struggles and successes of British Muslim women. Where Muslim women are mentioned, it is within the context of 'fundamentalism' – a term that recurs in popular and academic discourse, but exists without coherent definition (cf. Patel 1997) in pejorative reference, mostly towards Muslims.[9]

At a personal level, an assertion of a Muslim identity has, on occasions, elicited some interesting responses from both academic colleagues and other associates. Since I do not wear the *hijab* myself, first impressions will classify me as an Asian woman; but what follows is generally an assumption that my very presence within an elitist institution such as a university signals secularization and an assimilation of Western ideals. My religious sensitivities manifest themselves in other ways, such as a rejection of alcohol or of non-*halal* meat. In response to my refusal, for instance, of a 'proper' drink, a typical reaction would be to request further confirmation before the issue of 'why' enters the conversation. Once the religious basis is established, some academic colleagues have commented, 'I didn't realize you were a *proper* Muslim!' The issue, of course, is not my actual abstention from a social drink; it is the cited reason behind it. Were I to adopt a secular identity as an 'Asian woman' or a 'black woman', some interactions would almost certainly be more accommodating.

The strength of a term such as 'black' as an indicator of identity and as a political signifier of group solidarity was made apparent to me in my first formal research post in an academic social work department many years ago; and this, in the process, also highlighted to me how weak in comparison the term 'Asian' was and how labels have an all-assuming power to define and objectify, masking real and potential tensions that exist within the labelled group. An acceptance of being 'black' does not guarantee immunity from harbouring deeply ingrained preconceptions and suspicions of other 'black' people based on ignorance, objectification and 'Othering'.

While I was working as a research assistant to two women who described themselves as 'black feminists', we convened a conference on black student experiences in social work. A participant at a plenary session asked about the rise of Islamophobia in social services. Following a long uncomfortable silence, one of my senior colleagues asked the participant to explain what 'Islamophobia' was. He responded by saying that if she did not know what 'Islamophobia' was, she had no business sitting on a panel as an 'expert' on racism. My colleagues wanted to dismiss his question as irrelevant, and later described the participant who posed the question as a 'troublemaker'. Their response draws attention to two main issues: one is the lack of significance attributed to faith and spirituality issues in mainstream social work as a result of secular anti-racist and superficial multicultural policies; the other is the personal unease and ignorance my former colleagues exhibited to the mere question of 'Islamophobia' and their own rejection of this form of discrimination as even germane to the discussion.

More recently, I presented a paper at a conference organized by a social services department to mark International Women's Week on 'forced marriages'. I was asked to give a 'Muslim' perspective, which simply involved quoting a few Islamic laws stating a woman's right to choose her marriage partner (which is explicitly stated) and then proceeded to highlight some other rights women have within Islam. Sharing the platform was an Asian woman presenting a paper, based on anecdotal evidence, of a link between forced marriages and self-harm. She presented herself as a 'black feminist' and applauded my summary of women's rights (within Islam) until a question on the rules governing marriage to people from other religions was posed. When I stated that Muslim women were only permitted to marry Muslim men, while Muslim men were permitted to marry 'women of the book', that is, Jewish or Christian women, she openly sniggered and told me that I had 'ruined' an otherwise eloquent paper.

My purpose in citing these personal examples is not simply to draw attention to the ignorance of particular colleagues or associates, but to highlight how black feminism and some who identify as black feminists can also contribute to the 'Othering' process when talking *about* Muslim women. By situating Muslim women outside normative discourses, they thereby fail to credit Muslim women with the capacity of speaking independently and overlook the centrality certain frames of reference hold, *even* if they are perceived by them to be regulative and patriarchal. Other concepts of 'feminism', or perhaps more appropriately, 'female empowerment', such as 'Islamic feminism', are far more complex than feminists from a 'Western' perspective (black or white) seem to credit. Empowerment, many Muslim women would argue, is not simply a matter of making a 'choice' between religion and gender; for them it hinges on the accept-ance of a fundamentally and politically distinct ideology of gender relations. It is one that enables Muslim women both to offer critiques of oppressive practices and 'patriarchal relations' within their own communi-ties and also simultaneously to maintain a positive religious identity *as Muslim women* (but see Brah 1996).

Views from 'Within'

There is something of a general tentativeness associated with researchers 'doing research on their own communities'. We have to define and ques-tion whether we are, or want to be, identified as 'part of the community' – a term that in itself implies spatial diffuseness. Should we then wish to locate ourselves as active subjects within 'the community'? However, how we view and rate our own work and that of others who also choose to define themselves as part of 'the community' is an issue that is often overlooked.

As an 'insider', for instance, there may be concerns that our 'insider knowledge' is not 'good enough knowledge'. This may well be reflective of both the nominal status we occupy within academia and the legacy of anthropological traditions that defined us as research objects,[10] who at their best can only be social documentators. As researchers, this can impact on the kind of research questions we want to focus on, the support we receive from those in positions of influence, the perceptions those in our local communities or social networks have of academia and the way they view our research and our own power to define ourselves. As we are all aware, the focus of so much of academic activity is not about dissemin-ation to the communities we study; our points of reference and profes-sional validation are sought from our academic colleagues. When we do embark on research that does situate us as 'part of the community', whether we define ourselves as occupying this position or not, and espe-cially if our work presents challenges to accepted 'ways of thinking', a number of reactions can ensue. Our work is dismissed as 'too involved', 'defensive' or 'apologetic', or anecdotal and incidental. Our knowledge becomes marked. For instance, the Muslim journalist Faisal Bodi was recently told by the BBC that he had to add a 'qualifier' to all his reports stating his 'bias as a Muslim reporter' (Bodi 2001). Personal communi-cation with a Muslim documentary film-maker working in the mainstream confirms the lack of confidence the liberal white intelligentsia hold about our abilities to remain 'neutral' and to produce noteworthy work without supervision.[11] The irony is clear – while 'we' make for good objects of social research and scrutiny, once we claim our piece of the academic terrain, our knowledge ceases to be viewed as properly 'academic'.

Issues of Social Responsibility

Another hurdle (or limiting framework) in need of addressing is accusations that we may have 'sold out', either because we are successful or because we have publicized 'our communities' 'dirty linen'. While we recognize our own minority positions within academia, we also need to be aware of our responsibilities and the political power we wield as women representatives of 'South Asianness' (or, in the case of this chapter, 'British South Asian Muslimness') within the academy, whether we want to be recognized for this or not, and the reverberations this academic fallout has for our personal relationships and locations within our families, neighbourhoods and 'communities' – mythical or other. Research on sensitive issues such as domestic violence and forced marriage provide notable examples where such difficulties arise. Our own aspirations and our motives for delving into sensitive areas of research are also then brought into question.

The Application of Western Concepts to Non-Western Groups

Marnia Lazreg (1988) and Chandra Talpade Mohanty (1988) draw our attention to the broad influence of Western ideologies that not only construct fixed representations of the non-Western world, but also wield authority over third world women who similarly utilize these ideological tools themselves when writing about their own communities. This can be exemplified when South Asian Muslim women are problematized and when the tools of Western objectification are implemented by South Asian or Muslim women themselves. 'Patriarchy theory' in particular is a good example of a 'grand' and over-arching Western feminist concept that is often discussed in relation to non-Western families. In the diasporic space South Asian families occupy in the UK the application of this theory raises some important questions.

Bhopal's work on South Asian women in East London, which draws heavily on Sylvia Walby's theories of patriarchy, and has usefully highlighted a process of rapid social change and self-empowerment amongst

younger South Asian women through the appropriation of higher qualifications and professional employment – in itself a challenge to stereotypes
of South Asian women. However, her interpretation of the significance of
links between, say, higher education and lifestyle choices, particularly in
relation to marriage, can be debated. For instance, her general application
of patriarchy theory as a framework would imply that *all* South Asian
family structures and gender relationships are inherently oppressive, and
suggests that individual 'agency' can only be exercised once the subject
has consciously dissented from the familial and cultural group. By re-
introducing the polarized dichotomy between 'traditional women' – those
possessing few or no qualifications – and 'single, independent women',
seen as 'deviant women' (1999: 129) who benefited from 'a high level of
education' (1999: 132), Bhopal's analysis would indicate that to be
'successful' South Asian women have little option but to 'turn their backs
on their religion and culture' (Bhopal 1997a, b, 1998).

Apart from masking the diversity of experiences and differences within
South Asian communities in respect of practices and beliefs centred
around marriage and failing to situate her work within a wider social
context (for example, by referring to social class differences and racism),
the binaries alluded to above bear little resemblance to the differing forms
of agency exhibited by South Asian women in other research studies,
including my own (Ahmad 2001), and obscure the potential for other,
alternative avenues of expression. They ignore the fluidity and diversity
of male:female relationships, which is regrettable, since the positive aspect
of Bhopal's thesis, namely, its emphasis on the impact of higher education
as a tool for empowerment, has become secondary to its interpretation.

My aim in voicing my brief critique of Bhopal's perspective is not just
to emphasize how restrictive regulative discourses such as 'patriarchy' in
post-modern contexts are, but specifically to raise concerns over the ways
in which Western structural theories, when operationalized to describe
non-Western societies, can act to pathologize these groups and silence
forms of agency and difference that do not conform. To be 'educated' and
South Asian, it seems, is to be 'Westernized', 'modern' and secular; to be
'traditional' is to be 'uneducated' and backward. These binaries are not
just restricted to everyday stereotypes employed by the media as part of
their ongoing selective and Orientalist discourse, but are deeply ingrained
misconceptions that extend into the academic working environment. In
the body of work cited above, the very fact that extreme binaries are
presented, that cultural diversity not just within South Asian ethnic groups
but within individual families is not accounted for, and that ultimately, the
only route to achieving success is for women to 'turn their backs on their

religion and culture' is a product of a Western hegemonic discourse that requires an urgent response.

Interrogating Representations

'Agency' in the context described above can become a concept dependent upon cultural 'assimilation'. Gayatri Spivak (1999) questioned why women of South Asian origin were still subjected to only two kinds of 'validating agency' – loosely referring to the 'traditional–modern' dichotomy. If neither form of validating agency were accepted by a South Asian woman, she would be 'without validation' – in a sense, 'subaltern'. In the contemporary moment, as researchers exploring South Asian women's *identifications,* especially if we are South Asian in origin ourselves, we may want to vocally to reject these limiting dichotomies as impractical. Where, after all, would those of us who exhibit and embrace both 'traditional' and 'modern' traits and who acknowledge our marginalities, differences and commonalities within the social structures we are a part of, locate *ourselves*?

In my research with young Muslim South Asian women in higher education, I have engaged with Muslim women who stress visible difference and religious affiliation by wearing the *hijab*, and others who display more secular beliefs and practices (and one with a strong leaning towards Christianity), through to one young *salwaar kameez*-wearing student who was an unmarried mother to a half-Jamaican child, but at the time of the interview living with her white partner. All these women volunteered themselves for interview as 'Muslim women' (of South Asian origin), yet we can already see that the political aspects to both self-affirmation and structural positioning with respect to a certain set of terminologies can be loaded with other complexities. What are the differences between a 'British South Asian Muslim woman' and a 'British South Asian *practising* Muslim woman'? How do I begin to address and discuss the similarities and diversity of educational experiences for South Asian Muslim women with vastly differing practices and levels of religious belief without falling into the trap of reductionism? Here, it might be helpful to consider the suggestions of Shahnaz Khan (1998) whose work on Muslim women in Canada draws heavily on the work of cultural theorists such as Hall (1992), Gilroy (1992), Spivak (1999) and especially Homi Bhabha, with his notion of hybridised subjectivity in the third space. Khan advocates problematizing the term 'muslim', reminding us of the power the term 'Muslim' holds in our imaginations, and asserts that this is 'in an attempt to recognise the fluidity of cultural expressions, particularly those within diasporic communities' (1998: 465).

Alternative Spaces?

Perhaps much of my unease about the texts that are published thus far stems from the fact that 'we' as South Asian women are still developing a discourse, and that the theoretical tools that are available to us have yet to be integrated into the fieldwork produced. Articulations about say, racism, sexism, religion, class and sexuality in both the public and private domains still fail to locate themselves as dynamic moments in regional and temporal time. A critical engagement with methodology that links local and globalizing forces still appears to be confined and compounded by a number of 'stumbling-blocks' that have yet to be resolved. 'We' remain 'in progress' as a thesis, and are still arguing against generational accounts, or against geographically specific locations that claim representational licence. Deeper, psychic manifestations of 'culture' are denied any further extensive exploration of the relationships between and within macro and micro contexts. In short, the research that continues to identify 'us' in the wider, public domain is either limited by essentialism, or limited in the linking of theory with fieldwork, with both arguing for the 'authenticity' of their accounts.

Notes

1. The paper on which this chapter is based was originally presented as, 'Articulating The Void – Methodological Dilemmas in Theorizing South Asian Women' at *Theoretical Considerations on Gender & the South Asian Diaspora*, a seminar organized by Nirmal Puwar at the Department of Sociology, University of Leicester, June 1999.
2. As a result of persistent lobbying by Muslim organizations such as the *Muslim Council of Britain* for the inclusion of a voluntary question on religious affiliation, the 2001 Census may provide more reliable figures as to the size of Britain's faith communities. However, this data was not available at the time of writing.
3. For recent examples, see Bradby (1999), Butler (1999), and Jacobsen on young Pakistani British Muslims in Waltham Forest, east London

(1998). The latter is an informative study that seeks to explore the 'survival of religious tradition' (p. 1), namely Islam in Britain. Religion is enunciated as a product of various boundary processes (ethnic, social and parental), and gender, class and racism were treated as background features. However, this framework led to the researcher's making a number of assumptions on behalf of her respondents, *'my aim has been to understand what I have deemed to be the significant role played by religion in the lives of my young British Pakistani respondents'* (p. 121). My concern here is that despite academic postmodernist inspired accounts of localized narratives, pluralized identities and discourses of agency, for example, the prevalence of reductive categories persists in public discourses, particularly within the media, but also, more disturbingly, within academia. At an institutional level these are manifested through a determination of research agendas; but they also influence personal relationships.

4. The case of Shakeela Naz, the mother who murdered her daughter, Rukhsana, for an illicit affair from which she became pregnant (Jason Burke, *Observer*, Sunday 8 October 2000).

5. The Ouseley Report, 'Community Pride, Not Prejudice' (2001), was commissioned prior to the riots but was launched just after the riots in Bradford. It stressed the issue of citizenship education and described Bradford as a town exhibiting 'virtual apartheid' along racial and religious lines (though the report itself erred in failing to distinguish between 'Muslim' schools and schools with a majority of Asian Muslim students).

6. Young Asian Muslim male disaffection was characterized in a report submitted to the above commission with the cringe-worthy title of, *'Between Lord Ahmed and Ali G: Which future for British Muslims?'* (Lewis 2001).

7. *Jihad* in its fullest meaning means 'struggle', and is more often applied to individuals in their own internal struggles to achieve moral and spiritual well-being through prayer and devotion to God.

8. Yuval-Davis implies that those who actively mobilize and seek empowerment as Muslim women are 'using popular religious traditions' (1997: 123) in order to achieve rights that would not accrue to them otherwise.

9. Anthias and Yuval-Davis (1992) maintain that British multicultural policies, with their emphasis on cultural differences, have, especially in the wake of the Rushdie affair, promoted a rise in Muslim 'fundamentalism' and militancy that have had detrimental effects on women.

10. Academia is not immune from a sense of its own cultural superiority. A disturbing discourse exists that centres around 'these people' without the simultaneous realization that 'these people' are in fact, colleagues, albeit junior. It is extremely uncomfortable to sit in a conference, as I myself and others have done, and hear senior colleagues debate in this way.
11. Many Muslim organizations and Muslim individuals working within the media or known as specialists on British Muslim communities were, during the 11th September crisis, frequently called upon by Western journalists as having assumed 'sources' of knowledge as to the whereabouts of alleged terror cells and terrorist suspects! This raises some serious issues about media responsibility and highlights how ill-equipped the Western media have been in dealing with Muslim communities and Muslims in general.

Acknowledgements

A huge note of thanks to the editors for their support and patience and advice, and especially Nirmal Puwar for initially creating the original space for dialogue where these themes were first aired.

References

Ahmad, F. (2001), 'Modern Traditions? British Muslim Women and Academic Achievement', *Gender and Education*, 13 (2): 137–52.

Ang-Lygate, M. (1997), 'Charting the Spaces of (Un)location: On Theorizing Diaspora', in H. S. Mirza (ed.), *'Black British Feminism, A Reader'*, Routledge: London.

Anthias, F. and Yuval-Davis, N. (1992), *Racialised Boundaries, Race, Nation, Gender, Colour and Class and the Anti-Racist Struggle*, Routledge: London.

Anwar, M. (1998), *Between Cultures, Continuity and Change in the Lives of Young Asians,* London: Routledge.

Ballard, R. (ed.) (1994), *Desh Pardesh, The South Asian Presence in Britain,* London: Hurst & Company.

Basit, T. (1997), *Eastern Values; Western Milieu: Identities and Aspirations of Adolescent British Muslim Girls,* Aldershot: Ashgate.

Berrington, L (1993), 'Islam Sheds Its Image As Purely Eastern Religion', *The Times,* 9–10 November.

Bhachu, P. (1988), 'Apni Marzi Kardi', in S. Westwood and P. Bhachu (eds), *Enterprising Women, Ethnicity, Economy and Gender Relations,* London: Routledge.

Bhopal, K. (1997a), 'South Asian Women Within Households: Dowries, Degradation and Despair', *Women's Studies International Forum,* 20: 483–92.

—— (1997b), *Gender, 'Race' and Patriarchy, A Study of South Asian Women,* Aldershot: Ashgate.

—— (1998), 'How Gender and Ethnicity Intersect: The Significance of Education, Employment and Marital Status', *Sociological Research Online,* 3 (3): 1–16.

—— (1999), 'South Asian Women and Arranged Marriages in East London', in R. Barot, H. Bradley and S. Fenton (eds), *Ethnicity, Gender and Social Change,* Basingstoke: Macmillan.

Bodi, F. (2001), 'Why I Was Banned by the BBC', *The Guardian,* 21 May.

Bradby, H. (1999), 'Negotiating Marriage: Young Punjabi Women's Assessment of their Individual and Family Interests', in R. Barot, H. Bradley, and S. Fenton (eds), *Ethnicity, Gender and Social Change,* Basingstoke: Macmillan.

Brah, A. (1996), *Cartographies of Diaspora,* Routledge: London.

Bullock, K. (2002), *Rethinking Muslim Women and the Veil,* London: IIT.

Bunting, M. (2001), 'Can Islam Liberate Women?', *The Guardian,* 8 December.

Burchill, J. (2001), 'Some People Will Believe Anything', *The Guardian,* 18 August.

Burke, J. (2000), 'Love, Honour and Obey – Or Die', *The Observer,* 8 October.

Butler, C. (1999), 'Cultural Diversity and Religious Conformity: Dimensions of Social Change among Second-Generation Muslim Women', in R. Barot, H. Bradley and S. Fenton (eds), *Ethnicity, Gender and Social Change,* Basingstoke: Macmillan.

Chrisafis, A. (2001), 'Under Siege', *The Guardian,* 8 December.

Dejevsky, M. (2001), 'Lifting the Veil Does Not Liberate Women', *The Guardian,* 20 November.

Dwyer, C. (1999), 'Veiled Meanings: British Muslim Women and the Negotiation of Differences', *Gender, Place and Culture* 6 (1): 5–26.

Evening Standard (2001), 'Race Row MP Vows To Speak Out', Associated Press, 13 July.

Gilroy, P. (1992), 'The End of Anti-Racism', in J. Donald and A. Rattansi (eds), *'Race', Culture and Difference,* London: Sage.

Hall, S. (1992), 'New Ethnicities', in J. Donald and A. Rattansi (eds), *'Race', Culture and Difference*, London: Sage.

House of Commons (1999), *Hansard*, 10 February, Columns 256–9.

Jacobsen, J. (1998), *Islam in Transition. Religion and Identity Among British Pakistani Youth*, London: Routledge.

Khan, S. (1998), 'Muslim Women: Negotiations in the Third Space', *Signs: Journal of Women and Culture in Society,* 23 (2): 463–94.

Khan, V. S. (1977), 'The Pakistanis: Mirpuri Villagers at Home and in Bradford', in J. L. Watson (ed.), *Between Two Cultures: Migrants and Minorities in Britain,* Oxford: Blackwell.

Knott, K. and Khokher, S. (1993), 'Religious and Ethnic Identity Among Young Muslim Women in Bradford', *New Community*, 19 (4): 593–610.

Lazreg, M. (1988), 'Feminism and Difference: The Perils of Writing as a Woman on Women in Algeria', *Feminist Studies,* 14 (Spring): 81–107.

Lewis, P. (1994), *Islamic Britain: Religion, Politics and Identity among British Muslims,* London: I. B. Tauris & Co.

—— (2001) *Between Lord Ahmed and Ali G: Which future for British Muslims?* Report submitted to the Bradford Race Review chaired by Lord Herman Ouseley.

Lyon, W. (1995), 'Islam and Islamic Women in Britain', *Women: A Cultural Review*, 6 (1): 46–56.

Mirza, H. S. (ed.) (1997), *Black British Feminism, A Reader,* London: Routledge.

Modood, T., Berthoud, R., Lakey, J., Nazroo, J., Smith, P., Virdee, S. and Beishon, S. (1997), *Ethnic Minorities in Britain: Diversity and Disadvantage*, London: Policy Studies Institute.

Moghissi, H. (1999), *Feminism and Islamic Fundamentalism, The Limits of Postmodern Analysis*, London: Zed Books.

Mohanty, C. T. (1988), 'Under Western Eyes: Feminist Scholarship and Colonial Discourse', *Feminist Review*, 30 (Autumn): 65–88.

Patel, P. (1997), 'Third Wave Feminism and Black Women's Activism', in H. S. Mirza (ed.), *Black British Feminism, A Reader*, London: Routledge.

Salih, R. (2001), 'Confronting Modernities, Muslim Women in Italy', *International Institute for the Study of Islam in the Modern World Newsletter*, 7:1

Shah-Kazemi, S. N. (2001), *Untying The Knot: Muslim Women, Divorce and the Shariah,* London: Published with the support of the Nuffield Foundation.

Shaw, A. (1988), *A Pakistani Community in Britain*, Oxford: Blackwell.

—— (1994), 'The Pakistani Community in Oxford', in R. Ballard (ed.),

Desh Pardesh: The South Asian Presence in Britain, London: Hurst & Company.

Spivak, G. C. (1999), 'A Critique of Post Colonial Reason', Speech given at Goldsmiths College, London University, May 1999.

Sudbury, J. (1998), *'Other Kinds of Dreams': Black Women's Organisations and the Politics of Transformation*, London: Routledge.

——— (2001), '(Re)constructing Multiracial Blackness: Women's Activism, Difference and Collective Identity in Britain', *Ethnic and Racial Studies*, 24 (1): 22–49.

Toynbee, P. (1997), 'Why I am an Islamophobe', *The Independent*, November 1997.

Werbner, P. (1988), 'Taking and Giving: Working Women and Female Bonds in a Pakistani Immigrant Neighbourhood', in S. Westwood and P. Bhachu (eds), *Enterprising Women, Ethnicity, Economy and Gender Relations,* London: Routledge.

Wilson, A. (1978), *Finding a Voice – Asian Women in Britain*, London: Virago Press.

Young, L. (2001), 'What Is Black British Feminism?', *Women: A Cultural Review*, 11 (1/2): 45–60.

Yuval-Davis, N. (1997), *Gender and Nation*, London: Sage.

– 4 –

Fashioning the South Asian Diaspora: Production and Consumption Tales
Parvati Raghuram

Existing paradigms for understanding cultures and economies both provide limited understandings of the economic agency of South Asian women. In this chapter I use the example of the role being played by one Asian woman entrepreneur in serving an emerging niche market – Asian designer retail wear – in order to highlight some of the intricacies of production and consumption of clothing in the diaspora. I argue that using a biographical approach can provide one way of understanding the historical and geographical complexities of making and selling clothes in the South Asian diaspora.

Production Tales

The imposition of a neo-liberal agenda has led to the freeing of some forms of trade across the globe. While the greater part of the literature on the consequences of this globalization has focused on the role of transnational corporations, more recent work has begun to recognize the significance of *émigrés* from the South in the North who enable linkages between and across rich and poor nations in the North and South and thus facilitate globalization (Dicken, Kelly, Olds and Yeung 2001; Bhachu and Light 1993). As a result there is a growing literature on the mobilization of transnational networks by members of the Chinese diaspora, the archetypal entrepreneurial diaspora in Cohen's classification of diasporic populations (Cohen 1997; Olds and Yeung 1999; Mitchell 1995), that highlights the social embeddedness of economic transactions.

In Britain, another body of work that has tried to address these issues is that of 'ethnic minority entrepreneurship'. Although most literature in this vein has discussed the problems faced by ethnic minority entrepreneurs,[1] more recent accounts recognize that *émigrés* may benefit from locating themselves in 'ethnic minority niches' and 'ethnic minority enclaves'. Here they can cater to:

> specialised fields of demand ideally adapted to the cultural and business practices of ethnic firms . . . in which they enjoy a competitive edge, even a monopoly advantage over non-minority firms . . . perhaps the most obvious of such niches is that provided by the customer potential of the ethnic minority population itself (Ram and Jones 1998: 35).

Examples, therefore, might include the production and/or distribution of specialist foods or fashions. However, as Hardill, Raghuram and Strange (2002) have argued, this local embeddedness of retailing is accompanied by a more global embeddedness in production linkages that have been facilitated by longer-standing social relations.

The importance of 'ethnic minority entrepreneurs', 'live links' with both labour and markets in other parts of the world for national economies, is also being recognized by policy makers. Pen Kent, Executive Director, Finance and Industry, Bank of England, urging delegates at an Ethnic Minority conference to evaluate their strengths, said:

> Now what are the strengths? . . . You know you have and one of them is 'Global Links' which was mentioned yesterday. Has the African-Caribbean Community got some links which gives you a start point, an entry point to import, to export, to build, to create, to do things etc.? Has the Asian community got those? I believe and know the answer is yes because I've met some of the people who do actually use their Global Links. They are often like a small inheritance of your own family histories and those can be built upon (Global Consulting 1996, section 8, 9).

These accounts of 'busy' people and successful businesses are not gender-neutral. Gendered notions of 'entrepreneurship' and 'success' are threaded through these stories. Marlow and Strange in their study of 'white' women entrepreneurs argue that entrepreneurship research has been 'largely gender blind' (Marlow and Strange 1994: 1) with 'entrepreneurial theories . . . created by men, for men, and ¼ applied to men' (Holmquist and Sundin 1989: 1). Women rarely appear as actors in this literature, and where they do appear, it is in the form of unpaid family labour, as cultural and social reproducers who facilitate the 'real work' of economic production undertaken by men. Even gender-sensitive research, however, ignores the presence of self-employed women among ethnic minority groups in Britain, although the proportion of women in self-employment is substantially higher than for the white population. For example, in 1991 8.2 per cent of minority ethnic working women were self-employed, as opposed to 6.8 per cent for white working women (Owen 1995). This invisibility of women entrepreneurs is particularly marked in the case of South Asian businesses.

Some feminists have, however, highlighted women's contributions to ethnic minority entrepreneurship; but these insights have been predominantly in the context of the unskilled labour market, with women featuring as home-workers, in sweatshops, and as hidden labour in businesses owned by 'ethnic minorities' (Phizacklea and Wolkowitz 1995; Phizacklea 1988; but see Phizacklea and Ram 1996). For instance, Annie Phizacklea's (1990) study of women in the fashion industry highlights the importance of 'ethnic minority' women's labour in producing fashion clothing; but such women never activate networks of production. This is characteristic of the picture of the multiply disadvantaged woman that dominates feminist literature on women migrants in Europe in the 1970s and 1980s.

Consumption Tales

So often South Asian women are conceived as consuming agents within the context of their reproductive role; an activity they engage in, in order to support the family, to feed the husband, to buy clothes for the children and so on. Here, consumption is not for pleasure but is part of a duty, a part of women's caring roles. In this discourse consumption of personal products may only be justified through the pleasure it provides others.

Significantly, the choices that women make about what to consume, and what not to consume, also carry with them symbolic value. Theoretical frameworks that cast South Asian women as 'traditional' in the binary division between tradition and modernity will also by extension see them as purchasing goods that are 'traditional', as well as based primarily on their racialized identity. In such analyses material cultures are *preserved* through the consumption practices of diasporic women.

In response to these implied but unspoken notions of consumption working through the literature on South Asian women, young South Asian women in the diaspora have produced alternative accounts. They suggest through their narratives the significance of purchasing not for the family but also for oneself, not as part of caring for others but for pleasure. For instance, Bakirathi Mani's discussion of fashion in the US (this volume) disrupts the tradition–modernity binary by exploring the ways in which women mix and match different forms of clothing, Western and Asian, and through this problematizes the paradigmatic constructions of the referent geopolitical entities. Such research successfully challenges stereotypical representations both of the clothes and of those who wear them.

Importantly, this reconfiguration of what may be consumed is not just occurring in diasporic spaces. Rather, as Shoma Munshi argues, middle-class urban Indians too are negotiating modernity/tradition dichotomies in their consumption patterns. She points out that producers of visual media are conscious in their advertising strategies that enlarging the range of feminine subjectivities will alter and increase consumption. The 'modern' woman they target 'now in most cases combines both family and career, familial relationships and independence, selflessness and a little (long overdue) selfishness' (2001: 81). Advertisements emphasize the promise of individual pleasure and fuel the increasingly intensive investment in women's appearance. The products the women consume too draw upon both international styles and on 'international expertise', drawing on the notion of the 'international' to validate their usefulness and authenticity. While some advertisers may manipulate tales of modernity to sell products, others sell the image of 'Indianness' and the importance of that image in the context of new reconfigurations of gender in South Asia. As Munshi argues, 'the 'marvellous me' persona wears the 'international' look on the outside but is a real 'home' girl at heart' (2001: 91). Thus, highlighting women's agency in advertisements not only increases the sales of 'modern' products but also those that have longer histories of consumption in India.

Accounts that emphasize women's agency in their exercise of purchasing power (Nava 1991) challenge the productionism of the narrative in the previous section and suggest that meaning is not exclusively produced at the moment of production. However, although they highlight the extent to which women subvert patriarchy through their consumption practices, others have argued that this subversion has been achieved at the expense of control and domination by capitalism (McRobbie 1997). While consumption tales reconfigure patriarchy, they also solidify capitalism. In response people may produce their identities through consumption, addressing issues of style and ethnicity; but these styles are not wholly appropriated as the producers (often men) intended. Women in their purchasing subvert these styles and stereotypes through their clothing practices, as for instance, through cross-dressing, mixing, parody and excess, thus altering the meanings of the products they buy. They refigure sites such as shopping malls by hanging around without purchasing! Women's economic agency is therefore more complex than appears in these readings.

Bringing Production and Consumption Together – Issues of Method

The problematic relationship between economy and culture may be surmised from the discussions of production and consumption outlined above. Production studies have on the whole been heavily influenced by the political economy formulation, so that culture is ultimately economically determined. These studies often bear other markers of their political origins, a concern with structures and the global scale of analysis among others.[2] On the other hand, a focus on consumption attempts to overturn the economic determinism of production studies models, although they can sometimes be excessively culturally deterministic. For instance, it has been argued that culture can also be constitutive of social and economic formations. Cultural forms ultimately influence the ways in which the economy is represented, and these processes of representation and the meaning of representation (signs) exercise their own force, their own determinacy on how we understand these formations. One of the strengths of this position can be that it is more likely to recognize the spatio-temporal contingency of the products and processes we study. It aims to study meanings, but rarely posits those meanings as universal.

While, these two positions may be ultimately too simplistic, they continue to have currency in academic research. More nuanced attempts to bring culture and economy together have however been attempted by those who for example, embed or contextualize economic processes in the cultural. The problematic gap between production and consumption has been addressed by a number of cultural theorists (Appadurai 1986; Lash 1997; Du Gay 1997).

Much of the work produced in this vein, however, privileges *product* biographies. For instance, Scott Lash's research on the culture industries focuses on ten media products. His method involves an analysis of the 'transformations of cultural products as they move from one stage of production to the next: from production to distribution to sales to consumption, from one sector to another (1997: 4). Moreover, he traces these 'backwards' in time, from consumption through marketing back through cultural intermediaries all the way to the various stages of design and original production' (1997: 4). The focus on the products of consumer culture arises from the concern to reveal and explore the contradictions between the exploitative production processes of capitalism and the product's seamless appearance and symbolic value: the difference between appearance and reality, the processes whereby cultural artefacts conceal their origins ideologically (Johnson, Chambers, Raghuram and Tincknell, forthcoming). The focus on products has also been a corrective to an anthropological stance that has primarily been absorbed with social life, rather than the social life of things, but one consequence of this has been the object-centric direction that this research has therefore taken.

An attempt to address this, to include the role of the subject and to make it central has been made by Bruno Latour (1993) in his actor network theory or ANT.[3] Subjects are incorporated through their role in networks, as 'actants' in networks, but the notion of the subject is itself rewritten so that both humans and non-humans acquire agency. This theory has been utilized by cultural theorists to highlight the multiple forms of agency available to and mobilized by individuals acting at multiple nodes in order 'to develop, produce, distribute and diffuse methods for generating goods and services' (Callon 1991: 139). For instance, Lash suggests that ANT offers a method of understanding the extent to which 'and how key actors recruit, not just other actors but mobilize the cultural products themselves and the affordances which they, and technologies of distribution, offer as forces in such struggles' (1997: 5–6). However, Lash's own work adopts the product biography as the primary method, as the 'perspective or orientation within which a range of appropriate methods is deployed' (1997: 6). This emphasis on products I would argue ultimately objectifies the production–consumption chain. On the other hand, the ANT approach, by focusing primarily on the agency of entities (human and non-human), is in danger of reducing complex production and consumption systems into a mechanistic framework. Concentrating on agents operating at nodes within the network and focusing solely on the links between them can disembed these systems from social frameworks and processes within which these links are set (Dicken *et al.* 2001). The discursive framing of social relations and the pre-existing rationalities that underpin the networks may both be sidelined in such analyses.

What is also common to all these narratives is their location within a particular form of commodity culture, where Karl Marx would argue that labour is ultimately alienated. Whether the products are for an elite market or are those of mass culture, the producer and consumer are removed from each other. Hence, those who produce are never seen as consuming what they produce. The woman who produces clothes at home is only ever a sweatshop worker producing for global markets. This also effectively erases all 'pre-industrial' forms of production and consumption, so that the activities of women who produce their own clothes to wear never enter these debates. The forms of production that have come to be studied are themselves quite specific to urban, industrial and capitalist cultures. The experiences of people in the world that cannot be formulated within these models have largely been ignored. Moreover, not all women (or men) who produce for consumption may be cast as engaging in 'pre-industrial' activities. For many production may be an act of creativity, of pleasure, challenging current analysis, which largely identifies pleasure at the point of consumption. I would therefore argue that a focus on self-provisioning interrogates existing ways of thinking production/consumption. Focusing on those who produce in order to consume what they produce would provide an interesting methodological twist to such stories, and would entail a shift from product biographies to personal biographies, from circuits of production to histories and geographies of the producer.[4]

Self-provisioning is seen as the activity not of choice, but of survival. Hence, those who are 'forced' to produce in order to consume carry with them the 'burdens' of certain class positions. The image of a woman sewing her own clothes is particularly common in the development literature, where it is argued that self-provisioning is increasingly being adopted as a strategy by those who have been adversely affected by falls in income and increasing commodity prices due to Structural Adjustment Programmes. But these burdens may not just be of poor 'third world women'. It is also here that South Asian women find their place, at the nexus between production and consumption tales. South Asian women who participated in early waves of migration to the UK and who continued to wear *salwaar kameez* or saris found few stores from which to buy these clothes (see Puwar, 2002). Thus, for many women, sewing one's own clothes was the main route to wearing clothes of one's choice, a common enough practice not just among migrants but throughout the world[5]. What was distinctive about South Asian women's clothing shops was that they served a small niche market, so that differentiation of products to suit different aesthetics took longer and has depended on the growth of a market large enough to support these different tastes. Hence, self-provisioning continued to be a strategy for South Asian women, perhaps longer than for women wearing 'Western clothes', as the commodified 'ready-mades' market in 'Asian' clothes emerged later. More recently, the emergence of new niche markets to meet the demands of a population marked by a confident reconfiguring of ethnicity as well as by class has lead to the mushrooming of differentiated products and the growth of new retailing outlets (Bhachu 2000; Bhachu 1995; Raghuram and Hardill 1998).

In the rest of this chapter I aim to explore the ways in which one South Asian woman entrepreneur initiated a successful enterprise in order to meet her own clothing requirements. She identified a growing demand for particular forms of clothing on the basis of her own experiences and responded to this by initiating a production chain. While she did not produce her own clothes, the impetus to produce arose from a recognition of her own needs. Although this pattern is undoubtedly common in entrepreneurship, with many ideas for business start-up coming out of personal experience, there has been little work so far that recognizes the importance of this process, of how unsatisfied customers become pro-ducers who make 'what they want', and then become consumers of their own products. Methodologically, recognizing this pattern highlights the subjective elements to the production process and adds to current research, where we often come across subjectivities, at identity formation, only through the lens of consumption. Producers' identities are limited to their role in global capitalist economies.[6]

The personal biography method is strategic on two accounts. It high-lights the agency of South Asian women, placing them not just as pawns in the production cycles, while at the same time making more complex the histories of women's consumption within the South Asian diaspora. Although I am focusing on one woman's narrative, privileging the existen-tial setting, of the place and time, the histories and geographies of the producer enables me to extend the story to others who share similar spaces and times. Secondly, it highlights the multiple layers present in the economic relationships in which any individual engages, and thus draws together issues of power relations with those of agency.

Placing the Story

This chapter is based on the story of Malini, a 31-year-old East African Asian (Gujarati) businesswoman living in the Midlands.[7] Asian immi-gration to East Africa preceded British colonial policies, but was intensi-fied and transformed through colonialism. Until 1922 Asians, especially Gujaratis, were taken to East Africa as indentured plantation labour. After the abolition of the indenture system in 1922, subsequent migrations were largely voluntary, and migrants filled the middle strata of colonial society in Kenya, Uganda and Tanzania, between the more prosperous and politic-ally powerful white minority and the poorer rural African populations. The Asians, many of whom originated from rural areas, now engaged in business and administration in urban areas and acquired many of the markers of 'modernity': knowledge of English, urban behaviour and administrative skills.

While the Asian community in East Africa was never monolithic, capitalism operated to solidify their experiences in the context of the wider differences that existed between them and the other population groups, the Africans and the Europeans, in colonial East Africa's tripartite society (Bujra 1992). The Asians acted as the middle strata of business people who conduited the profits extracted from the African peasantry. Malini's family were late immigrants from India, having left Gujarat in 1948 and settled in Zambia, where they retailed children's clothing. Malini's father moved to Great Britain in 1954, before the large migration flows from East Africa, which were generated by the independence of many of these countries in the 1960s and the political changes that followed. He was joined by his wife and two children in 1958. Malini was born after the family settled in Leicester.

The experiences of Malini's family highlight the historical complexities behind the formation of diasporas. Diasporic populations are constituted not merely through the dispersion from the homeland but also through further dispersions and population movements. Also, these movements are not necessarily conditioned by the return to home. 'Multi-locale' dispersions have been particularly central in the case of the South Asian diaspora. Thus, diasporic populations retain linkages not only with 'home' but also with other parts of the diaspora.

The experiences and skills of East African Asians in Britain differ from those people who have directly migrated from the Indian subcontinent, for whom the migration to Britain has been their first migratory experience, as the East African Asians have considerable entrepreneurial experience and an urban base (see above). The Asian population – whether the result of direct or indirect migration – is very diverse, being marked by linguistic, religious, regional and sectarian differences. Furthermore, the 1980s and 1990s have also witnessed a growing social polarization between and within Asian communities, with those who were indirect migrants emerging as real 'winners' (Metcalf, Modood and Virdee 1996).[8] There also appears to be a strong gender dimension in this 'success' story: Asian men appear to have benefited more than Asian women.

Many of the labour migrants from India and Pakistan who moved to meet the post-war labour shortages in the 1950s and early 1960s, the family reunion migrants who followed, and the more numerous migrants from East Africa in the late 1960s and 1970s settled in Leicester, particularly in the Highfields and Belgrave areas (Nash and Reeder 1993: 27). Although suburbanization has led to dispersal of residence away from these areas (O'Connor 1995; Byrne 1998), retailing continues to be concentrated in these wards, particularly along the Belgrave and Melton Roads, which now represents the one of most important retail centre for

Asians in the East Midlands and for Gujaratis nationally, offering a central focus for celebrations such as Diwali.

Clothing and the Diaspora

Although there are large variations within clothing patterns in the Indian subcontinent, there has been a tendency for certain garments, such as the sari and the *salwaar kameez*, to gain a hegemonic status, both in the subcontinent and in its diasporic populations (Tarlo 1996).[9] As Jennifer Craik (1994) points out, these garments have acquired fashion status, and sit alongside 'Western' garments as markers of modernity. Hence, the fashion garment industry has concentrated on these two forms of clothing or variants of them, but has thus also reconfigured these 'traditional' garments as modern and desirable.[10]

Asian men are, on the whole, less likely to wear 'Asian clothes' every day,[11] as indeed is the custom and practice in the Indian subcontinent.[12] Asian women, on the other hand, are more likely to wear 'Asian clothing', and it is unlikely that they would wear 'Western clothing' for special occasions – for festivals or for social gatherings surrounding lifecourse events, such as birth, marriage or death. These generalized patterns, of course, do vary with religious affiliation and region of origin in the Indian subcontinent, as well as area of residence in the UK. Thus, for example, men appear to be more likely to wear a *salwaar kameez* in areas where there is a relatively substantial visible Asian presence, or when visiting such areas. The importance of changing dresses for different occasions particularly highlights the performative aspect of culture, the importance of dressing up, of knowing the appropriate social codes and of recognizing the historically and spatially dynamic nature of these codes. 'Keeping up' with fashion requires temporal sensibilities as well as spatial sensibilities.

These codes also intersect with economic processes, with particular forms of class stratification. The increasing social stratification within British society is also reflected (and perhaps even magnified) within the Asians. Thus, an increasingly important form of differentiation is emerging with the growth in the number of the Asian service-class of managers and professionals, leading to specific forms of consumption.[13] Along with the status value, there is also a symbolic value to the clothes they wear, which arises out of the meaning-making processes formed within reference systems bounded by class differences but also racialized and gendered differences. Forms of consumption become not only the tools for reflecting status but also means of gaining and negotiating status across these social hierarchies (Bourdieu 1984).

Malini's recognition of the complexities of differentiation and stratification, of the importance of consuming the 'right thing', of the rapid increase in the numbers who could engage in particular forms of consumption led her to establish a business in 1985. Her own location within this cohort meant that she could identify the needs of this group. She thus started the business because she was an unsatisfied customer. She targeted the group of 'conspicuous consumers', who cut across cultural, racial and ethnic communities.

She identified a new, innovative market niche, 'Asian' fashion clothing – ready-to-wear *salwaar kameez* – which were products that she herself wanted to wear for social occasions, but that were not available at the time. Malini therefore had a few garments made to order, which she then sold through a friend's retail outlet. The success of this venture encouraged her to enter into partnership with the owner of an existing business:

' I have always wanted to do clothes and I knew there was a potential for this industry . . . at the time we started it was so new. People didn't talk about readymades then . . . I knew it was going to take off in a big way so I got in at the right time.'[14]

She began retailing Asian fashion clothes (ready-to-wear *salwaar kameez*) to capture this market, a market that she identified as a consumer. She targeted those Asians who she felt had higher purchasing power: 'the classy Punjabis and the Malawi Muslims . . . they have got investments here and there . . . are major business clients . . . once you have got one or two families in the community you get the whole lot.' She also recognized the increasing number of professional Asian women: 'Fifteen- and sixteen-year-old kids . . . they are not really our clients, our clients are business people, we want the professionals.'

Malini bought into the company 'eight years ago'. It 'went limited and that's when I joined it'. The company has three retail outlets, but she also owns an export company . . . based in India. 'It is a British company but based out in India . . . every two months we are out in India.' Their garments are manufactured in India, but most raw materials are imported to India. The company employs forty-one persons in the UK and seven in an office in India, but also uses subcontractors in India and China. About 80 per cent of their production is for the 'British market', but they also export to other countries with significant Asian populations, notably South Africa and the USA, through the establishment of a parallel export–import firm. She also has buyers who retail her products in Europe. 'We export from India to . . . Mauritius, South Africa and America, it's better to do direct rather than going by Great Britain because the duties are too high in Great Britain.'

Their American client undertakes quality checks and orders during business trips, but as her parents also live in Great Britain such trips become family trips too. Malini thus actively uses diasporic connections to produce and sell her products; but she also recreates the diasporic culture through her production and marketing strategies. The European market has catered not just to the diaspora but also to the 'white population', where Indo-chic has become popular (see Puwar, 2002 for a discussion of Indo-chic). In Britain she notes that she has 'regular customers who are English, especially at Christmas time'.

The clothes she sells are designed in Great Britain – influenced by British designers – but manufactured in India. Malini feels that the skills required for the production of the clothes are only available in India: 'just [for] the labour [and] they produce what we want'.

In Hartwick's terms second-order meaning is crucial in fashion (2000). Arguably, images of fashion necessarily erase images of production, remembering only the processes of conceptualization and design. However, for diasporic fashions the place of production may not only hold meaning but may also be valorized, since a second-order meaning of 'authenticity' may be ascribed to the product precisely because of the location of its production and producers. Malini plays with this notion of authenticity through her production process, working the image of authenticity at the level of the sign. Thus production tales become central to consumption tales. At the same time, she is undoubtedly also able to access cheaper labour through a global economic position of privilege that we cannot overlook.

After the Indian economy was liberalized in 1992 it became possible for her to open an office in India (the company is registered in the UK) and to work more closely with subcontracting cut, make and trim (CMT) units. She travels to India every two months to manage the business. The upgrading of garments to fashion products is dependent on the aesthetic values of consumers, which are discursively produced in the locales of consumption. Hence her input into the production of the clothes is also necessary. 'Authenticity' must be mediated to meet consumer choice, and this is difficult to achieve in differentiated production locales without frequent visits to monitor production.

Malini only employs women in the retail outlets where she sells clothes. She argues that even customers who visit the one menswear department in an outlet in London, men '. . . value a woman's opinion of what they look like rather than a guy's, which is strange. We found that they prefer to be served by women, it's just worked out that it should be all women, and why not?'

Interestingly, although she and her customers wear Western clothes on weekdays they wear Asian clothing on Saturdays. Retail centres are spaces of consumption as well as performative spaces, spaces that not only reproduce but also create a sense of identity. Just as people 'go shopping' not merely to buy or even to see but also to be seen, so too, those who sell clothes also dress in order to be seen. But differentiating between different days also requires a sensitivity to who comes shopping and when. If Malini wears a *salwaar kameez* in her shop on Saturday, it is probably a recognition that the nature of the shopping area changes at the weekends, with members of the Asian community coming from further afield. The ethnic mix of the shopping area changes, and the dressing up forms part of the creation of a milieu and the articulation of one version of a 'group identity'. Everyone is therefore 'on show' in a very particular way at the weekend, when people are more likely spontaneously to meet relatives, friends and neighbours.

At the same time, the practice of dressing up in Asian clothes to go shopping/selling on Belgrave Road must be seen in conjunction with exclusionary processes operating elsewhere, to the racism of the 'high street', where wearing a *salwaar kameez* may lead to racist comments such as 'Paki'. Thus, just as people may dress in Asian clothes to go shopping in Wembley, they also wear Western clothes to go shopping in the high street. Inclusionary and exclusionary processes are simultaneously juxtaposed in the creation of specialist retail centres. The terms of participation within such retailing centres are not wholly celebratory or autonomous, but must be situated within the contingent contextuality of the spaces and places from which such participation is excluded.[15] Thus, producing and wearing clothes requires a sensitivity not simply to ethnicity, or to class and gender, but also to spatially situated racialized codes.

Conclusion

This chapter explores the possibility of using personal biographies along with product biographies at the multiple points that they intersect, including design, production and consumption, in order to challenge the product-centricity of much current analysis of production/consumption. By utilizing the story of an Asian woman, I also aim to highlight the agency of South Asian women at all these multiple points, challenging reduced understandings of such women's roles in the global economy.

Through a focus on clothing in the South Asian diaspora I have attempted to highlight the ways in which links with a 'home country' condition consumption and production for some entrepreneurs. Women's bodies are marked as gendered and racialized, bearing markers of 'tradition' and reconfigured through modernity, and dressing up is one way in which these racialized and gendered identities are performed. However, women who identify the consumption needs implicated by this 'burden' may utilize this knowledge in order to produce for themselves and for others. Thus in my study Malini initiated production of fashion clothing because she found her consumption needs unmet by current forms of production and distribution. The clothes she produces are for a niche that is differentiated by race, gender and class; but this niche occurs not only in the UK but in multiple locales across the diaspora. Focusing on production and consumption processes and their relation with the 'homeland' makes the cartography of north–south inequalities more complex and disrupts simple notions of global and local. South Asia becomes the production locale, but also the space the links to which generate consumption needs.

At the same time the disparities within the diaspora, in the nature of shops, clothing and the nature of the clientele, question the cohesiveness of the diaspora. A diasporic sphere of retailing assumes a homogeneity of experiences based on place of origin as well as of migratory experiences, but, as this study shows, both these may vary, leading to heterogeneous communities with heterogeneous consumption patterns.

Notes

1. Ethnic minority entrepreneurial niches are characterized by their concentration in low-income, high-labour-intensity industries, such as hairdressing among African-Caribbeans and grocery stores amongst Asians. Most studies on this topic rarely discuss the ways in which stereotypical images of minority groups direct people from certain groups to certain types of activity, by allocating or withdrawing start-up funding. Rather they portray sectoral niches as products of natural proclivities or of a lack of imagination. Breakout from ethnic niches becomes the key answer to success (Global Consulting 1996).
2. Because of its Marxist roots, even cultural studies has always located itself within capitalist economic systems, although it remains primarily critical of them. It has been much less interested in pre-capitalist or

feudal economic relations other than in terms of locating the historical processes that influence capitalist relations.

3. Another body of literature that has tried to bring these two processes that have for long been held apart together has been conducted under the rubric of 'global commodity chain analysis' (Gereffi 1994; Dicken and Hassler 2000). Here, too, the emphasis tends to be product-centred.

4. An interesting example of this, however, is the use of actor network theory as a means to understanding global commodity chains.

5. The occasional trips to the subcontinent presented another opportunity to 'stock up' on clothes. Although such trips are now more affordable and therefore becoming more common, the need to 'stock up' has on the other hand reduced.

6. This is undoubtedly influenced by the focus of production studies on large companies that fuel transnational capitalism, where the scale of the study means that access to those who initiate production may be limited.

7. This research was funded by The Nottingham Trent University. Other participants in the project were David Graham, Irene Hardill and Adam Strange. This chapter is based on a three and a half hour interview with 'Malini' conducted by me in 1996. The views expressed here are the author's alone.

8. At the same time, it must be realized that unemployment rates are much higher for minority ethnic populations: 8.3% for whites compared to 17.6% for all minority ethnic groups. These figures also vary between groups, ranging from 12.6% among Indians to 25.8% among Pakistani–Bangladeshi populations. Similar variations must also exist within the category 'White'. Such studies do not reveal the extent to which education is used to delay unemployment.

9. Both in India and in the Indian diaspora there has been a growing tendency to replace the sari with *salwaar kameez*, even for formal occasions. Hence a market for high-quality *salwaar kameez* has been created. The market in India is however already saturated, and Malini recognized this.

10. Other clothing, such as *lehngas*, have also become popular, although arguably the popularity of these garments waxes and wanes.

11. The use of turbans by Sikhs is an interesting exception to this pattern.

12. These patterns are mediated by class, religion and gender and by media representations of clothing.

13. The emergence of a South Asian minority with considerable purchasing power is not perhaps wholly new. For instance, I have argued

elsewhere (Raghuram 2000) that women have played an important part in skilled migration to the UK, but that their presence has not really been recognized in migration literature. What is new, perhaps, is the self-confidence of the generation of professionals who have been brought up here in the UK.

14. At the time shops largely sold fabrics that women bought and then tailored. The style of fabric and of the garments varied widely, depending on interesting intersections between age of the person buying and sewing and current fashions, amongst other factors.

15. Although some 'Asian' design elements have in the past two years been incorporated into Western fashion, I would argue that this has not increased the 'acceptability' of Asian clothing *per se*. Moreover, 'acceptability', if any, is always mediated by the consuming body, so that Asian women wearing *salwaar kameez* may be cast as 'traditional' at the same time that these garments are being adopted and adapted by Western women as a mark of their modernity, of their cultural openness.

References

Appadurai, A. (ed.) (1986), *The Social Life of Things: Commodities in Cultural Perspective,* Cambridge : Cambridge University Press.

Bhachu, P. (1995), 'New Cultural Forms and Transnational Asian Women: Culture, Class and Consumption among British Asian Women in the Diaspora', in P. van de Vere (ed.), *Nation and Migration: The Politics of Space in the South Asian Diaspora*, pp. 56–85 Philadelphia: University of Pennsylvania Press.

—— (2000), 'Dangerous Designs: South Asian Fashion and Style in Global Markets', *Public Lecture for ESRC Transnational Communities Project*, University College London.

Bhachu, P. and Light, I. (eds) (1993), *Immigration and Entrepreneurship: Culture, Capital, and Ethnic Networks*, New Brunswick, NJ: Transaction Publishers.

Bourdieu, P. (1984), *Distinction: A Social Critique of the Judgement of Taste,* Cambridge, MA: Harvard University Press.

Bujra, P. (1992), 'Ethnicity and Class: The Case of the East African Asians', in T. Allen and A. Thomas (eds), *Poverty and Development in the 1990s,* pp. 437–61. Milton Keynes: Open University.

Byrne, D. (1998), 'Class and Ethnicity in Complex Cities: Leicester and Bradford', *Environment and Planning A*, 30: 703–20.

Callon, M. (1991), 'Techno-Economic Networks and Irreversibility in a Sociology of Monsters', in J. Law (ed.), *A Sociology of Monsters: Essays on Power, Technology and Domination,* pp. 132–61. London: Routledge.

Cohen, R. (1997), *Global Diasporas: An Introduction,* London: UCL Press.

Craik, J. (1994), *The Face of Fashion: Cultural Studies in Fashion,* London: Routledge.

Dicken, P. and Hassler, M. (2000), 'Organizing the Indonesian Clothing Industry in the Global Economy: The Role of Business Networks', *Environment and Planning A* 32(2): 263–80.

Dicken, P., Kelly, P., Olds, K. and Yeung, H. (2001), 'Chains and Networks, Territories and Scales: Towards a Relational Framework for Analysing the Global Economy', *Global Networks,* 1(2): 89–112.

Du Gay, P. (ed.) (1997), *The Production of Culture/Cultures Of Production,* London: Sage.

Gereffi, G. (1994), 'The Organization of Buyer-driven Global Commodity Chains: How US Retailers Shape Overseas Production Networks', in G. Gereffi and M. Korzeniewicz (eds), *Commodity Chains and Global Capitalism,* pp. 95–122. Westport, CT: Praeger.

Global Consulting (1996), *Ethnic Minority Businesses National Conference: Conference Report and Best Practice Guide,* Leicester: Global Consulting.

Hardill, I., Raghuram, P. and Strange, A. (2002) 'Diasporic Embeddedness among Asian Women Entrepreneurs in the UK', in M. Taylor and S. Leonard (eds), *Social Capital and the Embedded Enterprise: International Perspectives,* London: Ashgate.

Hartwick, E. (2000), 'Towards a Geographical Politics of Consumption', *Environment and Planning A,* 32: 1177–92.

Holmquist, C. and Sundin, E. (1989), 'The Growth of Women's Entrepreneurship: Push or Pull Factors?' Paper presented to *EISAM Conference on Small Business,* University of Durham Business School.

Johnson, R., Chambers, D., Raghuram, P. and Tincknell, E. (forthcoming), *Practices of Cultural Research,* London: Sage

Lash, S. (1997), *The Culture Industries: Biographies of Cultural Products.* Available at http://www.goldsmiths.ac.uk/cultural-studies/html/cultural.html

Latour, B. (1993), *We Have Never Been Modern,* Hemel Hempstead: Harvester Wheatsheaf.

Mani, B. (2002), 'Undressing the Diaspora', in N. Puwar and P. Raghuram (eds), *South Asian Women in the Diaspora,* Oxford: Berg.

Marlow, S. and Strange, A. (1994), 'Female Entrepreneurs: Success by Whose Standards?', in M. Tandton (ed.), *Women in Management: A Developing Presence* , pp. 172–84. London: Routledge.

McRobbie, A. (1997), 'A New Kind of Rag Trade?', in A. Ross (ed.), *No Sweat: Fashion, Free Trade and The Rights Of Garment Workers*, pp. 275–89 New York: Verso.

Metcalf, H., Modood, T. and Virdee, S. (1996) *Asian Self-employment: The Interaction of Culture and Economics in England*, London: Policy Studies Institute.

Mitchell, K. (1995), 'Flexible Circulation in the Pacific Rim: Capitalisms in Cultural Context', *Economic Geography*, 71(4): 364–82.

Munshi, S. (2001), ' Marvellous Me: The Beauty Industry and the Construction of the Modern Indian Woman', in S. Munshi (ed.), *Images of the 'Modern Woman' in Asia: Global Media, Local Meanings*, pp. 78–93 Richmond: Curzon.

Nash, D. and Reeder, D. (1993), *Leicester in the Twentieth Century,* Stroud: Alan Sutton Publishing in association with Leicester City Council.

Nava, M. (1991), 'Consumerism Reconsidered: Buying and Power', *Cultural Studies*, 5, 2: 157–73.

O'Connor, H. (1995), *The Spatial Distribution of Ethnic Minority Communities in Leicester, 1971, 1981, and 1991: Analysis and Interpretation,* Leicester: Joint Publication of the Centre for Urban History and the Ethnicity Research Centre, University of Leicester.

Olds, K. and Yeung, H. W. (1999), '(Re)shaping 'Chinese' Business Networks in a Globalizing Era', *Environment and Planning D* 17 (5): 535–56.

Owen, D. W. (1995), *Ethnic Minority Women and Employment,* Manchester: Equal Opportunities Commission.

Phizacklea, A. (1988), 'Entrepreneurship, Ethnicity and Gender', in S. Westwood and P. Bhachu (eds), *Enterprising Women*, pp. 20–33. London: Routledge.

—— (1990), *Unpacking The Fashion Industry: Gender, Racism, and Class in Production,* London: Routledge.

Phizacklea, A. and Ram, M. (1996), 'Being Your Own Boss: Ethnic Minority Entrepreneurs in Comparative Perspective', *Work, Employment and Society*, 10 (2): 319–39.

Phizacklea, A. and Wolkowitz C. (1995), *Homeworking Women: Gender, Racism and Class at Work*, London: Sage.

Puwar, N. (2002), 'Multicultural Fashion . . . Stirrings of Another Sense of Aesthetics and Memory', *Feminist Review*, 71: 63–87.

Raghuram, P. (2000), 'Gendering Skilled Migratory Streams: Implications for Conceptualizing Migration', *Asian and Pacific Migration Journal*, 9 (4): 429–57.

Raghuram, P. and Hardill, I. (1998), 'Negotiating a Market: A Case Study of an Asian Woman in Business', *Women's Studies International Forum*, 21 (5): 475–84.

Ram, M. and Jones, T. (1998), *Ethnic Minorities in Business*, London: Small Business Research Trust.

Ramji, H. (2002), 'Engendering Diasporic Identities', in N. Puwar and P. Raghuram (eds), *South Asian Women in the Diaspora*, Oxford: Berg.

Takhar, S. (2002), 'South Asian Women and the Question of Political Agency', in N. Puwar and P. Raghuram (eds), *South Asian Women in the Diaspora*, Oxford: Berg.

Tarlo, E. (1996), *Clothing Matters: Dress and Identity in India*, London: Hurst and Co.

Conceptualizing *Emigrant* Indian Female Subjectivity: Possible Entry Points
Mala Pandurang

This chapter explores a possible meeting-ground of interests between theorists of the South Asian Diaspora located in India and those in other locations. It is exploratory, and aims to identify entry points for a discussion between intellectuals working in the area of gender studies.

The Politics of Location: The Home Critic

I am located in a Women's University in Mumbai, India. I would therefore like to shift perspective in my discussion, from the *host* to the *home* or the *sending society*, which in the context of this chapter is the modern Indian nation-state. For the home nation, it is the phenomenon of *emigration* and not *immigration* that is of central interest. The West is therefore not the site of enunciation. The Indian is the subject rather than the object of investigation.[1]

I suggest three broad critical locations *vis-à-vis* responses to gender and the phenomenon of migration from the Indian subcontinent. First of all, there is the category of scholars who are located within Western metropolitan centres of 'knowledge' and whose interests arise from the experience of others in the diaspora – parents, neighbours, etc. Much of the analysis is directed at the emergence of a 'new world culture' within these geographical spaces and the emergence of contemporary cultural hybridities. It is not surprising, therefore, that the primary focus of these critics is on narratives that relate female subjectivity to issues of displacement and new states of belonging; and on syncretism and hybridity, within a specific cultural-racial paradigm. Second-generation subjectivities have increasingly offered an insider's view of the processes of what it is to be female, and to grow up in a multiracial/cultural milieu, by focusing on processes of translating between cultures and renegotiating traditions.

The second category of critics is that of postcolonial intellectuals of the third world who have re-located from their 'home' country and are now in the first world. Lavie and Swedenberg (1996) point out that these critics tend to concentrate on Western expressive culture. The 'time zones' of their cultural studies are usually North American or European. They define their condition as the transition from an 'elsewhere', to the 'centre', and highlight aspects of multiple subject positions (1996: 19). One cannot take members of this group to be spokespersons of the migrant experiences of all third world peoples. As Homi Bhabha asks, 'caught between worlds that collide as often as they collude, are we representative of anything but ourselves?' (2000: 135).

The third category is that of the 'home critic' who operates from within the third world locale. I use the term 'third world' primarily as an econ-omic marker of nation-states that geographically constitute the parameters of a non-European developed world. The home critic operates from within the sending nation, and therefore engagements with racial interaction, and definitions of concepts of hybridity that are part of a Western matrix are not really the terms of their theoretical explorations. For instance, my area of concern is not with the analysis of modes of resistance to racial discrimination, but rather the systems of domination – political, economic and discursive – that are linked to the positions of emigrant Indian women.

The tremendous pressures of India's growing population, in combina-tion with the so-called free labour market today, continue to ensure large-scale mobilization of different categories of workforces outside the Indian geopolitical space. India may well have the world's largest expatriate citizenry by the next decade. If migration from the Indian subcontinent is largely predicated on economic inequities, and male migrants are looking for better opportunities to improve life chances, then one might ask, what are the pre-migration expectations of women?

Annanya Bhattacharjee suggests that the expatriate Indian woman carries 'seeds of an immigrant' in her 'deferred but nevertheless prospect-ive immigrant state' (1992: 3). Moreover, an increasing number of young middle-class women anticipate the possibility of emigration as a given. Working on this presumption, is it then possible to evolve conceptual and analytical tools that would allow access to the space of a pre-migration state of mind? Mary John comments; 'It is my belief that a good many postcolonial women, including self-identified feminists, find themselves gazing and going westwards for reasons that cannot be rendered intellig-ible in the language of a presumed or proposed international feminism alone' (1996: 16).

Contemporary Indian Emigration: *Understanding Departure*

The Indian nation-state has experienced swift social and cultural changes since the 1990s with the liberalization of the Indian economy. As a theorist located from within the *homeland*, my interests lie in culture narratives that reveal the mechanisms of a new global interaction, but with my own *local geo-centre* as the focus point. It is important to understand that the context of contemporary Indian emigration to the West, in the post-globalization era, differs greatly from that of earlier generations of Indian emigrants in the post-war period. Unlike the latter, today's emigrants also include those who do not have to 'burn the bridge and travel with a one-way ticket' (Rath 1999: 13). This in turn means that the paradigms for addressing the emigrant/host nation/home nation relationship also change. For example, prior to the 1990s, the approach towards professionals who chose to leave the country for greener pastures was in general hostile and accusatory. Today, however, the debate on the 'brain-drain' of knowledge workers is marked by an optimism that the increased frequency of contact with home, facilitated by rapid technology developments in information, communication and travel, will have a 'trickle-down effect on the sending countries' (Khadria 1999: 15). The middle-class diasporic therefore becomes more 'acceptable'.

It is crucial to formulate analytical tools to assess states of subjectivity, at the *point of departure*. It is only thus that we can arrive at any conclusion about shifts of identity and dilemmas of liminality that take place after *arrival*. Commenting on work currently available on the migrant experiences of South Asian women, Mary John observes that, by and large, in the theorizing that emanates from the host-nation, 'the language of arrival is truly valorized . . . one comes across less where women have come from, much more about what they have come to' (1996: 18).

Rajeshwari Sunder Rajan warns of the 'need to resist the homogeneous image of the "new Indian woman" which irons out differences of class, caste, community and language' (1993: 129). There are standpoints of women that are particular to their specific contexts. I keep this in mind when I take up the example of the category of middle-class Indian woman, whose position is marked by certain class privileges: for instance, women who in the US are wives of green-card-holding professional men are often highly qualified professionals themselves. Yet their dependence is sanctioned and even enforced by law because of technicalities of the visa issued to them. This status of dependency for educated women is bound to create complex material and emotional problems that cannot be de-linked from their own expectations of the receiving culture prior to emigration, especially since popular media images of the West cast it as a liberating space for women. Does the educated Indian middle-class woman, in the process of migrating, view the movement out of the geographical space of the home culture as an opportunity to go beyond her middle-class social status, and explore the possibilities of 'the agentive new woman', or is her role one of being a vital link in the continuation of the culture of the sending society, largely already pre-defined? For many of these young brides, the responsibility of balancing tradition with modernity also becomes a 'painful struggle' (Rajan 1993: 123). How well are women emigrants 'pre-prepared', through exposure to narratives of popular culture, constantly to negotiate identity within complex and shifting perspectives created by changes in both geographies and economics? It is here that theoretical discussions of feminists from within the South Asian diaspora have the potential to offer additional entry points to the familiar discourses of tradition and modernity in the context of the contemporary politics of emigration.

Also, the middle-class Indian woman located within the geographical space of the Indian nation-state already belongs simultaneously to a diversity of cultures. The act of emigration only adds to the complexity of her hybrid composition. Kumkum Sangari points out that hybridity 'need not be an east/west binary that is usually privileged by western based writers but should incorporate the complex cultural intersections of regional, linguistic, caste, class and gender affiliations' (1995: 146). It would be equally beneficial to examine how other South Asian feminist theorists engage with conflicting heterogeneity and the multiple articulation of different identities.

Spatial Connectors: *The Problematic Umblical Cord*

Over the past decade, there has been a growing realization on the part of the Indian Government that Peoples of Indian origin (POI) and Non-Resident Indians (NRI) have the potential to play increasingly important roles as catalysts in globalization processes within the Indian economy. It is however not absolutely essential that the return of human capital 'be conditional upon the return migration to the home country as long as the continuum of emotional bonding and affinity to the home culture is sustained' (Khadria 1999: 20). In this context, the issue of the subjectivity of the emigrant women gets 'inextricably linked to nation-ness' (Bhattacharjee 1992: 1). The collective networking that is integral to the survival of the *natio* beyond the geographical territory of the sending society is ensured through constructs of pre-defined roles that the woman is expected to perform. The strong popularity of Bollywood films (popular Hindi films), and innumerable websites hosted for and by Indians abroad, which offer viewing of television serials in Indian languages (sonytv.com, numtv.com), bring the visual presence of the homeland right into the domestic space of emigrant homes. This in turn allows for the continued internalization of patriarchal constructs and ensures that, while the new Indian citizen may be physically dispersed within the boundaries of another state, s/he will remain culturally part of the homeland. Robin Cohen in *Global Diasporas* (1997) points out that the strong retention of group ties sustained over an extended period of time could in turn lead to varying levels of social exclusion in the destination societies. Non-assimilative Asian diasporas in countries such as Uganda, Kenya and Fiji have had to face repercussions of sustaining such 'umbilical attachments'. A common accusation against these communities is that they deliberately engender a distance from host cultures, which in turn hinders identification with the adopted society in terms of political loyalty and cultural affinity.

My interest lies in the power of such spatial connectors that originate in the home culture, but continue to shape female subjectivity even after the act of emigration. Many of the interrogations I put forward to problematize the complex of mediations between the home and the community have origins in my own experiences of migrancy, and the complexity of the spaces that I myself inhabit. Therefore, I take the liberty of a personal intervention. Several of the spatial connectors I experienced about two decades ago continue to be reinforced powerfully, and therefore offer a rich resource for a common meeting-ground of analysis.

I was born in Bukoba, a tiny coffee-growing town on the shores of Lake Victoria in Tanzania. I grew up in post-independence Zambia of the 1970s, when cultural nationalism was still at its height. Yet all the programmes shown on the national television of Zambia were either American crime serials or English sit-coms. My closest friends were black Zambians, and yet I grew up in an atmosphere of only partial acceptance. At home, my parents had ensured that our Indian cultural baggage remained intact. My mother wore only the sari in the four decades she spent on the African continent, and had set a dress code for me, on reaching puberty, of long skirts and loose-fitting tops. This had served as a marker of difference from my African classmates, and created great discomfort on non-uniform days in school.

My parents returned to India in the 1980s. In the initial years of college education in the South of India, I found myself, to adapt that famous

Bhaba-ian phrase – 'almost but not quite' – a quasi-subject, a participant and yet marginal to the culture of the subcontinent. I reflect upon the complex combination of identifiers responsible for my multivalent identity and I ask: What was in the family's own *Gunny sack*, to borrow the metaphorical title of M. G. Vassanji's (1990) first novel, that made my 're-turn', my acceptability by and my own assimilation back into, the 'mother culture' a shade 'easier' than perhaps if my parents had chosen to emigrate to the West? Was it merely race and ethnicity? Or rather, was it the care taken by my family to carefully cultivate an 'Indian' and 'Hindu' female subjectivity, and therefore to preserve my marriageability? Stories of the epics of the *Ramayana* and the *Mahabharatha* were very much part of my childhood. Sita figured prominently as example of the ideal Hindu daughter and wife. Once a month, we would gather at the local Hindu Hall for a Hindi film screened by the Gujarati trading community. The powerful medium of Hindi (Bollywood) popular films continues to strengthen its overseas reach to date, and film producers still project a particular version of the 'good' Indian wife by resorting to the virgin/vamp dichotomy of the nineteenth-century and early twentieth-century cultural nationalists.

My own quest to work out a new identity of self, gradual as it was, was interwoven with a growing sense of affinity with other Indian women of my generation and background, who were also caught in an ambivalent bicultural situation. These young women have been educated in English in urban/metropolitan locations, and belong to a socio-cultural milieu that is being rapidly transformed by policies of economic liberalization and globalization. As I negotiated my way between the two variants of 'estrangement' and 'comfort', I increasingly identified with the politics of Indian women creative writers and artists oppositional to the patriarchal ideology of the larger, dominant 'Hindu' culture. This contributed to my own emerging sense of belonging to a marginalized community, albeit within a large nationhood.

Towards a New Meeting-ground: *The Politics of Information Dissemination*

I do believe that, differences in certain priorities of investigation notwithstanding, it is still possible to chart out a meeting-ground of conceptual and methodological issues raised by both scholars of the experience of women of the South Asian diaspora, and Indian 'home' scholars, in their exploration of gender-based issues. After all, both groups are primarily concerned with apparatuses of history, religion and collective myths used by dominant/ patriarchal ideologies. Their work veers towards the analysis of various levels of co-option; and offers sites of resistance to socio-political-cultural structures of oppression. In the early stages of Indian feminism, it was not uncommon for Indian critics to fall back on American and British paradigms with regard to women as subjects of analysis. By the 1980s, most Indian feminists had however rejected the homogenizing impulses of Western feminism (Tharu and Lalitha 1991; Sangari and Vaid 1989; Sunder Rajan 1993). This move was largely influenced by the wider postcolonial movement by women of colour to decentre the Western female subject by focusing on the specifics of their own marginal positions within Eurocentric cultures. Identity politics and the politics of location came to the fore. In the process, alternative ways of thinking of female subjecthoods emerged and also brought across cultural discussions into the arena of academic theorizing.

Yet, despite sincere moves to re-conceptualize parameters of feminism, the production, distribution and consumption of 'knowledge' on non-Eurocentric gender issues is still governed by what has the 'sanction' of Western academic centres of learning. A survey of library resources in the SNDT Women's University (Mumbai) and the University of Mumbai reveals that there is a significant absence of information on theoretical investigations into the experiences of women of the South Asian diaspora. The only literary text that is prescribed for study at postgraduate level is Atima Srivastava's *Transmission* (1992) in the paper on British writing at the University of Mumbai. Economics plays a crucial role in what texts and theory are available in third world locations. Choice of research topics by Indian academicians is often predicated on the funds made available to undertake projects.

In the 1980s, the Canadian government set up of Centers of Canadian Studies in select Indian Universities. In Canada, gestures of inclusion are encouraged as part of the multicultural policy, and grants are made available for research into certain visible minorities. The easy accessibility of these initiated dialogues between privileged women of colour in turn facilitated the shift from White Canadian mainstream to immigrant writing as a choice topic for research dissertations by Indian research students. At the SNDT for instance, there are more than a dozen M.Phil. and Ph.D. dissertations on Canadian minority writers, and amongst these are projects on South Asian Canadian women like Himmani Baneerjee and Uma Para-meswaran. Comparative cultural analysis of South Asian women in other non-Western locations is negligible. One of the few exceptions is Tejas-wani Niranjana's ongoing project for the SEPHIS south–south exchange programme entitled *Mobilizing 'India': Gender and Ethnicity in the*

Subaltern Diaspora. A Comparative Study of India, Trinidad and South Africa. On similar lines, one might ask to what extent do scholars within the host state have access to knowledge being produced outside the Eurocentre? How much of an initiative is being made to access research emanating from non-Western locations?

I return to my opening question of the complexities involved when the *home* attempts to understand other South Asian second-generation female subjectivities. What are the images of the immigrant woman of Indian origin that we receive, and how are these images constructed? The Indian media in English tends either to appropriate successful immigrants as 'Indian' achievers (Kalpana Chawla, a naturalized American citizen, is lauded as the first *Indian* woman in space); or to sensationalize women of Indian origin who are linked to Western male celebrities (Selina Setur as the sultry lover of Boris Becker). With the mushrooming of satellite television, cable channels offer a variety of programmes in English produced in the West. These are, however, productions that offer a mainstream perspective on the Western world – the immigrant presence remains marginalized.

It is here that cultural studies can play an important role of intervention. As Patrick White (1995: 4–5) puts it, literary narratives can offer 'exciting opportunities for analysis as inputs to research' and therefore 'allow for social scientists and humanities scholars to come together'. By bringing into the Indian classroom narrative representations of women's experiences across the South Asian Diasporas as resources for social analysis, Indian students may gain entry points to examine the real-life texture of the heterogeneous lives of immigrant women.

Note

1. The term 'South Asian' has much broader geographical connotations, and I will therefore use the term 'Indian' to demarcate the geopolitical space under review.

References

Bhabha, H. (2000), 'The Vernacular Cosmopolitan', in F. Dennis and N. Khan (eds), *Voices of the Crossing. The Impact of Britain on Writers from Asia, The Caribbean and Africa,* London: Serpentail's Trail.

Bhattacharjee, A. (1992), 'The Habit of Ex-Nomination: Nation, Woman, and the Indian Immigrant Bourgeoisie', *Public Culture* 5 (1) (Fall): 19–44.

Robin Cohen (1997), *Global Diasporas*, London: UCL Press

John, M. E. (1996), *Discrepant Dislocations. Feminism, Theory and Postcolonial Histories,* Delhi: Oxford University Press.

Khadria, B. (1999), *The Migration of Knowledge Workers. Second Generation Effects of India's Brain Drain,* New Delhi: Sage.

Lavie, S. and Swedenberg, T. (eds) (1996), *Displacement, Diaspora, and the Geographies of Identity,* Durham, NC: Duke University Press.

Rajan, R.S. (1993), *Real and Imagined Women: Culture, Gender and Postcolonialism*, London: Routledge.

Rath, S. P. (1999), 'Home(s) Abroad: Diasporic Identities in Third World Spaces', *Journal of Contemporary Thought*, 9 (Summer): 1–23.

Sangari, K. (1995), 'The Politics of the Possible', in B. Ashcroft, G. Griffiths and H. Tiffin (eds), *The Postcolonial Studies Reader,* 1, pp. 43–7. London: Routledge.

Sangari, K. and Vaid, S. (1989), *Recasting Women: Essays in Colonial History*, Delhi: Kali for Women.

Srivastava, A. (1992), *Transmission*, London: Serpent's Tail.

Tharu, S. and Lalita, K. (1991), *Women Writing in India: 60 BC to the Present*, Oxford: Oxford University Press.

Vassanji, M. G. (1990), *The Gunny Sack,* New Delhi: Penguin Books.

White P. (1995), 'Geography, Literature and Migration', in R. King, J. Connell and P. White (eds), *Writing Across Worlds*, pp. 1–19. London: Routledge.

Part II
Embodying South Asian Femininities

–6–

Romantic Transgressions in the Colonial Zone: Reading Mircea Eliade's *Bengal Nights* and Maitreyi Devi's *It Does Not Die*[1]

Nandi Bhatia

Introduction

Scholarship on the representation and construction of upper-class women in colonial India has identified the nationalist and colonialist positions, both of which attempted to secure female emancipation and liberation through a 'modern' education and women's control over their own sexuality as well as through a series of reforms that would ostensibly rescue women from the oppressive practices of Indian culture.[2] While the two positions were not necessarily at odds with each other, the oppositional projects of nationalism and colonialism came to debate the 'woman question' in ways that constructed and represented her role in accordance with their own specific requirements and benefits. As colonialists constructed Indian women as exotic yet oppressed, to justify their own 'civilizing mission', there emerged in response to such colonialist claims a patriarchal anticolonial nationalism, which endorsed women's education and social reforms, yet situated, according to Partha Chatterjee (1989), their ideal role in the realm of the spiritual, identified as the home or the inner sphere. Constituted as a domain of sovereignty free from Western influence, this sphere, argues Chatterjee, was in opposition to the material sphere of science, rationality and modern methods of statecraft inhabited by European nations, which gave Europeans the edge to rule over the colonized nations. Defining this sphere served the function of establishing the identity, superiority, and cultural distinctiveness of the national culture of the colonized over that of the West. Since the Indian woman was seen as the representation of this inner core of national culture, she was assigned the dubious honour of carrying the traditional values of the home. While her education, dress, food and cultural sophistication made her an equal to her Western counterpart, her preservation of the traditional domain of the home established her as superior to the former as well as to the lower-class Indian woman, and made her the perfect embodiment of the virtuous and chaste 'new woman'. In both cases, then – the colonialist and the nationalist positions – the actual question of the woman's condition was left out and specific roles were carved out for her, which, while emancipatory to some extent, also imposed certain limitations that kept her in subordination.

As exemplified by the writings of Bankim Chandra and Rabindranath Tagore, two centrally important nationalist writers of the nineteenth and twentieth centuries respectively, themes pertaining to the position of women came to be extensively debated in journalistic, vernacular, fictional and autobiographical writing, as well as in oral and visual forms of communication.[3] Since for the most part the writings of these male nationalists legitimized new controls over women, they also spawned a history of struggle against this new patriarchy on the part of women, a history that has been recorded in autobiographical writings by women. In a situation where they found themselves subordinated simultaneously 'to colonialism as well as to a nationalist patriarchy' (Chatterjee 1993: 140) women, through their autobiographies, sought to identify 'the distribution of power in intimate human relationships in gender-political terms' (Sarkar 1997: 47).[4]

The internationally acclaimed writer and activist Maitreyi Devi's academy award-winning autobiographical narrative, *Na Hanyate*, translated as *It Does not Die* (1972), can be seen as another significant addition to the corpus of autobiographical writing by women that urges us to reconsider and think through the impact of the multiple forces of race, colonialism, and nationalism on the position of women.[5] Written in direct response to a colonialist work titled *Bengal Nights* (originally published in Romanian in 1933 under the title of *Maitreyi*), Devi's narrative openly investigates both the Orientalist and the liberal reformist dimensions of colonialist and nationalist thought, and explores the implications of the complicated nexus of the two positions for women, such as herself, who were involved in an inter-racial romance.

A European living in India in the 1930s, Mircea Eliade, the author of *Bengal Nights* (1994), was a student of Maitreyi's father, and later became a reputed Professor of Religion at the University of Chicago. In a semi-autobiographical vein *Bengal Nights* details its protagonist Alaine's Orientalist fascination with India and his tragic love affair with the young Maitreyi in 1930.[6] In representing Maitreyi through his Oriental fantasy,

Eliade obscures the violence of colonialism as well as the violations entailed in the constructions of the native woman. Upon reading his narrative for the first time after more than forty years and feeling betrayed by its descriptions, Devi writes her own version, which does not deny her love for him but is attentive to the tensions and transgressions of a cross-racial romance. However, while countering Eliade's agenda of Orientalist cultural conquest, Maitreyi Devi also simultaneously reflects on the colonial and nationalist contexts that framed her relationship with him and reveals how, as a woman from an affluent, liberal, and educated family, she was deprived of a relationship with a European. To this end, she shows how her family's concerns with 'honour, duty, and obligation' (Devi 1995: 43) became the foundation on which they built her worth as a good and responsible daughter and wife and expected her to take on the role of the 'new woman'. Devi's careful exposition of the colonial and nationalist structures that controlled women's lives provides a greater understanding of the ways in which they were imagined, constructed, and represented. How Devi is constituted by her European lover and their intellectual and romantic interactions on the one hand, and by her nationalist father, on the other, in a space configured within asymmetrical relations of power, is one of the concerns of this chapter. Additionally, this chapter examines Maitreyi's response, which, written with tremendous emotional intensity and a powerful display of feelings forty-two years later, becomes an important intervention in such constructions.

Since their re-publication by the University of Chicago Press in 1994, both Devi's and Eliade's novels have attracted critical attention in the West and are viewed as narrative representations of a tragic love affair fraught with cross-cultural tensions. However, barring a few reviews, Devi's narrative has received rather short shrift. Additionally, the neglect of gender and race politics and how Devi is constructed in these two texts has obscured the politics of the representation and construction of the Indian woman in Orientalist texts, as well as the question of her own self-representation.[7] Analyses that leave out the racial, gendered, and political elements, not only obscure the complicated power dynamics of the romantic affair in a colonial situation but the sympathetic attention given to Eliade's narrative neutralizes the effect of his romantic tale in terms of its con-struction of the mysterious, exotic and oppressed Indian woman, through descriptions that subject her and her body to the gaze of the reader.

Since what is at stake in Eliade's text is the representation of the colonized woman in a forbidden romance that takes place within asym-metrical relations of power, Devi's narrative needs to be read in tandem with Eliade's *Bengal Nights*. Narrated in the first person, Eliade's narrative opens with his protagonist Alaine's recollection of his first meeting with Maitreyi Devi, and immediately draws the reader's attention to her body and her skin colour and his initial contempt for her 'ugliness'; he describes her as having 'eyes that were too large and too black, thick and curling lips and the powerful chest of a Bengali maiden who had developed too quickly' (Eliade 1994: 1). As the novel progresses, the narrative turns into a vivid description of Maitreyi and Alaine's romance and their hidden sexual encounters in her parents' home, where Alaine begins to reside upon the invitation of her father Surendranath Dasgupta. Their romance is ultimately exposed to her parents, who banish Alaine from their home. The novel ends with Alaine's inability to meet Maitreyi and is peppered with information about the regular beatings inflicted on Maitreyi by her father. Unable to bear the pain of suffering and separation, Alaine returns to Europe without meeting her again.

Romantic Transgressions and 'The Illustration to Some Oriental Tale'

Because the romance between Maitreyi and Alaine enters the forbidden zone on racial, spatial, and political levels, it becomes transgressive on several fronts. First, in the colonial space of forbidden interracial relationships, the act of consorting with a European results in a transgression of the racial boundaries required to be maintained between a European man and an Indian woman. Alaine, the protagonist of Eliade's novel, draws the reader's attention to this transgression by establishing the racial difference between himself and Maitreyi through explicit references to Maitreyi's skin, and by alluding to the numerous sarcasms inflicted upon him by his white friends once they discover his affair with Maitreyi. In fact, his descriptions of Maitreyi's body reveal his obsession with the racial body and his own racial prejudices (not surprising given that Eliade had turned fascist in the 1930s). His discussion of Maitreyi's blackness represents his preoccupation with a concern that the empire had developed in the 1890s regarding the spread of diseases among Europeans consorting with native women in India, a concern through which the empire worked 'to consolidate and secure an authority predicated on whiteness, maleness, and European-ness' (Levine 1996: 587).

The political situation of 1930 – the year of their romance – makes their relationship still more transgressive. It coincides with an emerging feminist movement in the wake of intensifying nationalism spurred by the Swadeshi movement of earlier decades. Swadeshi's call for the boycott of everything European, including European men and women, places moral and nationalistic demands upon Maitreyi that involve a rejection of her European lover on ideological grounds. Further, Gandhi's arrest in 1930, the sentencing of Nehru to six months imprisonment, and the mass-scale arrest of nationalist agitators would have made it equally dangerous for a European and an Indian to be seen together. Moreover, the romance begins in the home of her parents. Despite the liberal social codes of the household, which do not require women to observe *purdah* and in which Maitreyi has the freedom to discourse freely with men, discuss political affairs with her father and his friends and move between the different rooms, Maitreyi is required to observe social codes that forbid a romantic involvement with their guest. To add to this, Eliade's narrative description of the home constructs a spatial configuration emplotted by intrigue, deceit, and unknown forces engaged in voyeurism, thus providing their romance with a transgressive quality.

For Alaine, the protagonist of Eliade's novel (and his creator Eliade, with whom we find a striking resemblance in his autobiography (1990)), these forbidden spaces only intensify the pleasure and eroticism of their relationship, and allow him to construct an oriental fantasy. Enchanted by the 'landscape, the climate, the people, their languages and beliefs' he, in fact, enjoys transgressing all kinds of boundaries. Despite his own awareness and being warned by Maitreyi's father about the dangers of walking on the streets during the nationalist agitation, he takes relish from doing precisely that. Says Eliade in his autobiography: 'I was white and on the streets and in the street-cars the Bengalis looked at me with contempt and hatred. In Bhowanipur, children shouted after me, "white monkey" and sometimes threw stones. This contempt and aggressiveness fascinated me' (Eliade 1990: 180). It is evident in his autobiography that Eliade wants to channel this fascination into a book about the civil revolution in India.

In his fictional account, Eliade's yearning to know India and to become an Indian acquires a language that figures their romance initially in the form of descriptions of Maitreyi's body and careful observation of the customs and manners of Maitreyi's family. As the romance progresses, he constructs a fantasy in which she enters his room at night (something Maitreyi Devi denies in her novel) to engage in passionate lovemaking. In fact, he presents her as initially cautious and constructs her refusal to respond to him as an effect of being circumscribed by the Hindu codes of womanhood as he understands them, from whose shackles, he believes, she is unable to break free. In so doing, Eliade underscores much of the nineteenth-century Orientalist response that constructed the Indian woman as exotic yet socially oppressed. Additionally, his descriptions of Maitreyi's philosophical bent of mind, love for poetry, and liberal education fit the Orientalist descriptions of Indian women as they were perceived to be during the golden age of Hinduism, through which the author also conceptualizes for the reader the dominant social order of the Hindu ethos, and its social and psychic demands on women at the time of a rising nationalism that played on the mythology of the golden Hindu age.[8] Yet he turns Maitreyi's interest in poetry and philosophy, independent mind and spirit, and participation in public gatherings of men and women into another form of teenage romantic fulfilment, especially in his suggestions about her infatuation with her *guru*, Rabindranath Tagore. Maitreyi's devotion to her *guru* is explained by Alaine and presented to the reader as no more than a misplaced or pathologized form of sexual interest.

And when it comes to her relationship with himself, Alaine elevates her sexuality to a form of maturity and presents her as a goddess. For a reader well schooled in the lessons of Orientalist historiography, Alaine's own specialist knowledge of Hindu mythology and philosophy serves to convince the reader of Maiteryi's goddess-like qualities. Once Alaine elevates her to the level of goddess, he can then focus on her sexuality and even allow her to command authority when it comes to sexuality. Hence, in Eliade's novel it is Maiteryi who initiates all the sexual moves: she enters his room at night, initiates a secret marriage engagement, and participates in ferocious sexual fulfilment with him, transgressing, in the process, the norms of respectability that occupy her parents' home. While her sexuality may appear to be a subversion of conventional popular romance genres, which usually portray a passive and tame heroine, within the larger context of a colonial setting, such a portrayal is fuelled by the imagination of a western Orientalist mind that seeks to provide, in Eliade's words, 'the illustration to some oriental tale'. One instance that calls attention to his Orientalist sensibility is the evocation of Kalidasa's *Shakuntala*, a text that, as Tejaswini Niranjana argues, helped construct a 'powerful version of the "Hindu"' in Europe following William Jones's translation – a version that 'later writers of different philosophical and political persuasions incorporated into their texts in an almost seamless fashion' and used as evidence of the 'political arrangements and laws of the age' (Niranjana 1992: 128, 137). Like Jones, whose eighteenth-century renditions of *Shakuntala* had disseminated images in Europe of Indian women as exotic, Eliade's narrative also constructs a mythology about Indian women through a personalized romance.[9] This becomes evident not only in the successful reception of the novel in Europe, but also in the reverential response of Eliade's student to Devi decades later in India.

That Eliade is an Orientalist is evident both from his autobiography and his semi-autobiographical novel. His interest in India, to begin with, is the result of his engagement with Indian philosophy, which is encouraged by his Professor, who tells him to keep alive his 'interest in the Orient', especially India. Motivated by such urgings, he goes to India to study Indian philosophy under the patronage of Maharajah Mahindra Chandra Nandy of Kassimbazar and becomes a student of Maitreyi's father, Surendranath Dasgupta. In an autobiographical note, Eliade writes:

> I felt that the Orient meant, for me, much more than a fairy-tale landscape or an object for study, that it was a part of the world that deserves to be known for its secret history or for the grandeur of its spiritual creation. It held a strange attraction for me, in which I seemed to read my fate: a mysterious enchantment sprung from unknown sources. I sensed in it a minaret discovered unexpectedly at the end of the street, a shadow beneath an old wall, the sky glimpsed between the cypress trees (Eliade 1990: 147).

Given his orientation and training, it is hardly surprising that Alaine, Eliade's protagonist of *Bengal Nights*, retains an anthropological search for the 'authentic India'. In his search for India, Alaine treats Maitreyi initially as a 'rare document', makes notes of the 'primitive nature of her thinking', and calls her a 'child who has read too much' (Eliade 1994: 34–5). Although he is very unsure of how to behave with Indians, Alaine presents himself as a 'true' European scholar – educated in mathematical physics and engineering, interested in novels, essays on political economy, and history, who is now in search of the 'authentic India'. While as a liberal intellectual he reads with Maitreyi Kalidasa, Papini, Walt Whitman and Tagore, he suspects the freedom given to her by her father and the latter's hospitality towards him as trickery. And when they become intimate, he thinks of their relationship as that of 'civilized man and barbarian' (Eliade 1994: 32). These primitive/developed, child/adult, civilized/barbarian oppositions evoke the discourse of 'improvement' that combined the mainstays of earlier Orientalist and liberal scholars such as William Jones and James Mill (1820) respectively, with the former emphasizing the glories of an ancient Hindu civilization and the latter emphasizing the 'primitive', 'wild' and 'barbaric' qualities of Indians. Eventually, Alaine's Orientalist quest conflates Maitreyi's body with the body of the Indian nation. He affirms this fantasy at the end of Devi's novel in her final meeting with him in the library of the Divinity School at the University of Chicago, in which he cannot confront the flesh and blood Devi even forty-two years later, but instead sees her only in terms of an Indian goddess and as the daughter of 'immortal India'.

Finally, despite his construction of the racial and civilizational differences between Alain and Maitreyi, Eliade elevates Alaine's love into the realm of the transcendental and spiritual; he begins to imagine himself as a Hindu, and after being spurned from her home by her father, dons the persona of a suffering ascetic. The sentiment evoked in his romance through descriptions of his own mental anguish and the suffering inflicted on Maitreyi's body and mind by her family seeks to neutralize the terms of his Orientalism. Indeed, the horrible outcome of the affair that results in his expulsion from Maitreyi's home, the loss of his job and the loss of his European friends, who see him as contaminated, takes the shape of a terrible tragedy in which Eliade presents Alaine as the Aristotelian tragic hero whose quest for knowledge about India and romantic involvement with Maitreyi in unconducive circumstances lead to his downfall. In so doing, Alaine steps out of historical time, giving his affair an atemporal quality – something that was to bring eternal joy and eternal sorrow. As Eliade says in his autobiography:

> If 'historical' India were forbidden to me, the road now was opened to 'eternal' India. I realized also that I had to know passion, drama, and suffering before renouncing the 'historical' dimensions of my existence and making my way toward a transhistorical, atemporal, paradigmatic dimension in which tensions and conflicts would themselves disappear (Eliade 1990: 189).

It could be argued that Alaine's representation of himself as the tragic hero and his elevation of his love to the transcendental and atemporal is the only way for him to deal with his suffering. As he himself says in his autobiography,

> I was suffering terribly, all the more so because I knew that, along with the friendship of the Dasgupta family, I had lost India itself. All that had happened had arisen out of my desire to identify with India, to become, truly 'Indian'. After I read Dasgupta's letter, I knew that I would not soon be forgiven. This India that I had begun to know about, which I had dreamed about and that I loved so much, was now permanently forbidden to me (Eliade 1990: 186).

Such stepping out of historical time, however, is not devoid of consequences. First, his presentation of the failed romance in such terms obscures the historical and material realities of the difficulties of an interracial relationship in the vexed political context of 1930s India. While the pursuit of their romance was inhibited by the racial dynamics in the colonial economy, Eliade's novel constructs such inhibitions only in terms of familial and social pressures from Maitreyi's family. Doing so, his narrative masks the rigid segregation of the races demanded by colonial pressures. And secondly, his descriptions of Maitreyi's maltreatment at the hands of the family reinforce images of the harsh treatment meted out to Indian women – images on the basis of which the colonizers justified the colonial mission, and perpetuated a discourse about white men saving brown women through the script of romantic love – images that continue to be seen in stories such as M. M. Kaye's *The Far Pavilions* (1997). Eliade's narrative about his failed romance, then, is one that belongs in the discourse of liberal imperial ideology, which seeks to reveal the fate of the native woman in terms similar to those presented by European liberal thought. Scrutiny of Eliade's novel in these terms helps reveal its centrality to the continuing production of contemporary liberal ideologies that regard the native woman as exotic and mysterious, as one who, as Chandra Mohanty (1995) argues, continues to be seen as oppressed by familial and social ideologies.[10]

Finally, Eliade's representation also gives Maitreyi limited agency, constructing her capacity to act in sexual or in philosophical discourses in his own terms. His refusal to grant her agency and power comes with his insistent spurning of the letters that Maitreyi sends through her cousin Khoka. In fact, Alaine's own fantasy and commonplace knowledge refuses even for a minute to call in question Khoka's stories about the physical and mental abuse inflicted on Maitreyi. On the contrary, he channels the assertion of his own moral fibre into the virtues of male self-control and the ideals of honouring his (imagined) promise to her father never to see her again. Doing so, Alaine seeks to secure for himself the same codes of virtue, rationality, and duty that the colonizing male ostensibly observed in order to justify his own civilized status.

Eliade's novel was written only a few years after Rabindranath Tagore's *The Home and the World*, and one finds many parallels, especially between Maitreyi and Bimala, Tagore's fiercely independent heroine, who transgresses the boundaries of home and marital conventions to have an affair with her husband's friend, the dynamic and forceful freedom fighter Sundeep. Like Bimala, whom Tagore likens to Kali, Eliade also treats Maitreyi's independence and fierce sexuality as an embodiment of Kali. When placed against the political and literary backdrop, both romances provoke questions about the particular ideological and social functions they might perform. At the time, when the nationalist movement had fostered the participation of women, who came out in large numbers, the male nationalist, seeing in women's independence a threat to the domestic order, also sought to contain them. In this context, Tagore's romance narrative, *The Home and the World*, contains the woman's freedom by giving her a sexual identity that invokes her proper role within the domestic order. Once she crosses the boundaries set by the author, she is punished.[11] While Eliade's narrative performs a somewhat dissimilar function, in that, unlike Tagore's Bimala, Alaine sees no transgression in Maitreyi's independence and evokes sympathy from the reader for the treatment he is told she receives at the hands of her father, as a European Eliade's representation of Maitreyi's subjugation becomes a way of presenting Alaine as the enlightened man who believes in women's freedom. In so doing, his romance demonstrates the overlaps between Orientalist and nationalist thought on the question of women's emancipation.

Maitreyi's Story

In recalling her affair with Eliade through her own narrative, in which she challenges Eliade's assertions, Devi writes of her personal experience of pain and loneliness and does not deny her love for him. However, her self-conscious and carefully crafted story also situates their romance in a much more complex layering and intersection of Orientalism, of upper-class Hindu orthodoxy, and of a patriarchal anti-colonial liberal nationalist outlook symbolized by her 'half-westernized, half-orthodox' father who encouraged women's emancipation through education on the one hand, and carved out fixed social and domestic roles on the other (Devi 1995: 3). The inextricable linkages of these socio-political factors with the personal also makes her response a manual of the social codes that governed upper-class Indian women in the 1930s.

As the daughter of an affluent and intellectual household and a student of the eminent nationalist writer Rabindranath Tagore, who also writes the foreword to her first book of poems, Maitreyi consciously reveals her connections with liberal and nationalist circles of the time. She visits the opera, spends time attending lavish tea-parties, frequents the European 'empire theatre' instead of the Indian 'nautches' that were never mentioned in 'good society', and engages in the activities that went into the making of a lifestyle of leisure and pleasure (Devi 1995: 109). Her class is also indicated by material markers such as her chauffeur-driven Chevrolet car, the Victorian furniture in her home, and a room of her own, and through comparisons with her child-widow cousin. The intellectual influence of her father is evident in his library of seven thousand books and his encouragement to her to begin the study of Sanskrit with Kalidasa's *Sakuntala*, take lessons in music and violin, and learn French from

Alaine. Her rationalist father also encourages her to mix freely with men and to debate with them. She mentions the ways in which she enhances this inherited condition through her own restless energy and intellectual efforts. Thus she recalls conversing freely with her father's Indian and foreign students, and even going to the boys' college on her father's recommendation 'to recite poetry on different occasions', a 'rebellious act for both her father and herself' (Devi 1995: 25). Her father views this freedom as a 'revolution' within the domestic sphere, where his wife and daughter are allowed to speak freely with Europeans, and that, too, unveiled.

In highlighting the social, material, intellectual and class privileges available to her, Devi shows her readers the preoccupation with modernity among nationalists such as her father and the ways in which her own household becomes a site for its construction. However, to emphasize how this modernity complicates her life, she also renders visible its peculiar paradoxes and contradictions. While, as an upper-class woman who is encouraged by her 'inga-banga' father to write and read poetry, discourse and debate publicly on philosophical subjects and learn French, painting, and dancing, she fulfils the role of the 'new woman' that her father desires, she tells her readers how he forbids her to have any personal or sexual interactions (Devi 1995: 25). As she recalls, she 'seldom spoke with the boys – an unseen veil covered our faces'. 'Purdah' she remembers, 'affected both men and women. The effect of a taboo coming through the ages persisted obstinately' (Devi 1995: 25–6). Says Devi:

> In higher middle class families like ours, sex remained completely hidden. Nobody talked about it, no books dealing even remotely with sex were allowed. We never saw any expressions of sex, leave alone outrageous acts of necking or kissing – we never saw men and women hold hands. Even novels were selected by elders, and some including those of Bankim and even Tagore were banned (Devi 1995: 25–6).

Having grown up with an awareness of these codes of social propriety, then, she is initially cautious, and often questions whether her relationship with Alaine is a sinful act. Finally, when she expresses the desire to marry the European Alaine, her father renders her completely powerless in this decision-making process. In exposing her father's contradictory attitudes, Devi turns her narrative into a space where she self-consciously comments on the contradictions of patriarchal liberal thought as exemplified by her father, who, under pressure to resist colonization, rejects European-ness and is simultaneously driven by the nationalistic need to educate women.

In rewriting the story of her affair with Eliade and responding to what she identifies as 'half-truths' in his novel, Devi then consciously identifies the mediation of these multiple factors that are crucial to providing complicated meanings to her subjectivity as a woman, a daughter, and a future wife. As a matter of fact, in order to reconstruct her romance, Maitreyi finds herself compelled to recall these subtle yet intricately linked aspects of her life.

The view that these and the events of 1930 are inextricably tied to the outcome of her romance is reinforced by her memory of historical time, which is marked by tremendous precision. Even though Devi defines her love for Eliade as an 'experience that cannot be measured by time', and calls it 'timeless, sublime, existential and transcendental', she is very specific about recording dates and historical events (Devi 1995: 111). She provides a detailed commentary on the nationalistic movement and patriotic attitudes: Gandhi's Dandi March and her own experimentation with Swadeshi, in which she unable to participate publicly because of her father's disapproval, but which nevertheless, she tells her readers, 'stirred us to depths'. To this end, Devi's narrative reveals the contradictions of modernist aspirations for elite families who saw female education as essential for emancipation, yet envisaged this emancipation only in terms of their duty towards their families and nations as mothers and wives. The *bhadralok's* concern with respectability transformed women in such families into 'guardians of culture, a heavy burden on women in a situation in which bhadralok identity depended to a large extent on this very culture' (Engles 1996: 10). Notwithstanding her father's disapproval, she gives up the use of foreign goods. Despite her references to transcendental time when she recalls her love for Eliade, the reference to 1930, her interest/involvement in Swadeshi, the patriarchal demands of nationalism in the form of her father, and the armoury raid in Chittagong reveal that these incidents must have affected her lived experience and the personal aspects of her life. For, as she recalls the freedom movement and the revolutionary fervour of 1930, she also highlights Eliade's frivolous reaction as he goes out in search of the 'Revolution' – to witness it – so that he can tell his countrymen about seeing the 'real' India. Her constant and self-conscious separation of contemporary time and the historical past, recollected and rendered as it is into writing, forces us to consider the ways in which political and historical events structure the personal, which we as readers are provided a glimpse of through her descriptions of her state of mind as she recollects moments of pain, submission and excitement, her guilt over being a nationalist on the one hand and consorting with a European on the other, the fear of disclosure of her affair to her family, and critical analysis of her father. To this end, she not only points out how, despite her 'modern' education and freedom, she was subjected to severe disciplining, but also mentions her father's mistreatment of her mother, whom he ultimately abandons when he marries a much younger woman.

That Devi's narrative is written forty-two years later is also significant. In 1972, she was no longer the young Maitreyi of 1930 but a respectable grandmother in an upper-class household, a mother-in-law, and a devoted wife. She commanded a position of relative power over her daughter-in-law and other members of the household. At this point she also understood the impact her book would have on her family and relatives, who, as she writes, were very angry with her for publishing the book. Yet perhaps she realized that as an established intellectual she could also intervene in the mores of Orientalist and nationalist thought through her narrative. Hence, she takes advantage of her established position as an intellectual and ensures that, in choosing to counter Eliade's fantasies, she also critically evaluates the consequences of the paradoxes of liberalism and colonial modernity for women such as herself.

On one level, thus, Devi's romantic relationship, and the accompanying desire and longing that existed in tension with colonial and nationalist codes that imagined the two races as strictly apart, makes us re-think the question of representation in the colonial zone. Yet in situating the failed romance in a much more complex layering and intersection of political forces, each of which provides complicated meanings to her subjectivity as a woman, a daughter, a wife, a nationalist activist, an upper-class Hindu woman with a liberal education, and the lover of a white European, Devi not only challenges what she identifies as 'untruths' in Eliade's Orientalist account; her keen attentiveness to the political contexts of 1930, the racial difference, and the familial complications that occur as a result of this difference, remind us of the need for historical investigation of the complex implications of interracial codes for colonized women and the ideological underpinnings of transgressing such codes in a colonial economy. Her self-revelation of her personal life, accompanied as it was by its particular freedoms and entrapments in the 1930s, thus becomes a critical intervention in both Orientalist constructions of Indian women and in the contradictions of a liberal anti-colonial nationalism that, in its bid to emancipate the nation from the clutches of imperial rule, also reconfigured social codes of honour and duty that were ultimately disempowering for women.

As the above discussion shows, Devi's response to Eliade's narrative is important because it exposes the overlaps between and the contradictions of nationalist and colonialist claims to modern and traditional values that circumscribe her role in the world. As such, it highlights her role in questioning her own social subjectivity, which is fuelled by such claims. Her response can thus be seen as her refusal to produce herself as a victim of Orientalist and nationalist discourses. However, what makes her narrative even more significant is its disruption, additionally, of the continuing production in liberal feminist discourse of what Mohanty has called the 'average third world woman' who, in contrast to the implicit 'self-representation of Western women as educated, modern, as having control over their sexualities, and the freedom to make their own decisions', is represented as leading 'an essentially truncated life based on her feminine gender (read: sexually constrained) and being "third world" (read: ignorant, poor, uneducated, tradition-bound, domestic, family-oriented, victimized, etc.)' (1995: 261). Devi's keen attentiveness to the different temporal, spatial and familial contexts and the dictates of her own class background serves as a reminder that any analysis of South Asian women must be 'formed in concrete, historical, and political' terms and analysis (Mohanty 1995: 262).

Additionally, her narrative acquires a continuing relevance to the representation and construction of South Asian women in the postcolonial diaspora, because the historical encounters with colonial, nationalist and Orientalist discourses have spilled over into the West, especially in Britain, where not only has the vexed history of race-relations in the wake of immigration and relocation from the Indian subcontinent relied on stereotyping of South Asian women on the part of the dominant communities to emphasize the inferiority of South Asian communities, but also the South Asian community's defence against discourses that put them in a position of subordination has resulted in an intensification of regressive social and familial codes for women.[12] Nationalist aspirations manifested through a yearning for 'imaginary homelands' then lead to patriarchal drives that, at times, reproduce the victimization of South Asian women from within the communities. As has been shown in critical, theoretical and sociological analysis as well as in popular culture such as Gurinder Chadha's 1992 film *Bhaji on the Beach* (inspired by the lives of South Asian women in contemporary Britain), the legacies of colonialist and nationalist thought on the question of women have become deeply embedded in eurocentric consciousness and patriarchal relations, and continue to dominate the popular imagination as well as institutional practices and policies.[13] In forcing open the complex interconnections between past histories and present sensibilities in her narrative, Devi makes the past relevant to an understanding of the multiple manifestations of popular and institutional stereotyping as well as ongoing representations of South Asian women in the present.

Notes

1. Earlier versions of this chapter were presented at the 1999 Modern Languages Association Meeting at Chicago and at the South Asia Women's Conference in Los Angeles in 2000. My thanks to participants for their comments and feedback. Thanks also to Preet Aulakh for his careful reading of the chapter.
2. For seminal work and insightful analyses in this direction see Uma Chakravarty 1989; Partha Chatterjee 1989; Tanika Sarkar, 1997.
3. For more discussion on this issue see Chapters 6 and 7 in Partha Chatterjee (1993).
4. Some of the key examples mentioned by Sarkar include women writers such as Kailashbashini Debi in Bengal in the 1860s, and Tarabai Shinde and Pandita Ramabai in Maharashtra in the 1880s. For a discussion of women's autobiography, see also Chatterjee's 'Women and Nation' (1993), and Sarkar (1999), which provides another useful example of a colonized woman's autobiography.
5. Maitreyi Devi (1914–1990) was a poet and a lecturer. She founded the Council for the Promotion of Communal Harmony in 1964 and served as Vice-President of the All-India Women's Coordinating Council. Her first book of poems, for which Rabindranath Tagore wrote the foreword, appeared when she was sixteen. She published poetry and essays on philosophy and social reform. *Na Hanyate* brought both fame and fortune to Maitreyi Devi, and was translated into several European languages, including Romanian.
6. Eliade's novel won a literary prize and is considered to be one of the classics of Romanian literature. It has also been translated into several languages and made into a film starring Hugh Grant.
7. In her review of the two novels titled, 'O Calcutta', *New Republic* (15 August 1994): 43–5, Anita Desai describes Eliade's novel as 'a disturbing mixture of racial and colonial attitudes of the day and a lush romanticism' (p. 43). She describes the novel and its racist description of Maitreyi and her family as exemplifying the fascist influence of 1930s Europe on Eliade. Ann Irvine's short review in the *Library*

Journal 111 (15 April 1994), on the other hand, describes the stories as providing 'a wonderful study in contrasting cultures as well as an engaging love story'. Azim Firdaus in *The Journal of Asian Studies* 55. 4 (Nov. 1996): 1035–7 points out how Eliade portrays Maitreyi as a passive object who is subjected to an anthropological inquiry. Ian Buruma in *The New York Review of Books* 41. 15 (22 September 1994) provides an interesting analysis arguing that the relationship between Maitreyi and Eliade reflects a 'tension between rationalism and a fascination for the irrational' (p. 27). However, the asymmetries created by gender, race, and colonialism are not evoked in the analysis. K. E. Fleming's review, 'He Said, She Said', *The Nation* (10 October 1994): 390–3, identifies the archetypal literary Orientalism in Eliade's text, yet reinforces Eliade's eurocentric assertion when he says that Maitreyi and Eliade 'have done the *Kama Sutra* proud. The Maitreyi of Eliade's fantasy, no shy coquette tossing flowers across the threshold knows no inhibition . . . The erotic abilities of the experienced Alaine pale in comparison' (p. 91).

8. Chakravarty (1989), in her essay 'Whatever Happened to the Vedic Dasi?', contends that with the loss of self-esteem following the British conquest of India, the mythology of the past golden age of Hinduism enabled the emerging middle class to deal with the 'burden' of the present. At the centre of this mythology was the idea that the men of the age were 'free, brave, vigorous, fearless', civilized, noble, and spiritual, and the women were highly learned, free, and cultured.

9. For a detailed and insightful discussion of William Jones's *Sakuntala*, see Thapar 1999.

10. See Mohanty 1995. For a detailed version of the essay see Mohanty, Russo and Torres (eds) (1991).

11. First published in 1915, *Home and the World* was written in the context of Swadeshi (1903–1908) and the partition of Bengal. For a discussion of the novel see Michael Sprinker 1996.

12. See Bhachu 1993; Brah 1996; Yuval-Davies 1993.

13. For a discussion of *Bhaji on the Beach,* see Bhatia 1998.

References

Bhachu, P. (1993), 'Identities Constructed and Reconstructed: Representations of Asian Women in Britain', in G. Buijs (ed.), *Migrant Women: Crossing Boundaries and Changing Identities*, pp. 99–118. Oxford: Berg.

Bhatia, N. (1998), 'Women, Homelands, and the Indian Diaspora', *Centennial Review* (Fall 1998): 511–26.

Brah, A. (1996),. *Cartographies of Diaspora: Contesting Identities*, London and New York: Routledge.

Buruma, Ian (1994), 'Indian Love Call', *New York Review of Books*, 22 Sept.: 27.

Chakravarty, U. (1989), 'Whatever Happened to the Vedic Dasi? Orientalism, Nationalism, and a Script for the Past', in K. Sangari and S. Vaid (eds), *Recasting Women: Essays in Colonial History*, pp. 27–87. Delhi: Kali for Women.

Chatterjee, P. (1989), 'The Nationalist Resolution of the Women's Question', in K. Sangari and S. Vaid (eds), *Recasting Women: Essays in Colonial History,* pp. 233–53 Delhi: Kali for Women.

——. (1993), *The Nation and its Fragments. Colonial and Postcolonial Histories*, Princeton, NJ: Princeton University Press.

—— (1993), 'Woman and Nation', in P. Chatterjee *The Nation and its Fragments. Colonial and Postcolonial Histories,* pp. 135–57. Princeton, NJ: Princeton University Press.

Desai, A. (1994), 'O Calcutta!', *New Republic*, 15 August: 43–5.

Devi, M. (1995), *It Does Not Die: A Romance*, Chicago and London: University of Chicago Press.

Eliade, M. (1990), *Autobiography Volume I: Journey East, Journey West 1907–1937*, Chicago: The University of Chicago Press.

——. (1994), *Bengal Nights*, Chicago: University of Chicago Press.

Engles, D. (1996), *Beyond Purdah? Women in Bengal 1890–1939*, Delhi: Oxford University Press.

Fleming, K. E. (1994), 'He Said, She Said', *The Nation*, 10 October: 390–3.

Irvine, A. (1994), Review of *Bengal Nights* and *It Does Not Die*, *Library Journal*, 15 April: 111.

Kaye, M. M. (1997), *The Far Pavilions,* St Martin's Press.

Levine, P. (1996), 'Rereading the 1890s: Venereal Disease as "Constitutional Crisis" in Britain and British India', *Journal of Asian Studies* 55 (3): 585–612.

Mill, J. (1820), *History of British India* (1817), second edn. Published in 6 Vols. London: James Madden.

Mohanty, C. T. (1991), 'Under Western Eyes', in C. T. Mohanty, A. Russo and L. Torres (eds), *Third World Women and the Politics of Feminism*, pp. 51–80. Bloomington, IN: Indiana University Press.

——. (1995), 'Under Western Eyes', in B. Ashcroft, G. Griffiths and H. Tiffin (eds), *The Post-Colonial Studies Reader*, pp. 259–263. New York and London: Routledge.

Niranjana, T. (1992), 'Translation, Colonialism, and the Rise of English', in *Rethinking English. Essays in Literature, Language, History*, pp. 124–45. New Delhi: Trianka.

Sarkar, T. (1997), 'Women in South Asia: The Raj and After', *History Today* 47 (Sept.): 54–9.

——. (1999), *Words to Win: The Making of Amar Jiban. A Modern Autobiography*, Delhi: Kali for Women.

Sprinker, M. (1996), 'Homeboys: Nationalism, Colonialism, and Gender in Rabindranath Tagore's *The Home and the World*', in H. Schwarz and R. Deinst (eds), *Reading the Shape of the World. Toward an International Cultural Studies*, pp. 202–23. Boulder, CO: Westview Press.

Thapar, R. (1999), *Sakuntala. Texts, Readings, Histories*, Delhi: Kali for Women.

Yuval-Davis, N. (1993), 'Gender and Nation', *Ethnic and Racial Studies* 16 (4): 621–32.

7

Undressing the Diaspora
Bakirathi Mani

The clothing practices of diasporas in metropolitan cities of industrialized states – so often assumed to be congruent with histories of 'national origin', representative of a culture and tradition removed, in a faraway place – prompt an examination of clothing as a vehicle for the performance of ethnic identity. In the midst of *kurtas* worn over khakis, and *dupattas* veiling tank tops, the salience of fixed ethnic and national identities inscribed on to prediscursive biological entities must be called into question. The proposal of ethnic identity as a performative act at this juncture is an attempt to work through conversations in queer and performance theory on the one hand, and studies of South Asian diasporas and globalization on the other. Rather than proclaiming a transcendental transnational subject, I propose that the clothing practices of diasporic youth – the juxtaposition of shorts and tie-dye tops, slacks and embroidered shawls, and the layering of headresses, nose-rings, and anklets with jeans – produces a situated reading of 'diaspora' as a localized cultural form. Hence, the greater concern of this essay is to posit 'diaspora' as a critical point of inquiry in studies of globalization.[1]

As a theoretical, rather than ethnographic, endeavour my observations of the clothing practices of diasporic youth are almost entirely confined to those individuals I read (and racialize) as 'South Asian' on college campuses across the United States: men and women in their late teens and twenties, raised if not born in the US. It is therefore a peculiarly cosmopolitan, middle- and upper-class section of youth that I refer to, who participate in bourgeois consumption patterns and possess cultural capital generated by this practice of consumption. I also allude to representations of clothing practices in diasporic South Asian film, in the hope of providing a more tangible visualization of what a performative ethnic identity looks like. In this way, my examination of clothing choices and practices is by no means an ethnographic survey of South Asian youth in the United States. Instead, in the brief readings that follow, I ask two primary questions. First, what are the ways in which young South Asians in diaspora generate a sense of history and belonging? Second, how might a 'South Asian' identity engage with the disciplinary effects of state policies on ethnic multiculturalism?

I introduce the multivalent term 'diaspora' here as a means to contend with the transnational imaginaries of South Asian immigrant populations in the United States. The term 'diaspora', as I use it, refers not to sites of post-national study, but as Paul Gilroy (1987) suggests, to social formations located within the histories and institutions of national racial economies. To conceive of South Asians in the United States as a diaspora, therefore, is to broaden the theoretical and methodological paradigms used to think through immigration from the Indian subcontinent to the United States, and to situate the formation of subjectivities and communities within movements of labour, capital, and commodities that characterize the global economy in the early twenty-first century.[2] The use of the term 'diaspora' here is not meant to gloss over the multiple discursive ways in which ethnicity and community are constructed, nor to skim past the specific historical geneaologies behind the usage of the term.[3] Yet to the extent that diasporas can also mark those people implicated into a narrative of ethnicity rather than an analysis of racialization in their incorporation as immigrants to America (Shukla 1997: 306–12), I use the word to indicate the discrepancy between the performance of ethnic identity and systems of racial codification in the United States. Given the specific context of this racial economy, it is my contention that it is within the dialectical movement of diasporas that convenient narrativizations of immigrant history must be contested, and racial imaginaries of the US nation-state interrogated.

Simultaneously, my use of the word 'South Asia' rests upon the irony of its invocation. As a phrase that refers to immigrants from the Indian subcontinent, the category of 'South Asian' makes sense as a racial/cultural referent *only* in the United States. While 'South Asia' denotes the territorial construct of the Indian subcontinent – a remnant of US foreign policy during the Cold War – the term 'South Asian' circulates among second-generation immigrant youth on American college campuses as a common denominator that references a racial/political category as well as a cohesive cultural history. Thus, to identify as 'South Asian' more often than not invokes a post-1965 history of immigration in which South Asians are consistently named the 'model minority', immigrating to the United States as skilled professionals. In the process, the history of Sikh farm labourers in the United States in the early twentieth century, and the currently rising numbers of working-class South Asian immigrants are eclipsed. The political viability of the term 'South Asian' is thus para-doxically contingent upon the overdetermination of histories of immigra-tion from the subcontinent. As such, to identify as 'South Asian' gestures multiply: to an imagined homeland, as well as the racialized location of immigrants in the US state.

I begin with the premise that the clothing choices of youth in the South Asian diaspora are a distinctly political act, with implications that disturb the assumed coherence between categories of race, nation, and culture. By examining the effects of combining so-called 'native costume' and West-ern clothes, I trace the processes through which ethnic identity is enacted in and through dress, and examine the discursive possibility of 'coming out' as South Asian. I propose that ethnic identity is produced through performative acts that disrupt naturalized assumptions of biologically-inscribed racial (and hence cultural) identity. Concurrently, however, I also argue that performative acts that appear to rupture precisely this syn-chrony of race and culture may in fact reaffirm essentialized identities based on notions of cultural authenticity and nostalgia. As such, perform-ances of ethnic identity may not necessarily be read as acts of resistance, but rather, as a commentary on regimes of ethnic multiculturalism in the United States.

A Short History of Saris and Sneakers

An examination of clothing as a vehicle for performative ethnic identity necessitates not only a historicization of cloth as commodity culture, but also an examination of the theatres and modes of performance. My understanding of ethnic identity as a performative act refers not to the staged combinations of 'east–west' clothing paraded on Paris runways, but to the everyday practice of dress by diasporic youth. The study of fashion has to be wrestled out of ready-made semiotic systems of transcendent transnational understanding,[4] and from the easily-labelled category of 'subculture', which relegates clothing practices, particularly of youth, to the sidelines of traditional academic inquiry (Hebdige 1979). Conse-quently, I concentrate on a reading of historical and anthropological essays on clothing practices through the lens of performance and queer studies, in so far as the latter methodologies interrogate the naturalized correlation between biology and subjectivity. Adjacent to this is my concern with articulating a mode of performance that resonates clearly within specific historical trajectories of the use of clothing in South Asia, while simul-taneously working to understand the transformation of those trajectories in the movement of diasporas.[5]

Bernard Cohn's (1996) study of the production of authority and racial difference in 'Cloth, Clothes and Colonialism: India in the Nineteenth Century' provides a valuable starting-point by indicating the imbrication of clothes in the construction of a state-sponsored racial order. Taking his cue from the case of G. S. Sagar, an immigrant Sikh in Britain who protested for the right to retain his turban while wearing the mandatory uniform of public transportation employees, Cohn spins back on Sagar's protest to discuss a series of colonial attempts to delineate visible differences between British authorities and their Indian subjects. Locally-observed rituals, customs, and clothing practices were stratified as 'tradition'; the turban became one part of the colonial injunction on native presentation, identifying Sikhs as a 'martial race'. Behind the turban lay further negotiations over dress that demarcated the divide between imperial authority and colonial subject: the investiture of heavenly power in cloth by Mughal rulers, uneasily evaded by British traders; instructions for Indians to be attired in 'native costume' in front of their British superiors at the imperial *darbar*; the disapproval of British men who 'went native' after the formalization of colonial rule over India; and the construction of the 'Indian' into a visibly Oriental subject through the codification of caste, religion, and class hierarchy. By demonstrating the tense negotiations over gifts of cloth, changes in uniform, and expectations of ceremonial as well as everyday dress, Cohn demarcates the ambivalent space that clothing occupied in the imperial apparatus, and its role in the creation of a taxonomy of racial difference. Cohn's argument demonstrates not so much the role of clothes as a symbol of power, but the constitution and enactment of power and authority through racializing difference via the everyday use of cloth.

Particularly important to note in the racialization of the colonial subject is the highly gendered texture of the production of difference. Not only did cloth stand as a testimony to the Orientalization (or conversely, modernization) of the native, but very often the ground of contention for marking native 'progress' was the female body. Himani Banerjee (1995) illustrates the manner in which the changing clothing practices of middle-class Bengali gentlewomen became the site for the constitution of an indigenous intellectual (male) nationalism out of the discursive strands of colonial sexual and social ideology.[6] The high-collared blouses of the female landed classes, the lace-edged sari, and the brooch came to signal, in addition to dramatic revisions in the drape of the sari, the advancement of the Indian 'race' in the British colonial narrative of social Darwinism. In the loss of the translucent cloth that covered women's bodies, a new transparency was found: a nationalist ideology that substituted for heathen clothing practices a supposedly de-sexualized form of dress that policed the moral, sexual, and corporeal figure of Indian women.[7]

Perhaps the most exemplary historical indicator of the performative effect of clothing in South Asian history is M. K. Gandhi, whose strategies of dress literally embodied a form of Third World nationalism in the twentieth century. Emma Tarlo's (1996) demonstration of Gandhi's sartorial slippages – beginning with the dandy English top-hat and silk accoutrements that he wore while a student in London, to the simplified forms of Western attire and Kathiawadi peasant garb that he and his family adopted in South Africa, and then the increasingly more bare dimensions of dress that Gandhi adopted on his return to India – demonstrates the imbrication of cloth in the production of aesthetic and political value in multiple colonial racial economies. Men like Gandhi, who had the option of choosing between costumes, attempted to syncretize at each moment different semiotic systems, and to fuse together culturally disparate referents of identity. In his charged historical performance from minuteman to messiah, Gandhi's dress signalled the national imaginary of an independent India, altered aesthetic capital through the advocacy of *khadi*, and brand-named Indian nationalism with a loincloth.

Gandhi's successful enactment of modernity and a nascent nationalist movement through dress emphasizes the importance of a receptive audience in the performance of ethnic identity. The use of *khadi* cloth, for example, could not have performed its symbolic resistance had it not been overdetermined as such by a wider Indian and Western audience. As Judith Williamson (cited in Gaines 1990: 2) writes, it is 'as if the sexy black dress made you be a femme fatale, whereas 'femme fatale' is, precisely, an image; it needs a viewer to function at all'. As I transpose this historical survey of commodity culture on to a reading of diasporic South Asian youth cultural practices, my interests lie as much in the clothing choices made by South Asian American youth as in the receptivity to those choices of a wider array of audiences. I argue that the performative effect of 'diasporic dress', though resting largely within hegemonic notions of aesthetic capital, is generated out of a history of clothing practices that denote both colonial attempts to contain the potentially disruptive implications of cloth, and also nationalist/postcolonial attempts uniformly to dress – and thereby to represent – the nation.

Queering Diasporic Clothing Acts

What, then, are the peculiarly diasporic implications of clothing practices? In what ways do the clothed figures of diasporic South Asians interrupt metanarratives of the state that are based on racialized 'givens'? I begin with the assumption that the clothing practices of cosmopolitan diasporic youth – be it the simple drape of a sari over sneakers, or the casual twirling of a *dupatta* over denim – prompt a visual confusion of epistemologies of categorization. The apparent disjuncture between national referents suggested through a uniquely diasporic style produces '. . . a space of possibility structuring and confounding culture: the disruptive element that intervenes, not just a category crisis of male and female, but the crisis of category itself' (Garber 1992: 16).

If the clothing practices of South Asian diasporic youth, marked by various combinations of *kurtas* and jeans, the slip of sandals under a skirt, or an abundance of silver anklets and earrings can be considered akin to drag or cross-dressing more generally, it may be possible to highlight the extreme limits of performance theory. By playing with the supposedly stable structural entities of nation, culture, and ethnicity, diasporic dress responds to seamless state narratives that position 'ethnic' peoples as authentic vessels of their 'native' cultures – perfect representatives of a more 'global' community.

In effect, I argue that the clothing practices of diasporic South Asian youth are a response to Judith Butler's (1990: 137) notion of 'heterosexual coherence', denaturalizing the assumed link between raced skin and ethnic identity. By clothing the body in a *mélange* of ethnicized accessories, ethnic identity becomes a process of signification enacted through – though not contained within – the material history of commodity exchange. Consequently, the juxtaposition of cultural referents in the clothing practices of cosmopolitan South Asian American youth puts in motion a performance of ethnic identity that both confounds and confirms state-sponsored narratives of ethnic pluralism.[8] To quote Butler: 'There is no gender identity behind the expressions of gender; that identity is performatively constituted by the very 'expressions' that are said to be its results (Butler 1990: 25).[9]

If ethnicity is substituted for gender – albeit with difficulty – in this paradigm, ethnic identity becomes a series of temporally-bounded performative acts that are enacted in synchrony with (though not congruently to) the construction of racial order in the United States. Ethnic identity is thus produced in excess of a regime of racial taxonomy: the clothing practices of diasporic youth signal outwards towards an imagined community of 'South Asia', but also inwards to the very real fault lines in the racial paradigms of industrialized states. As a body produced through the deliberate attempt to resignify notions of home and places of belonging – reminding the observer of Queer Nation's slogan 'We're here, we're queer, get used to it' – the practice of diasporic dress begins to destabilize the space of performance, thereby interrogating the limits of reproduction of national narratives.

I turn here to the intimate relationship between queerness and diaspora suggested by David Eng (1997), who writes, '[diasporas are] a function of queerness – queerness not just in the narrow sense of sexual identity and sexual practices, but queerness as a critical methodology for evaluating Asian American racial formation across multiple axes of difference and in its numerous local and global manifestations.' (Eng 1997: 39).

While I cannot fully subsume diasporas into a 'function' of queer theory, my use of the word 'queer' here denotes the implications of Eng's 'critical methodology' for the re-inscription of metanarratives of the state. In agreement with Eng, I suggest that a more 'capacious set of Asian American locations' (1997: 43) hinges upon the location of the cross-dressed South Asian in the public sphere of the US nation-state, re-signifying – and thereby queering – the national narrative of America in its simultaneous citation of 'South Asia'. Playing upon assumptions of embodied cultural identity, and enacting temporary, contingent acts of ethnic identity, the clothing practices of diasporic South Asian youth riddle the epistemology of classificatory practices and bring into relief the racial taxonomy that underlines multiculturalism in the United States.

In order to demonstrate how a queer methodology may denote one form of re-territorialization, I pose here the discursive possibility of 'coming out' as South Asian in white America. In a racial economy where the metaphor of the closet manifests itself multiply – as a 'shaping presence' (Sedgewick 1990: 68) that ghettoizes minority discourse, structures legal discourse in the form of immigration laws, and thereby maps out a topography of power – coming out as South Asian dismantles disciplinary state practices that see race as being authentically representative of the 'ethnic' in a reflecting pool of whiteness. Following Eve Kosofsky Sedgwick's example of the ACT-UP tee-shirt that announces the homosexuality of its wearer (1990: 4), the conscious combination of 'ethnic' cloth and accessories with everyday Western clothes constitutes a deliberate performance of ethnic identity speaking in excess of the racialized body. Like Sedgwick's own history of coming out as a fat woman (1990: 63), identifying as South Asian is 'meant to do for the wearer, not the constative work of reporting that s/he *is* out, but the performative work of coming out in the first place' (1990: 4, italics in original). Coming out as South Asian, therefore, is not simply to have recourse to a nativist claim to cultural identification. Instead, it is a move towards recognizing one's production and location in the US nation-state through reterritorializing the coloured space of nationhood. By gesturing towards multiple national referents, the performative act of coming out as 'South Asian' dislodges attempts to stabilize the diasporic body in the US racial economy.

I extend my proposal of coming out by referring to films that take as their central subject the coming of age of diasporic South Asians. In Mira Nair's film *Mississippi Masala*, the rhetorical implications of coming out as South Asian are made tangible in the figure of Mina, played by Sarita Chowdhury. *Mississippi Masala* opens with Mina wearing clothes out of the neighbourhood K-mart; upon meeting her lover Demetrius (Denzel Washington) she quickly abandons her 'American' dress and clambers into bright *salwaar kameezes*, mirror-spangled shawls, and *dupattas*. Asked who she is, Mina replies, 'I'm . . . I'm a mix, masala'. In the heartland of the Mississippi, Mina has chosen to produce herself as an exotic ethnic commodity. The self-identification of Mina – in a replay of the clothing/unclothing choices of many diasporic South Asians – outlines a historical trajectory of ethnic identification through a changing aesthetic mode of dress, enacted within the liberal narrative of rainbow-coalition America. Mina begins her relationship with Demetrius in clothes indistinguishable from those of her black friends at the neighbourhood bar; midway through the film she walks on to the beaches of Mississippi in an orange *kurta*; and finally, the movie closes with Mina (in a *salwaar kameez*) embracing Demetrius (in *kente* cloth) in the pastureland of middle America. The production of a distinctly 'South Asian' identity –note that the immediate referent here is not the Indian subcontinent, but rather the trajectory of Mina's departure from Uganda, stopover in England, and subsequent arrival in America – is one that carries with it the stakes of identifying as both a person of colour and an exotic other. It is a move that Mina chooses to make precisely because her coming out as a South Asian woman makes her particularly desirable for Demetrius (and no doubt to a larger white audience), while allowing her to draw resources from a (somewhat spurious) 'cultural heritage' no longer confined to her family's diasporic movements.[10]

While Nair's portrayal of Mina's coming of age – as a woman, as a diasporic South Asian, as a person of colour – is deliberately staged through changes of dress, I think also of Srinivas Krishna's movie *Masala*, and the portrayal of Rita, defiantly outfitted in Himachali caps and miniskirts; Michelle Mohabeer's film *Coconut, Cane, and Cutlass*, and Mohabeer's self-depiction in coolie headdresses; and Nisha Ganatra's short film *Junky Punky Girlz*, whose central character deliberates over the complex sexual and ethnic implications of getting her nose pierced. I am particularly interested in the conscious performances by women in these films that attempt to produce a distinctly 'South Asian' body in an ethnically 'diverse' north America. As diasporic South Asian women choose particular combinations of 'ethnic' and 'Western' wear, the centrality of gender in the reproduction of national narratives is reiterated. Clothing in the diasporic context is recognized as one way in which cohesive cultural and religious histories are reproduced; thus their 'proper' appearance on the bodies of South Asian women is of paramount importance within patriarchal South Asian communities. The choice of some South Asian women to wear Himachali caps, or *kurtas* with their otherwise 'Western' clothes, denies precisely those patriarchal attempts to demand perfect reproductions of nation and tradition. As such, the choices of clothing that can be made by young South Asian women in metropolitan cities in the United States loop back into the history of attempts by nationalist men to mould women into representations of the modern Indian nation. For those women who are allowed to choose their clothing, coming out as 'South Asian' troubles not so much the stability of American multiculturalism, but rather the nostalgic ambitions of patriarchal diasporic communities to cling on to 'authentic' replicas of their cultural heritage.

As such, the consideration of ethnic identity as a performative act must reside at the heart of the riddle of racial/cultural authenticity. If identity politics is understood as the space from which the American nation-state assimilates immigrants into a hierarchy of ethnic pluralism, benevolently re-couping its spatial integrity and celebrating a narrative of state-sponsored whiteness, then it is only by deconstructing the foundations of authenticity that a theory of ethnic performativity can begin to act against coercive regimes of multiculturalism. Disturbing the synchrony of ethnicity and nationhood through clothing practices allows the cross-dressed South Asian to be marked not only as 'un-American' (Newton 1972: 1), but outside what is normatively called America.

Here I return to Eng's (1997) call for a more capacious set of Asian American locations, and attempt to elucidate the sites from which performative acts of ethnic identity can bring into relief the crooked lines of multicultural narratives. In this context, Esther Newton's (1972) pioneering work on drag queens in the United States has been particularly valuable. Newton's comparative ethnography of drag queens and street fairies demonstrates that the theatre of performative acts has major repercussions for the performance of so-called 'resistant' identities. Drag queens, professional female impersonators who perform on stage in clubs for a largely heterosexual audience, rigidly separate their work attire from their private life, appearing on stage with beaded dresses and wigs, only to strip off their make-up at home to cultivate a middle-class sensibility. The objective is to 'pass' in heteronormative cultural systems; consequently drag is denied visibility offstage while being flamboyantly, but finitely, performed onstage (1972: 13). In contrast, the clothing practices of street fairies (derisively known as 'nellies') elide the distinction between the public and the private spheres, so that they 'are never off stage' (1972: 8). Thus the attempt to perform within the normative frameworks of American society (for the benefit of the male heterosexual gaze) marks the ambivalent posturing identity of the drag queen; while the risk of eliding gender boundaries completely, of claiming and redefining sign systems, is the act of the nellie on the street.

The two radically different forms of drag speak to the potential for clothing practices to transgress hetero-normative systems of control. Literally contained within the demarcated space of the stage, drag queens are prevented from having a larger impact on their viewers, as the stage 'promote[s] the idea that there is a secure space between the stage and the floor . . . In other words, the deviates are all on the stage and the audience's honor is never threatened' (1972: 118). Street fairies, on the other hand, are always in full drag, performing perhaps not so much for a stage audience as for themselves. The collapse of the public and private sphere in the performative act of the street fairy situates the fantasy of performance in the 'real world', directly threatening assumptions of masculinity and modes of patriarchal discipline. For their constant visibility in public spaces, street fairies are chastised by both gay communities and mainstream heterosexual society. In Newton's ethnography, it is the everyday performance of the nellie, rather than the exotic spectacle of the drag queen, that constitutes a transgressive act.

The effect of diasporic clothing practices must similarly be called into question. If, like the drag queens, cross-dressed diasporic South Asian youth stage their clothing choices in order to cater to a hegemonic (white) gaze, then their clothing practices are complicit in the popular desire to consume 'ethnic chic'. Yet if the performative acts of young South Asian Americans slip between and across 'performance time' and 'real time',[11] the transgressive potential of diasporic clothing practices can effectively push beyond the normative paradigms of multicultural state narratives.

The project of outlining a theory of performative ethnic identity through dress is thus a means of reading the local as a site of the transnational, with its own emancipatory possibilities and resistant politics – but also with its own myths and hegemonizing tendencies. While it is all too easy to label the clothing practices of diasporic South Asian youth as 'avant-garde', narrativizing as transcendent those so-called transgressive acts that only circulate in the same medium of racial authenticity,[12] Kath

Weston is correct to point out that 'to destabilize is not always to subvert' (Weston 1993: 17). Unless performative acts of ethnicity respond directly to the axis of cultural authenticity, they remain in the service of state-sponsored representations of model minorities and consumable melting-pots.

In the light of current fashion trends where 'ethnic' commodities have suddenly become emblematic of a new cosmopolitan chic, the perform-ance of ethnic identity also brings into question the circuits of cultural commodification in first-world states. In the face of white youth who mark their bodies with reference to a brown Orient, what do the coloured, clothed bodies of diasporic South Asian youth produce? The preponder-ance of *bindis* and hennaed hands among urban youth today is a constant reminder of the fact that for a coloured body to wear 'ethnic' garb requires a display of what Johanna Schoss calls 'cultural competence' (1996: 161) with European aesthetic norms. In this demonstration of cultural capital, diasporic South Asian youth operate in a closed circuit of exchange, often enacting (like Mina in *Mississippi Masala*) precisely those ethnic perform-ances that are intended to be received by the white gaze. Hence the South Asian in Orientalized dress very often only serves to reaffirm comfortable categories of ethnic pluralism; instead of allowing for a 'multiplicity of cosmopolitanisms' (1996: 184) aesthetic capital is made multicultural. In this revival of a 60s nostalgia, a twist of 90s late capitalism allows for the reinvention of tradition as a 'new aesthetic mode' (Tarlo 1996: 298). Yet what shapes my study is the nagging premise that the participation of white bodies in 'ethnic' clothing is a markedly different parody from the citation of 'South Asia' in the clothing practices of diasporic South Asian youth – and it is the performance of the latter that testifies to the boomer-ang effect of the exchange of cultural commodities across nation-states.[13]

Coming to terms with what Tarlo calls 'the problem of what to wear' is, therefore, a highly strategic practice. The clothing practices of youth in the South Asian diaspora are imbricated in the history that clothes have occupied on the Indian subcontinent, and are enacted through a notion of aesthetic capital that allows the audience to comprehend performative acts of ethnic identity entirely within the normative paradigms of national narratives. The attempt to interrogate the performative qualities of dia-sporic clothing acts is thus a means of challenging synchronies of race and culture, while also acknowledging the disciplinary effects of state-sponsored multiculturalism. In a postcolonial world order, the clothing practices of South Asian diasporas are not only a 'performance of modernity' (Hendrickson 1996: 13), but are also an indication of a gend-ered and sexualized modernity; a modernity produced within an imperialist landscape; and a performance that may work to affirm the trope of assimilationist immigration rather than transform it.

Looking Through Glass: Diasporas and Globalization

In the wake of intensified attempts by the US government to reproduce technologies and taxonomies of racial order,[14] the diasporic dress of South Asian youth raises a spectre that problematizes the convenient narrativization of the multicultural US state. By pulling the third world into the space of the first, the clothing practices of South Asian youth uproot the notion of 'rooted' cultures (Malkki 1997), existing in excess of a single optics of national narration. My theoretical inquiry into diasporic clothing acts thus focuses on their potential to rupture the assumed isomorphism between space and culture (Gupta and Ferguson 1997: 34), and thereby comment on the narrative paradigms of transnationalism.

Working through ethnic performativity to trace the parameters of national narratives is both a localizing project – requiring the consideration of specific sites of performance – and a global one, implicated into imperialist histories of the production, circulation, and consumption of cultural commodities. Though they are often polarized as contesting units of analysis, it may be more productive to consider instead the mutually imbricated nature of globalization and localization. In so doing, my objective is to reconceptualize sites of capital and cultural production. By 'site', I do not intend a return to the bounded ethnographic field of the anthropologist; rather, I wish to suggest here a definition of space that constantly reproduces itself. To be positioned in a site that allows for the observation of the global-in-the-local takes up Arjun Appadurai's call for the 'production of locality' (1997b), and works towards an understanding of transnationalism that contests spatialized and racialized notions of culture.

If the cultural cross-dressing of diasporic South Asian youth rests in part on an essentialized nostalgia, calling towards an imagined 'South Asia' that is somehow strangely displaced on to the Indian subcontinent, then it also transcends the polarities of 'East–West' geographies. It is particularly important to note how the figure of the diasporic South Asian performs an ethnic identity that simultaneously acts within national narratives of America and yet also, more generally, tends to prefigure a collapse of first world – third world binaries. In the absence of stable epistemologies of the nation-state, South Asian diasporas are fore-grounded by an 'ethnoscape' of cultures-in-motion, thus proposing the task to ethnography of unravelling the conundrum: 'What is the nature of locality as a lived experience in a globalized, deterritorialized world?' (Appadurai 1997b: 52).

The urgency of reworking cartographies of the nation-state with reference to diasporas highlights the futility of working within static geographical units. In so far as 'South Asia' is a construct produced by the diasporic imagination, it has very real political possibilities and consequences. To identify as South Asian is at once to make reference to a geographical area demarcated and controlled by the US state department, and also to make reference to a space that exists outside the white American imagination. In this gesture of multiple reference lies the potential for resistance to narratives of racialization, for it outlines the space from which political geographies are suddenly destabilized. Through the performative act of coming out as South Asian, state-sponsored policies of ethnic containment are inverted to display how and what is incorporated and assimilated into the nation; and also, how much is excluded and excreated from that story.[15]

The production of locality through the figure of the cross-dressed South Asian thus points towards the need to work against the grain of triumphant theories of transnationalism while reaffirming the salience of locality. If the mix-and-match clothing practices of South Asian American youth confound neat demarcations of culture and citizenship demanded by the US nation-state, they also respond to the increasingly dangerous production of essentialized racial/national/religious identities performed within diasporic communities. For example, in Indian Independence Day or Pakistan Day celebrations across the US, the ability to perform 'South Asia' is increasingly and more intricately linked to visual (physical) markers of history and heritage, bringing back into play the colour-coded principles of nationhood. It is only when cultural cross-dressing is no longer emblematic of a celebratory fusion of two national cultures, or the token sign of being 'ethnic', that dressing the diaspora becomes a site from which to critique the ideological moorings of national subjectivity, refract the hegemonic gaze of the state, and produce a notion of culture uprooted from biological myths of racialized bodies.

The possibility of a conversation between cross-dressed South Asian youth and the clothing practices of youth subcultures in other countries yields another point of inquiry. Joe Woods' 1998 essay on the 'Yellow Negro', Japanese youth who dress in black hip-hop fashion, is a case in point (1998: 73). Looking at the clothing, speech, and social practices of Japanese youth, Wood writes a contemplative ethnography that at once unravels the parameters of the US racial economy as it begins to interrogate the supposedly uniracial construct of Japan. Woods' immediate reaction to Japanese youth in hip-hop clothes is to assume that they are trying to be black while trying to be white, their bodies speaking to white America through commodified blackness (dark skin perfected in tanning salons, the acquisition of a 'black' body language, etc.). Yet this is a hypothesis that proves to be unsustainable, as the shifting spaces occupied by 'black' Japanese youth also appears to be a manner of response to the Japanese state's own attempts to erase otherness. I am reminded here of the many South Asian men, and some women, who dress in hip-hop fashion, staking out their own 'hoods' in Queens and the Bronx, or in the more suburban locales of New Jersey. This particular mode of diasporic dress may speak to the reconstruction of masculinity among South Asian diasporic youth, and/or undermine the coalition of 'ethnic minorities' produced by liberal political rhetoric – for wearing gangster clothes is not simply a mimicry of black 'cool', but the self-styled proclamation of arrival of new boys and girls in the hood. Consequently, my contention that the clothing choices of the South Asian diaspora are a strategic performance rests upon the parallel assertion that studies of diasporas are a crucial intervention in redefining the field of transnational practices.

Undressing the diaspora, therefore, is a proposal to look beyond diasporic populations as assimilated immigrant communities, singularly narrated through the structures of first world states. Instead, it is a venture to revisit the site of cultural formation. In the process of generating new notions of locality, the clothing practices of diasporic South Asian youth are not immediately contestatory: they are liable to be consumed by a white Orientalist commodity chic, while veering dangerously towards the side of constructing homogeneous and hegemonic understandings of 'South Asia'. Yet if performative acts of ethnic identity can speak, at least in part, to the urgent need to chart out a theoretical apparatus that takes into account precisely the dialectics of this movement, the problem of what to wear shifts from being a constant dilemma for diasporic South Asian youth, to an epistemological confrontation with the narrative paradigms of multicultural states.

Notes

1. David Scott's (1996) call for generating a 'contrast effect' in academic inquiry has been particularly valuable in structuring my research in this area.

2. Arjun Appadurai's (1997a) model of 'scapes' – ethnoscapes, finance-scapes, ideoscapes, mediascapes, and technoscapes – has been especially instructive in this regard.

3. The attempt to define 'diaspora' as a conceptual tool seems constantly to lapse into categorical definitions of 'ideal types': see Ganguly 1992; Clifford 1994; Brah 1996.

4. This is particularly apparent in Barthes' (1983) treatment of fashion as a coherent semiotic language, and is in contrast with my argument that clothing practices in themselves are not a 'sign' of ethnicity: rather, it is the very act of wearing the clothes that becomes something in excess of a tokenized ethnicization, and as such neither cloth nor the body can be taken as a given sign.

5. Karen Hansen's (1995) work on used clothing practices in Lusaka, Kenya, highlights 'kinks' in the cultural production, consumption, and exchange of cloth. While examining the renewal of used clothing imported from the US among the lower middle class in Lusaka, Hansen observes the simultaneous manufacture of new cloth in Kenya exclusively for export to diasporic African communities. It is out of these production sites that ideas of 'chic' are generated for the urban population of Lusaka.

6. For a contemporary examination of the dilemmas posed by female bodies adapting masculinist nationalist identities, see Bastian 1996.

7. The tense management of women's sexuality and nationalist ideology is exemplified by the refusal of many Bengali women to wear fully European gowns (Banerjee 1995). For the reiteration of the centrality of women's bodies in the construction of post-colonial national narratives, see Nag 1991.

8. One only needs to go to shops like Urban Outfitters to see the public pronouncement of a chic Orientalism, as garments, accessories, and household goods are visibly ethnicized, and the imaginary idea of South Asia is materially realized in the form of silver jewellery, block-printed bedsheets, and cotton skirts. The aesthetic value generated by these items of clothing – which, importantly, are also consumed by diasporic South Asian youth – is predicated on a liberal version of hegemonic whiteness, thereby making it increasingly difficult to articulate resistant performances of ethnic identity. I refer here to Bourdieu's (1982) study of aesthetic capital, and to an understanding of commodity aesthetics outlined by Haug (1986).

9. I realize that Butler has since revisited the premises of *Gender Trouble*; however, her argument for the consideration of the performativity of sex and gender, and her subsequent elucidation of 'the body' within

performance theory only compel me to continue with my argument for performative acts of ethnic identity. For an extended discussion of the production of 'material' bodies within the discursive parameters of performativity, see Butler 1993.

10. The desire for a cogent history traceable to a single point of origin is often decisive in prompting diasporic youth to come out as South Asian. Like Shahid in The Black Album (Kureishi 1995) (1995) many South Asian youth – tokenized as native informants – find themselves unable to recuperate a stable referent of national identity. 'These days everyone was insisting on their identity, coming out as a man, woman, gay, black, Jew – brandishing whichever features they could claim, as if without a tag they wouldn't be human. Shahid, too, wanted to belong to his people. But first he had to know them, their past . . .' (1995: 102). The naming of one's 'people', and the construction of a history of home is, of course, a performative act in itself.

11. For an extended and illuminating account of the slippage between performance space and real space/time, see Bruner and Kirshenblatt-Gimblett 1994.

12. Dorinne Kondo's (1997) book *About Face* includes a section on 'avant-garde' Japanese fashion and its implications for the production of a nationalist identity. Kondo attempts to extricate a pure performance of modern Japanese identity from the seemingly unconventional cut and weave of the clothes, refusing to consider the value accrued by cloth as it is draped over the bodies of white European models and paraded on the confined stage of the Paris runway. I would argue that a more substantial transgression lies in the manner in which high fashion percolates on to the streets of Tokyo in more affordable versions for Japanese youth, thus reacting against the sphere of aesthetic capital within which the 'avant-garde' is normatively produced and consumed. See Kondo 1997: 105–186.

13. I refer here to the shuttle-effect of musical production in the movement of South Asian diasporas, as club beats mixed in Manchester travel to Toronto and Manhattan; and then go 'back' to India, where they are broadcast to the urban elite: see Gopinath 1995.

14. Proposition 187, surveilling and controlling 'illegal' immigration to California (passed in 1994) and Proposition 209, banning affirmative action programmes in the state (passed in 1996) are two striking – but by no means singular – examples of the attempt to discipline the racial order of the United States. The orchestration of a metanarrative of America, invoked through hetero-normative family institutions and capitalist modes of production, recalls the reactionary rhetoric of an

editorial on Proposition 187 in *U.S. News and World Report*, which declares: 'The very identity of America is at stake.' See Zuckerman 1994.

15. The media coverage of France's victory in the 1998 World Cup is a case in point. Prime Minister Chirac's jubilation at the French team's victory was expressed in terms of the multicultural appearance of the team: clad in the colours of the French flag, the descendants of Algerian, Tunisian, and Moroccan immigrants who scored some of the most eye-catching goals constituted a 'new France' that Chirac aggressively sought to promote.

References

Appadurai, A. (1997a), *Modernity at Large,* Delhi: Oxford University Press.

—— (1997b), 'The Production of Locality', in A. Appadurai (ed.), *Modernity at Large*, pp. 178–200. Delhi: Oxford University Press.

Banerjee, H. (1995), 'Attired in Virtue: The Discourse on Shame (*lajja*) and Clothing of the *Bhadramahila* in Colonial Bengal', in R. Bharati (ed.), *From the Seams of History: Essays on Indian Women*, pp. 67–106. Delhi: Oxford University Press.

Barthes, R. (1983), *The Fashion System,* New York: Hill and Wang.

Bastian, M. (1996), 'Female "Alhajis" and Entrepreneurial Fashions: Flexible Identities in Southeastern Nigerian Clothing Practice', in H. Hendrickson (ed.), *Clothing and Difference*, pp. 97–132. Durham, NC: Duke University Press.

Bourdieu, P. (1982), *Distinction,* Cambridge, MA: Harvard University Press.

Brah, A. (1996), *Cartographies of Diaspora,* London: Routledge.

Bruner, E. M. and Kirshenblatt-Gimblett, B. (1994), 'Maasai on the Lawn: Tourist Realism in East Africa', *Cultural Anthropology* , 9 (4): 435–70.

Butler, J. (1990), *Gender Trouble,* New York: Routledge (at p. 137).

—— (ed.), (1993), *Bodies That Matter,* New York: Routledge.

—— (1993), 'Critically Queer', in J. Butler (ed.), *Bodies That Matter*, pp. 223–42. New York: Routledge.

Clifford, J. (1994), 'Diasporas', *Cultural Anthropology,* 9 (3): 302–38.

Cohn, B. (1996), *Colonialism and its Forms of Knowledge*, pp. 106–62. Princeton, NJ: Princeton University Press.

Eng, D. L. (1997), 'Out Here and Over There: Queerness and Diaspora in Asian American Studies', *Social Text* 52/53, 3/4: 39.

Gaines, J. (1990), 'Introduction: Fabricating the Female Body', in J. Gaines and C. Herzog (eds), *Fabrications: Costume and the Female Body*, New York: Routledge.

Ganguly, K. (1992), 'Migrant Identities: Personal Memory and the Construction of Selfhood', *Cultural Studies*, 6 (1): 27–50.

Garber, M. (1992), *Vested Interests: Cross-Dress and Cultural Anxiety*, New York: Harper Perennial, (at p. 16).

Gilroy, P. (1987), *There Ain't No Black in the Union Jack: The Cultural Politics of Race and Nation,* Chicago: University of Chicago Press.

Gopinath, G. (1995), 'Bombay, U. K., Yuba City: Bhangra Music and the Engendering of Diaspora', *Diaspora*, 4 (3): 303–21.

Gupta, A. and Ferguson, J. (1997), 'Beyond Culture', in A. Gupta and J. Ferguson (eds), *Culture, Power, Place: Explorations in Critical Anthropology*, Durham, NC: Duke University Press, (at p. 34).

Hansen, K. (1995), 'Transnational Biographies and Local Meanings: Used Clothing Practices in Lusaka', *Journal of Southern African Studies*, 21 (1): 131–45.

Haug, W. (1986), *Critique of Commodity Aesthetics,* Minneapolis, MN: University of Minnesota Press.

Hebdige, D. (1979), *Subculture: The Meaning of Style,* New York: Methuen and Company.

Hendrickson, H. (ed.), (1996), 'Introduction', in H. Hendrickson (ed.), *Clothing and Difference*, pp. 1–16. Durham, NC: Duke University Press.

Kondo, D. (1997), *About Face: Performing Race in Fashion and Theater,* New York: Routledge.

Kureishi, H. (1995), *The Black Album,* New York: Simon and Schuster.

Malkki, L. (1997), 'National Geographic: The Rooting of Peoples and the Territorialization of National Identity among Scholars and Refugees', in A. Gupta and J. Ferguson (eds), *Culture, Power, Place: Explorations in Critical Anthropology*, pp. 52–74. Durham, NC: Duke University Press.

Nag, D. (1991), 'Fashion, Gender and the Bengali Middle Class', *Public Culture*, 3 (2): 93–112.

Newton, E. (1972), *Mother Camp,* Chicago: University of Chicago Press.

Schoss, J. (1996), 'Dressed to "Shine": Work, Leisure, and Style in Malindi, Kenya', in H. Hendrickson (ed.), *Clothing and Difference,* pp. 157–88. Durham, NC: Duke University Press.

Scott, D. (1996), 'Postcolonial Criticism and The Claims of Political Modernity', *Social Text, 48*, 14, 3: 1–26.

Sedgewick, E. K. (1990), *Epistemology of the Closet,* Berkeley, CA: University of California Press.

Shukla, S. (1997), 'Building Diaspora and Nation: The 1991 "Cultural Festival of India"', *Cultural Studies,* 11 (2): 306–12.

Tarlo, E. (1996), *Clothing Matters: Dress and Identity in India,* New Delhi: Viking (at pp. 62–93).

Weston, K. (1993), "Do Clothes Make the Woman?: Gender, Performance Theory, and Lesbian Eroticism", *Genders* 17 (5): 1–21.

Woods, J. (1998), 'The Yellow Negro', *Transition,* 73: 40–66.

Zuckerman, M. B. (1994), 'Beyond Proposition 187', 12 December 1994. Available at < http://www.usnews.com/usnews/wash/187oped.htm > (Accessed on 19th January 1999).

8

Re-producing South Asian Wom(b)en: Female Feticide and the Spectacle of Culture

Tej Purewal

'Faced with the dialectically interlocking sentences that are constructible as 'White men are saving brown women from brown men' and 'The women wanted to die', the postcolonial woman intellectual asks the question of simple semiosis – What does this mean? – and begins to plot a history (Spivak 1993: 297).

Introduction

Hegemonic modes of understanding South Asian women have relied upon the reproductive sphere as a means of locating South Asian women's perceived cultural and gender locations. This chapter is concerned with the ways in which South Asian women have been reproduced in debates relating to son preference and sex selection. By focusing upon reproductive technologies relating to sex selection, I examine these two areas in tandem in their contributions towards defining discourses on South Asian women. The perception of South Asian women as both victims and actors in the act of female feticide has been a problematic one. On the one hand, health practitioners from within the liberal health establishment in Britain have in some instances intervened as protectors of the unborn child by discriminantly not disclosing the sex of the fetus to expecting parents with the 'knowledge' that some clients upon revelation of female fetuses may consider sex-selective abortions. The production and reproduction of this knowledge is, of course, imbricated in paternalistic colonial and postcolonial discourses. On the other hand, South Asian women themselves have a multiplicity of views on the subject, which can neither be defined in cultural terms nor removed from wider issues in the (Western) women's movement that have clearly couched women's reproductive rights in terms of in the enhancement and defence of women's choice. I use the term 'South Asian woman' *inclusively* to acknowledge differences of location, origin, nationality, ethnicity and the plethora of other ways in which women's identities are constituted. The South Asian woman in this chapter is a figure whose identity and agency have evolved and travelled through histories and geographies, and in this case, through mediated experiences of pregnancy.

The contiguity between discourses of reproduction and son preference in South Asia and the South Asian diaspora is, of course, problematic. How South Asian communities scattered around different parts of the world fit in (or do not fit in) with these discourses is subject to variables of class and race (Clarke, Peach and Vertovec 1990) as well as gender (Bhachu 1995) and the differential experiences of settlement and consolidation of South Asian communities within the diaspora. The need to address issues of son preference and sex selection and to challenge patriarchal practices without having recourse to the long history of racialized constructions of South Asian women underlies my concerns in this chapter.

This chapter is produced on the basis of interviews with South Asian women in Britain, conducted over a period of six months in 2001 with old and young, married and unmarried women, some of whom were born in Britain while others came to Britain after marriage or through marriage to men already living in Britain. The interviews illustrate some of the challenges that women's views on sex selection and son preference in the South Asian diaspora present to dominant modes of understanding this cultural 'spectacle', which, as is argued in this chapter, is not exclusively a 'South Asian thing', but is rather a product of wider patriarchal household and societal forms, not merely South Asian. However, at the same time, this is not to deny that son preference exists or that sex-selective abortions occur in South Asian diasporic communities. Son preference can be located in very real terms in many South Asian women's lives, and the challenges and responses to son preference that women make in their own communities and households represent important, diverse and not commonly represented (feminist) perspectives on the subject. Culturalist analyses rely upon and ultimately contribute to the sustenance of rather fixed notions of the ways in which women and indeed gender relations intersect and interact with 'culture.' In the case of South Asian women's reproductive rights, one cannot begin to address the complexities of women's experiences without first moving beyond a narrow view of culture as the defining factor in their lives. The attention given to the narratives of women in this chapter privileges the interpretations offered by South Asian women of their locations, highlighting complex and not easily defined attitudes towards sex selection and son preference[1].

Re-producing Discourses

Central to the 'civilizing mission' in British colonial India was the intrusion of the colonial state into both public and private gendered spheres. The representations of particular discriminatory aspects of Indian society were highlighted by the colonial state and flagged up as a clear indication of the need for social reform in the interests of the oppressed Indian woman. To ban certain traditions, of course, meant to define them first. The Abolition of Sati Act of 1829 and the Widow Remarriage Act of 1856 and the Female Infanticide Act of 1870 were a show of the British colonial project's mission to ban and reform cultural and traditional practices (Mani 1990). However, one only needs to look beyond the apparent intentions of the civilizing exercise to see that the actual effects of the colonial state's actions upon women from different caste and class groups were far from beneficial (Kumar 1994). On the one hand, most women did not have access to the legal machinery that would supposedly enforce the new laws. On the other hand, in the process of outlawing these practices, they came to be defined in rather narrow, often *Brahminical*, terms that gave specific, local practices national and more general connotations. Even more crucially, as the colonial administration proceeded to legitimize itself through the civilizing mission in this respect, it was largely unconcerned with the more immediate social and economic issues such as famines, agricultural production and literacy, so exposing its narcissistic objectives of gaining legitimacy in the region.

The guise under which most colonial social reform took place was the emancipation of the Indian woman from oppressive cultural practices. Female infanticide came to be highlighted as yet another cultural practice that had devastating impacts upon gender relations across the north of India. Hence the British 'discovery' of female infanticide in 1789 in Benares, which eventually led to the Female Infanticide Act in 1870, made it illegal to kill newborn female babies, a practice that was identified in particular regions where groups at the top level of their respective caste groups were thought to have viewed girls as liabilities. The practice was specifically located amongst large landowning, upper-caste Hindu and Sikh families, specifically in Rajasthan, Uttar Pradesh and Punjab, who presented a challenge to colonial authority in those regions. In Punjab a report by Major Lake in the mid-nineteenth century expounded that not a single girl child had survived over several generations within the Bedi caste, who were willing to take girls as daughter-in-laws in marriage but were unwilling to give them away to other caste groups below them (Visvanathan 1998). A similar 'discovery' was made in eastern Uttar Pradesh in 1835, when a British official, James Thomason, in a discussion with landowners referred to one of the men by mistake as a son-in-law, rather than as a son. The landowners' immediate correction of the impossibility of this led to an explanation that there were in fact no daughters born in the village. In this case, neglect rather than murder was given as the method of eliminating new generations of females – both, however, would eventually be considered as infanticide by the British. As a result of these findings, the practice was outlawed and a legal fine established for anyone found guilty of committing female infanticide. Without disputing whether or not the claim of this report was true or not, which is an issue in itself, the more interesting aspect of this period is why the British authorities were so interested in the practice of infanticide in the first place. Amongst a range of many other pressing social, economic and political issues which required attention, such as famine, agricultural output and literacy, why, we may ask, was the fate of newborn baby girls such a concern for the British? Were they in fact promoting a feminist or at least a gender-sensitive agenda, albeit within the colonial framework? The explanations for the British interest in female infanticide in the late nineteenth century lie in the fact that the impulse to 'civilize' these communities was inspired by the colonial mission's desire to control both its (male) allies and opponents. Baby girls became the focus of much missionary activity in these areas, being seen as representative of the barbarism of the South Asian male-dominated society. Thus, the interpretation and manipulation of culture was an important part of the knowledge production exercise in which the emancipation of the South Asian woman became the pinnacle of the British colonial mission (Rajan 1993). One only needs to scratch the surface of imperial Britain's own history to see that the English *memsahib* in India was hardly an emancipated woman herself; nor did Victorian England offer much else in this direction.

With the end of colonial rule in South Asia over fifty years ago, the resilience of colonial constructions in postcolonial Britain has continued to provide the foundation for racialized discourses showing stark continuities with respect to the subjecthood of the South Asian woman over time (Brah 1992; Parmar 1982; Wilson 1978). The continuities between colonial and postcolonial constructions of South Asian women *vis-à-vis* culture are striking (Bumiller 1989), showing evidence that the civilizing mission has continued well beyond the period of formal colonization. As 'post'-colonial subjects South Asian women in the diaspora often fall between the respective discourses on reproductive choice and reproductive health in the 'Third World' and in the 'West'. They are neither 'Third World women' nor are they comfortably seen as 'Western', with the reading that they have an altogether different set of cultural constraints. Readings of women in the South Asian diaspora are continually negotiated between these two constructions, where we are either seen as objects for development projects or social work cases. Our reproductive health concerns tend to be dominated by the population question and cultural tendencies towards son preference; while in mainstream discourses the concerns, namely around reproductive health and women's rights, lie around 'choice' and autonomy (Bandarage 1997; Purewal 2001). The implications of these readings are that they present a picture of South Asian women's reproductive experiences within a framework largely informed by culture rather than by feminism or women's movements, as is the case within more mainstream discourses. The utility of the South Asian woman in this respect has allowed for the continued characterization of communities as under colonialism. So, for instance, in postcolonial 1970s Britain, the characterization of East African Asians as potentially dangerous 'breeders' was an implicit part of the far right's racist mobilizations against the influx of these communities into Britain as they were being expelled from Uganda. On the other hand, the helpless South Asian woman restricted by the institutions of family, community and marriage came to personify the experiences of South Asian women as citizens in a so-called liberal, 'multicultural' Britain in the 1980s and 1990s, though, of course, not without challenge and response (Wilson 1978; Bhachu 1992; Patel 2001).

Scanning through the Lens of Culture

The reproductive sphere, *vis-à-vis* the household, has been critical as a means of placing South Asian women's perceived cultural, gender and racialized locations. When one steps outside the racialized discourses of gender in 'other' communities, we see a convergence of culture and patriarchy. The conflation of culture and patriarchy unduly pathologizes South Asian women under a double burden of culture and sexism, whereas other Western/white women only confront sexism. Concepts of culture and patriarchy have often problematically been applied interchangeably in cases relating to third world contexts and to various diasporic communities (Anthias and Yuval-Davis 1992). Particular tropes of subjectivity have been a common way of understanding and positioning women of colour: where the trope of 'race' has been used to mark African American women's reproductive rights (Bower 1995), the trope of 'culture' has been applied to South Asian women's reproductive rights. Implicit in the trope of 'culture' is the perception of South Asian culture as patriarchal and misogynist (Parmar 1982; Brah 1996; Narayan 1997). These simple readings shape the attitudes and actions of many policy-makers and practitioners towards South Asian communities. For example, the problematic cultural perception of South Asian women by some medical employees of the National Health Service in Britain has been noted in a study of record-taking and maternity care, in which an interview is highlighted that the author observed between a midwife and a British-born woman of South Asian descent.

Midwife:	What's your country of origin?
Woman:	Well, Britain, I'm British.
Midwife:	Yes, but where were you born?
Woman:	In Birmingham.
Midwife:	Yes, but your parents. They can't have been born in Britain.
Woman:	My parents were born in India.
Midwife:	OK (Bowler 1995: 43).

The study notes how the woman's country of origin was recorded as India, reflecting how perceptions of race and ethnicity become inculcated into even the most routine procedures such as record-taking. The tendency to want to typify women into easily understood, and in this case inappropriate, categories puts into question the assumptions behind the subjective perceptions that create the very categories themselves. Michel Foucault's (1973) elaboration of the medical gaze is most pertinent here. His examination of the power associated with the construction of medical knowledge and authority throw into question the interactions between patients and doctors as predominantly one-way dialogues in which patients are reduced to a function of the collective power of the medical establishment.

In this observed interview between midwife and patient/client, the *gaze* is clearly one that was both calculating and intent on connecting its categories of knowledge to the patient at hand. This trend to typify also resonates with an interview with one woman in *this study* who commented on her experience of wanting to know the sex of the fetus at the time of the scan: 'I wanted to know the sex of my child just to know for myself. I didn't care if it was a boy or girl, just that it was healthy. But the person who did the scan didn't tell me . . . she said it was hospital policy not to tell.' Ironically, this hospital did not in fact have a policy of not disclosing the sex information at the time of the scan, and therefore the refusal to reveal the sex of the *fetus*, it could be presumed, resulted from the wish of the sonographer to 'protect' the baby and woman from the presumed cultural interpretation of the information. The approach by this sonographer is not uncommon in other large South Asian catchment areas in Britain, where hospitals have either chosen to go along the path of selective denial of information or of blanket non-disclosure. That many women individually would opt to know the sex of the child, if they were given the choice, is by no means surprising in any constituency of women. Many women simply do not wish to know the sex of the fetus until the time of the birth as, to quote one respondent in this study 'it is a wonderful surprise at the end of a very long, dark tunnel'. However, this preference needs crucially to be seen within a wider discourse of choice that should not be seen to be discriminatorily prescriptive of choices for women of different class, culture, ethnic and racial backgrounds whose own particular choices do not necessarily reflect their perceived or constructed identities.

Cultural essentialism is clearly illustrated in assumptions made about the connection between cultural practices such as dowry and brideburning both in India and in the South Asian-American diaspora (Bumiller 1989). Contrary to the notion of culture as a set of continually changing processes (Brah 1996), culturalist generalizations have sought to construct more comfortable universal categories of comprehensibility ('Indian women,' 'Third World women,' 'Muslim women,' 'Western women') (Narayan 1998). But how 'Indian' are 'Indian' cultural practices? The location and status of cultural tradition according to fixed notions dispenses, as Narayan (1998: 94) argues, with 'excavating the historical colonial context that "produced" this status'. Hence, the issue at hand is not about whether particular cultural practices exist or not, but rather out of which context their existence or status came to the fore. Particular spectacles of culture, such as female infanticide and feticide, have offered an oblique lens through which South Asian women have been understood. In this sense, culture for South Asian women has been seen as a sort of anti-feminist noose, as opposed to their perceived Western feminist counterparts for whom (Western) culture has been the umbilical cord to a 'universal' feminism (Grewal and Kaplan 1994).

Analysis of the ultrasound scan lends itself to cultural explanations for its close associations with son preference and its utility in reinforcing patriarchal tendencies. One widely highlighted effect of the ultrasound scan, as well as of amniocentesis, is sex selection and skewed sex-ratios against females. A distinct body of literature on this subject in South Asia has emerged over the past two decades as, the initial and long-term impacts of sex selection through the facilitation of technology are still unfolding (Das Gupta 1987; Das Gupta and Bhat 1997; V. Patel 1988; Khanna 1995). There have been profound changes in demography and gender relations seen in many parts of the world, with places such as South Asia, with its 'missing women' (Sen 1990), being particularly highlighted for its enthusiastic adoption of the technologies in the context of its predominantly patriarchal backdrop.

However, the discourses and critiques of reproductive technologies in Western contexts mark a noticeable departure in terms of cultural readings of the application of reproductive technologies that assume a homogeneity of culture and largely focus upon the perceived growing tension between Western feminist notions of 'choice' and the dangers of technology further relegating women to the role of 'baby machines' through a tightening relationship between science, technology and capitalism (Strathern 1992; Wacjman 1991; Corea *et al.* 1985; Hanmer 1985; Mies 1987; Rowland 1992). Such studies have crucially interrogated the ways in which child-bearing has become increasingly commodified through the influence of capitalist medical interests and new sex-selective technologies, and highlight the fact that the new reproductive technologies can be seen as just another service available to consumers, further complicating the socio-economic context of women's value, the biological and the commercial. While I would not dispute these analyses in themselves, I argue that there is an unqualified double standard in the ways in which the impacts and interpretations of reproductive technologies in various cultural or geographical contexts have been understood and explained. While the patriarchal context is often given as the backdrop to the (ab)use of reproductive technologies against women, implicit in dominant discourses around the topic of sex selection and female feticide is the tendency to pathologize particular communities for son-preference, which assumes not only that boys are preferred, but also that women act with little power in the patriarchal project to ensure strong male households. Both of these assumptions give little agency to the women themselves. As might be imagined, the picture is far more complicated than this. Not only are women not merely victims, but they are also agents within the patriarchal project. One only has to look at the stereotype of the South Asian mother-in-law, whose own position is bolstered by her ability to control the household through her sons and, even more importantly, daughters-in-law. Women's agency in the most patriarchal of household contexts is routed through the valuation of women by their ability to contribute to the household in its reproductive capacities (Dyson and Moore 1983; Caldwell 1999).

Nonetheless, the choices available to women to collude, play on or challenge patriarchal mores and ways are vast. The pressure to have sons, for instance, is one that has roots in the marriage economy and the political economy of inheritance, which historically has put an unequivocal amount of burden upon the parents of females, who incur costs for wedding and dowry expenses and who generally end up passing on all their inheritance to sons. There is a significant body of anthropological literature that has analysed South Asian kinship systems in order to develop an understanding of the relationships between property ownership, inheritance, marriage, roles, household organization and the gendered valuation of girl and boy children (Jeffery, Jeffery and Lyon 1989; Jeffery and Jeffery 1996; Sharma 1980; Sheel 1999; Carroll 1991). There has also been a considerable amount of discussion about South Asian women's gender locations in the diaspora, which has looked at some of the ways in which women have negotiated through classed, racialized and gendered labour, community and family structures in postcolonial Britain (Gupta 1988; Brah 1992 and 1996: Bhachu 1986 and 1992; Wilson 1978; Parmar 1982; Westwood 1984). These threads of research have been influential in charting some of the experiential dimensions of South Asian women's location in the diaspora and have laid the foundations for further research. However, cross-generational challenge and change in the diaspora, particularly that of second-, third- and fourth-generation women (and men), which I argue is essential to moving on from culturalism, is in need of augmentation from the inside out.

Clifford (1999: 226) aptly states, 'diaspora experiences are always gendered'; but his ensuing question of whether gender subordination is reinforced or loosened through diaspora is best answered by the differential accounts of women themselves in the diaspora. Thus to draw out these types of negotiations as experienced rather than as merely perceived or theorized by, generally speaking, remote academicians, is critical to further engaging with and embarking on a more reflexive 'charting of the journey' (S. Grewal 1988). The challenge that Rey Chow (1993: 68) poses to 'third world' feminists (and academics) is to go beyond 'animating the oppressed women of their cultures but of making the automatized and animated condition of their own voices the conscious point of departure in their intervention'. It is precisely at this point of departure that the thrust of this book attempts to connect South Asian feminist/women's voices with the complexities of (self-) representation and agency in the 'post'-colonial West or 'first world'.

Critical engagement with gender and the South Asian diaspora in this manner is a long-term, indeed an indefinitely defined, project. Gender politics and social change are continually being negotiated, and the constitution of gender in the South Asian diaspora has thus far undergone a dynamic history of change. For instance, the whole notion of dowry in the diaspora (Barot 1999; Jhutti 1998) has evolved, with many young South Asian women working outside the home, which in itself can constitute a contribution to both their own families and their potential husbands' families, hardly rendering them as burdens or liabilities. Conscious of the implications of dowry, many women choose not to consider marriage to families who demand dowries. However, paid work and opposition to dowry do not necessarily result in the re-negotiation of women's gendered location in families and communities. Other choices that South Asian women have, such as whether to marry within the community or at all, and whether or when to have children and how many, also have implications on how and if son-preference is expressed. The desire to have sons is not a trait primordial to all South Asian women wanting to find a place within their communities. It is a constructed one, just as gender roles in their families and communities are; they do not necessarily follow or for that matter defy phallocentric logic in the designation of symbolic power. Thus, if the choices that South Asian women have are constructed ones, and if, as Brah's advice tells us, culture is a dynamic set of processes constantly undergoing change, then, son-preference in South Asian diasporic contexts also represents a range of choices, attitudes and actions. Some of these 'choices' indeed coalesce with the dictates of patriarchy's requirements for male heirs, while others challenge the discriminatory attitudes against female children by preferring to have girls as oppositional and empowering symbols for women.

Different Choices, Different Voices

'Knowledge' about pregnant (South) Asian clients by medical practitioners in Britain has led to improvised policies in some hospitals to (in)appropriately deal with the issue of son-preference. There is no conclusive evidence for the medical establishment to presume that South Asian couples prefer sons and would medically act upon this preference to ensure that they had sons. Uneasy about this sensitive subject, local hospitals, with *ad hoc* practices of information disclosure or non-disclosure, have made an effort to give the appearance of equal treatment of all patients through equality and diversity statements posted on the entrance bulletin board to their reception desks. One hospital has a sign posted in the waiting area of the ante-natal ward on 'sexing your child' that reads: 'the sonographer will only be able to tell you the sex of your child within the available given time . . . it is not always possible to tell the sex of the child depending on the position of the baby at the time of the scan . . . no extra time will be spent on this'. This hospital could be said to be covering itself from any potential accusation that it is somehow discriminatory when the sex of the fetus is not revealed. This is also one of the hospitals that has a reputation for disclosing the sex of the child depending on the perceived ethnicity of patients.

Where information on the sex of the fetus has selectively not been disclosed, private 'baby and gender clinics' have filled this gap by providing scanning services regardless of culture, ethnicity and race, and offer their services on the basis of the ability and willingness to pay the private fee. These services are advertised widely in the South Asian vernacular press in Britain as well as in the US and Canada, not to mention the broad reach of the internet. The advertisements vary in terms of their target consumer populations: some are explicitly aimed at South Asian communities, while others are more mainstream in their appeal, reflecting the variety of cultural contexts identified by scanning clinics. The extent to which such services are being utilized is unknown. However, the proliferation of such clinics and an increased visibility of advertisement campaigns indicates an upsurge in demand. In the early 1980s one of the first clinics in India, based in the city of Amritsar, used an advertising slogan '500 rupees now or 5 lakhs later', connecting the potential economic liability of the birth of a daughter and incurring dowry costs with the option to scan and then abort (Gandhi and Shah 1991). However, there are problems with superficially linking obvious indicators such as advertisement campaigns to social attitudes. Many questions are left unaddressed, such as: Who is accessing these services? For what purposes? Do they act upon the information that the scan discloses? Whose choice(s) does the option to visit a private clinic reflect? How has the ability to detect the sex of the child impacted on gender relations? Thus, the spectacle of culture remains imprinted on the pages of advertisements and in the ensuing analysis of the controversy (Fair 1996).

The *Babyscan Ltd* Clinics opened several clinics in the UK, showing the shrewd marketing of these services to South Asian communities, who, as has been argued, have the same right to access these services as everyone else. *Babyscan Ltd* Clinics connect South Asian diasporic communities with sex selection by their very location in areas of high concentration: in San Jose, California, in Washington State, which is across the border from Vancouver, in Buffalo, New York which is across the border from Toronto, and now London, Birmingham and Glasgow. So while the sonographers and medical practitioners within the NHS ponder whether or not equal access to choice with regard to sex identification is the best strategy, those not given the choice can obtain the service from private clinics.

Importantly, it would be incorrect, of course, to assume that anyone discontented with not being vouchsafed information on the sex of the fetus, or all those attending private clinics, would be interested in knowing the sex of the fetus purely for the purpose of sex selection. As was stated earlier, the choices and preferences of South Asian women are not merely defined by culture (in this case, son-preference). Women's reproductive, productive and community roles (Moser 1993) are continually being negotiated, and while the patriarchal household is still a hegemonic form, it is continually being negotiated and bargained with (Kandiyoti 1997; Walby 1990). Whether women's choices reflect their roles in collusion with the family or in contestation with its structure, attitudes towards sex preference among children are by no means unitary. As one respondent in this study, an older woman with two children (two daughters) and several grandchildren, reflected on the ethics of son-preference and the use of technologies:

> It's all up to God. I don't think people have the right to interfere in what is supposed to be . . . As a child I was told of young baby girls who were suffocated just after birth. That was terrible, but it was a different time. This is England now. Why should we mind if it's a boy or girl? Our girls are working and are no less than any boy.

She clearly saw the experience of migration and the economic contributions of her daughters as evidence of increased gender equality in arguing against female feticide.

This particular woman had come to Britain in the late 1960s, and had since then, until only a few years ago, worked in the foundries of Birmingham. Her own narration of gender politics is largely informed by her sense of achieving and maintaining a balance between shift-working and family life as both a woman and an economic contributor to the household. For her, the question of the desirability of children, boys or girls, was less about preference than about the socialization of gendered roles through, in my interpretation of the interview, a subversive household gender politics:

... the children used to be waiting at home for me when I got home from work when I was on the late shift ... they would get home from school, have a little rest and then start cleaning the house or preparing dinner. It wasn't like I was the only one who would do the cooking or anything ... I brought them up to know how to do things for themselves and for the family. Even my husband, who was brought up in a traditional sort of way, helped out, and could even keep the house running and make *roti*.

The notion of 'culture' in this interview is one that is enmeshed with the ways in which work and gender roles can push the boundaries of how manhood or womanhood are constructed through household roles and responsibilities, which are continually subject to reworking.

Another woman of a similar age, however, fits closer to the bill of the stereotypical 'mother-in-law' in wanting to ensure her family's future through the birth of a grandson:

My son has two girls and his wife is pregnant now. I've told them to have the scan done to find out if it's a boy or girl ... there is no question that three girls would be a bad thing for our family ... What kind of future would that be for us? ... I've said to 'the wife' (daughter-in-law) that all I want is for them to bring a boy into this house.

This voice of the patriarchal agent, or perpetrator of feticide, exhibits one of the more extreme and important opinions, as it gives a sense of the insecurity and vulnerability that many women feel within the patriarchal project. The artificial nature of the power that patriarchy yields to collaborating women is exposed when expectations are not being met, in this case, through being left without a grandson. A crucial point of tension in patriarchal settings is woman-on-woman oppression, which organizes the cross-generation power relations between mother-in-law, daughter, and daughter-in-law, ensuring patriarchal order while also dividing alliances among women and with men. The opinion expressed in the above interview reflects some of the 'cultural' undertones of son-preference and the affinity toward son-preference that are reflected by the medical establishment and the advertising campaigns of the private clinics. However, it is only one of many opinions voiced on this subject, and of course does not reveal to what extent this mother-in-law is actually able to wield power or influence over her son and daughter-in-law. That the patriarchal agent's opinion is opposed, ignored or even challenged is an important feature of how women have resisted and continue to resist the mores of patriarchy. While one woman in her early twenties admittedly rallied to the idea that having at least one son is important and should be striven for: 'It doesn't matter what you think or how much you think that girls and boys are the same . . . it's just a fact of life that a mother needs to have a son'.

Another respondent, an unmarried woman in her late twenties, commented:

> I would use the technologies, but carefully and only if necessary. First of all, no one, including my mother-in-law or husband could ever force me to do anything I didn't want to do, and second of all, I think that if I would use the technology it would be to make sure that I had a girl!

The second woman here sees the potential for women's enhanced choice and autonomy through technologies; but also shows how her own sense of agency within the household is pronounced. The arrival of ultrasound scanning clinics can indeed bring the contestation of gendered relations to the fore, in that in some cases the precipitation of choices can equip women to challenge patriarchal norms while for others it can further entrench them. The quotation taken from this interview could be seen to support the idea that more choice enhances women's autonomy. However, this statement, like all the others quoted in this chapter, is expressed from a political location that offers the opportunity for women to voice the preference or oppositional desire for girls. Indeed, the accusation by a South Asian women's organization in Canada *Mahila* that 'sex selection equals son selection' conversely challenges the notion of more choice *vis-à-vis* ultrasound technology in a patriarchal context, as it would inevitably result in discriminatory practices against girls and women (Fair 1996).

The representation of female feticide is one that is commonly understood through the choice discourse. Boys can be chosen over girls, women and couples can choose to have a scan or a sex-selective termination, and the expansive market for sex-selective services offers consumers choices of types of services. That a more 'mainstream' pool of women and couples wanting to know the sex of the fetus is posed differently to that of a culturally defined market of South Asian women throws the debate into a quandary of feminist action versus cultural essentialism, with a plethora of complex tensions in between. The location of these choices needs to be understood in context, and the context needs to be understood in terms of the constructed choices. A respondent referring to a new clinic that had recently opened within a central South Asian retail area in the Midlands commented:

> I definitely don't believe in the scan. I think it's wrong and that those places should be shut down by the government. When I drive by it, I feel sick. Those clinics are targeting our people because they know that they can make lots of

money from people who want boys only. There are a lot of people like that. It's outrageous.

For this interviewee, there is no question of choice. For her, it is a matter of exploitation of gender bias through cultural essentialism that makes such private clinics seek clients and business. The clinic in question is highly visible to the community and has caught the attention of many. Such commercial landmarks represent themselves as providers of choice (for a fee, of course) to communities of men and women for whom the gender of their offspring is becoming an increasingly commodified prescription. The culturally defined objects of these sex-selection representations (i.e. advertisements) and scanning services constitute a knowing consumer market for whom the visibility and presence of these services presents a challenge from the inside and the out as to the ethical, political and gender implications.

Attitudes to these new technologies, of course, are not static. As seen in the interviews in this chapter, there are a diversity of views, voices and positions on son and even daughter preference in the various South Asian communities. A traditional attitude to girls as financial and social liabilities for the family may still be held by some, but there is also a strong sense, at least in rhetoric, that this once popular view is broadening into a spectrum of views stretching between a more equitable understanding of the value of girls and boys on the part of some and a more entrenched patriarchal support for the desire for male offspring among others. Hence, as popular views and voices have evolved and altered, so have traditions and cultural practices, with the constituents of tradition and culture continually being challenged. While through culturalist notions South Asian communities are seen as somehow uniquely sexist and patriarchal, voices of protest against these constructions are everywhere, but perhaps not present in the places where the dominant discourses are formulated and articulated.

For instance, it is not uncommon that in the same newspapers where the sex selection and scanning firms advertise their services there are also poems and editorials commenting on issues relating to gender relations in specific communities or the gender impacts of reproductive technologies. This poem written by Preet Neetpur appeared in an issue of *Des Pardes* (March 2001), a London-based weekly Punjabi newspaper with a global circulation. In Britain this paper is commonly sold in South Asian grocery shops. The poem takes the metaphor of the bird, as commonly referred to in wedding songs in relation to the temporary status of girls in their parental homes, towards a cutting feminist reading of the metaphor:

We girls, are neither sparrows,
nor doves nor magpies.
Actually, we are a concentrated source
of fragrance of human values
and sharp swords to protect them.

We girls, are neither sparrows,
nor doves nor magpies.
Actually, we are a concentrated source
of fragrance of human values
and sharp swords to protect them.

Who says . . . ?
that harvest is good and that the birth of daughters is a bad omen.
Sons can be useless, but daughters are invaluable.
Daughters are like support pillars of mud houses . . . dear mother . . .
We girls are not sparrows . . . .
(translated to English from Punjabi)

These narratives in wide circulation amongst South Asians are not only re-visioning what daughters represent, but they are also an immediate challenge to the notion of the South Asian woman as passive and without voice. Indeed, the voices are there, but are perhaps not comprehensible in the languages in which they are spoken, nor are they heard in the media and idioms through which they are voiced. Thus is the challenge of the, possibly untranslatable, space of 'otherness' that is not without its own alterity.

Note

1. My concerns with son-preference and sex-selection are shaped by an interrogation of the dictates of patriarchy within and outside of Asian 'communities' women as well as by the racialized gender constructions that scholarship has imposed and continues to impose upon South Asian women.

References

Anthias, F. and Yuval-Davis, N. (1992), *Racialized Boundaries: Race, Nation, Colour, Class and the Anti-Racist Struggle*, London: Routledge.

Bandarage, A. (1997), *Women, Population and Global Crisis: A Political-Economic Analysis*, London: Zed Books.

Barot, R. (1999), 'Dowry and Hypergamy among the Gujaratis in Britain,' in W. Menski (ed.), *South Asians and the Dowry Problem*, GEMS No. 6, Stoke on Trent: Trentham Books.

Bhachu, P. (1986) 'Work, Marriage and Dowry Among East African Sikh Women in the United Kingdom', in R. Simon and C. Brettell (eds), *International Migration: The Female Experience*, Totowa, NJ: Rowman and Allanheld.

—— (1992) 'Identities Constructed and Reconstructed: Representations of Asian Women in Britain', in Gina Buijs (ed.), *Migrant Women: Crossing Boundaries and Changing Identities*, Oxford and New York: Berg Publishers.

—— (1995) *New Cultural Forms and Transnational South Asian Women: Culture, Class, and Consumption among British Asian Women in the Diaspora*, Philadelphia: University of Pennsylvania Press.

Bower, L. (1995), 'The Trope of the Dark Continent in the Fetal Harm Debates: "Africanism" and the Right to Choice', in P. Boling (ed.), *Expecting Trouble: Surrogacy, Fetal Abuse & New Reproductive Technologies*, Boulder, CO: Westview Press.

Bowler, I. (1995), 'Further Notes on Record Taking and Making in Maternity Care: The Case of South Asian Descent women', *Sociological Review*, 43 (1), (February): 36–51.

Brah, A. (1992), 'Women of South Asian Origin in Britain', in P. Braham, A. Rattansi and R. Skellington (eds), *Racism and Anti-Racism*, London: Sage.

—— (1996), *Cartographies of Diaspora: Contesting Identities*, London: Routledge.

Bumiller, E. (1989), *May You Be the Mother of One Hundred Sons*, New York: Ballantine Books.

Caldwell, B. (1999), *Marriage in Sri Lanka: A Century of Change*, Delhi: Hindustan Publishing Co.

Carroll, L. (1991), 'Daughter's Right of Inheritance in India: A Perspective on the Problem of Dowry', *Modern Asian Studies*, 25, (4): 791–809.

Chow, R. (1993), *Writing Diaspora: Tactics of Intervention in Contemporary Cultural Studies*, Bloomington, IN: Indiana University Press.

Clarke, C., Peach, C. and Vertovec, S. (eds), (1990), *South Asians Overseas: Migration and Ethnicity*, Cambridge: Cambridge University Press.

Clifford, J. (1999), 'Diasporas', in S. Vertovec and R. Cohen (eds), *Migration, Diasporas and Transnationalism*, Cheltenham: Edward Elgar Publishing.

Corea, G., Klein, R. D., Hanmer, J., Holmes, H. B., Hoskins, B., Kishwar, M., Raymond, J., Rowland, R. and Steinbacher, R. (1985), *Man Made Women: How New Reproductive Technologies Affect Women*, London: Hutchinson & Co.

Das Gupta, M. (1987), 'Selective Discrimination against Female Children in Rural Punjab, India', *Population and Development Review*, 13: 77–100.

Das Gupta, M. and Bhat, P. N. (1997), 'Fertility Decline and Increased Manifestation of Sex Bias in India', *Population and Development*, 51.

Dyson, T. and Moore, M. (1983), 'On Kinship Structure, Female Autonomy and Demographic Behaviour in India', *Population and Development Review*, 9 (1): 35–60.

Fair, C. (1996), 'Female Foeticide Among Vancouver Sikhs: Recontextualizing Sex Selection in the North American Diaspora', *International Journal of Punjab Studies*, 3 (1): 1–44.

Foucault, M. (1973), *The Birth of the Clinic: An Archaeology of Medical Perception*, London: Routledge.

Gandhi, N. and Shah, N. (1991), *The Issues at Stake: Theory and Practice in the Contemporary Women's Movement in India*, Delhi: Kali for Women.

Grewal, I. and Kaplan, C. (1994), *Scattered Hegemonies: Postmodernity and Transnational Feminist Practices*, Minneapolis, MN: University of Minnesota Press.

Grewal, S. (1988), *Charting the Journey: Writings by Black and Third World Women*, London: Sheba Feminist.

Gupta, R. (1988), 'Women and Communalism: A Tentative Inquiry', in *Charting the Journey: Writings by Black and Third World Women*, London: Sheba Feminist.

Hanmer, J. (1985), 'Transforming Consciousness: Women and the New Reproductive Technologies', in Gena Corea (*et al.*) (eds), *Man-Made Women: How New Reproductive Technologies Affect Women*, Hutchinson: London.

Jeffery, P. and Jeffery, R. (1996) *Don't Marry Me to Plowman!: Women's Everyday Lives in Rural North India*, Oxford: Westview Press.

Jeffery, P., Jeffery, R. and Lyon, A. (1989), *Labour Pains and Labour Power: Women and Childbearing in India*, London: Zed Books.

Jhutti, J. (1998), 'Dowry among Sikhs in Britain', in W. Menski (ed.), *South Asians and the Dowry Problem*, GEMS No. 6, Stoke on Trent: Trentham Books.

Kandiyoti, D. (1997), 'Bargaining Patriarchy', in N. Visvanathan, L. Duggan, L. Nisonoff and N. Wiegeresma (eds), *The Women, Gender and Development Reader*, London: Zed.

Khanna, S. K. (1995) 'Prenatal Sex Determination: A New Family-building Strategy', *Manushi*, 86: 23–9.

Kumar, N. (1994), *Women as Subjects: South Asian Histories*, Charlottesville, VA: University Press of Virginia.

Mani, L. (1990), 'Contentious Traditions: The Debate on Sati in Colonial India', in K. Sangari and S. Vaid (eds), *Recasting Women: Essays in Indian Colonial History*, Piscataway, NJ: Rutgers University Press.

Mies, M. (1987), 'Why Do We Need All This? A Call Against Genetic Engineering and Reproductive Technologies', in P. Spallone and D. Steinberg (eds), *Made to Order: The Myth of Reproductive and Genetic Progress*, Oxford: Pergamon.

Moser, C. (1993), *Gender Planning and Development: Theory, Practice and Training*, London: Routledge.

Narayan, U. (1997), *Dislocating Cultures: Identities, Traditions and Third World Feminism*, New York: Routledge.

—— (1998), 'Essence of Culture and a Sense of History: A Feminist Critique of Cultural Essentialism,' *Hypatia*, 13 (2): Spring: 86–106.

Panigrahi, L. (1972), *British Social Policy and Female Infanticide in India*, Delhi: Munshiram Manoharlal.

Parmar, P. (1982), 'Gender, Race and Class: Asian Women in Resistance', in Centre for Contemporary Cultural Studies (CCCS), *The Empire Strikes Back*, London: Hutchinson.

Patel, P. (2001), 'Creating Alternative Spaces: Black Women in Resistance', interview by P. Parbha in S. Rowbotham and S. Linkogle (eds), *Women Resist Globalization: Mobilizing for Livelihood and Rights*, London: Zed.

Patel, V. (1988), 'Sex Determination and Sex Pre-selection Tests: Abuse of Advanced Technologies', in R. Ghadially (ed.) *Women in Indian Society*, pp. 178–85. New Delhi: Sage Publications.

Rajan, R. S. (1993), *Real and Imagined Women: Gender, Culture and Postcolonialism*, New York: Routledge.

Rowland, R. (1992), *Living Laboratories: Women and Reproductive Technologies*, Bloomington, IN: Indiana University Press.

Sangari, K. and Vaid, S. (eds), *Recasting Women: Essays in Indian Colonial History*, Piscataway, NJ: Rutgers University Press.

Sen, A. (1990), 'More Than 100 Million Women are Missing', *New York Review*, 20 December: 61–6.

Sharma, U. (1980), *Women, Work and Property in Northwest India*, London: Tavistock.

Sheel, R. (1999), *The Political Economy of Dowry: Institutionalization and Expansion in North India*, New Delhi: Manohar.

Spivak, G. (1993), 'Can the Subaltern Speak?', in P. Williams and L. Chrisman (eds), *Colonial Discourse and Postcolonial Theory*, London: Harvester Wheatsheaf.

Strathern, M. (1992), *Reproducing the Future: Essays on Anthropology, Kinship and the New Reproductive Technologies*, Manchester: Manchester University Press.

Visvanathan, L. S. (1998), 'Efforts of Colonial State to Suppress Female Infanticide: Use of Sacred Texts, Generation of Knowledge', *Economic and Political Weekly*, May 9: 1104–12.

Wacjman, J. (1991), *Feminism Confronts Technology*, Philadelphia: Pennsylvania State University Press.

Walby, S. (1990), *Theorizing Patriarchy*, Oxford: Blackwell Publishers.

Westwood, S. (1984), *All Day Every Day: Factory and Family in the Making of Women's Lives*, London: Pluto Press.

Wilson, A. (1978), *Finding a Voice: Asian Women in Britain*, London: Virago Press.

9

Gendered Embodiments: Mapping the Body-Politic of the Raped Woman and the Nation in Bangladesh

Nayanika Mookherjee

Introduction

There has been much academic work outlining the complex links between women and the nation (Yuval-Davis and Anthias 1989; Yuval-Davis 1997; Yuval-Davis and Werbner 1999). Women provide legitimacy to the political projects of the nation within particular social and historical contexts (Kandiyoti 1991; Chatterjee 1994). This chapter focuses on the gendered symbolization of the nation through the rhetoric of the 'motherland' and the manipulation of this rhetoric in the context of national struggle in Bangladesh. I show the ways in which the visual representation of this 'motherland' as fertile countryside, and its idealization primarily through rural landscapes has enabled a crystallization of essentialist gender roles for women.[1]

Gender and Middle-Class Aesthetics

The ideology of woman as mother is a dominant symbolic imagery through which the position of the woman becomes visible in national projects. It becomes crucial for national mobilization processes (Yuval-Davis and Anthias 1989). Pnina Werbner (1999: 221) argues that the overt space occupied by 'political motherhood' in the public domain enables a breaking down of public/private dichotomies in which women are stereotypically situated. It creates conditions for the 'feminisation (rather than essentialist definitions of male and female qualities) of citizenship which show that women are not victims but active agents of their destiny with a strong sense of concern for family and community' (1999: 231). Motherhood as a space of public agency for women is not however unproblematic. What for instance are the implications of using motherhood as the dominant image through which women are symbolized in the nationalist project for the imagery and subjectivities of women who are not part of that maternal mould? Does the nationalist project make its public, symbolic space available to women only within the confines of specific subjectivities? These questions may be best answered by analysing the processes of gendering that are drawn upon to secure 'political motherhood'. Focusing not just on manhood and womanhood but on the processes through which gender roles are embodied enables us to understand the contradictions inherent in the fraught relationship between gender and nation.

Furthermore 'political motherhood' must be located in class aesthetics in order to understand its influence on the construction of race and nation.[2] Explorations of the role of gender within colonialism have shown how gender constitutes a trope for race and sexuality through the feminization of the colonized (Nandy 1983; Sinha 1995). However, examining gendered subjectivity without its intertwinings with class and race does not allow the dynamic nature of the link between national interests and hegemonic masculinities to be explored. Moreover a focus on class aesthetics/sensibilities rather than class *per se* allows us to move to reading class not as a pre-constituted group but as an ongoing process of articulation.

In this chapter I explore the embodiment[3] of gendered roles as envisaged in the feminization of the land, which enables the body of the woman as mother to be available for the aestheticzsing impulse of the project of nationalism in Bangladesh. I argue that processes of gendering in Bangladesh operate as a trope for hegemonic middle-class (both female and male) sensibilities (discourses and practices). It makes available women's bodies as representative icons of nationhood within debates on nationalism through the use of the rhetoric and imagery of the 'mother nation', a symbol that was used extensively by the emancipatory and socially progressive anticolonial and democratic movements in Bangladesh. These images then had to be reconciled with the subjectivities of women raped during the Bangladesh Liberation War (*Muktijuddho*). I argue that this was achieved through the aestheticizing sensibilities of Bangladesh's middle class.

I use middle-class aesthetics/sensibilities in multiple ways here. The very notion of aesthetics involves, according to Daniel (1997: 309), the need to bring order out of disorder, to mould form from that in which form is absent. But even though this order may be posited only as a future hope – something to be achieved – it is drenched in nostalgia, in musings on the imagined glory that once was. In Bangladesh this nostalgia is rooted in the

Bengali identity, epitomized in the literary tradition, the main readership of which consists of the middle classes. The romanticism that emerges from this also finds its fruition in the 'glamour and sorrow' of the liberation struggle, the *Muktijuddho*, in which the middle classes were important players.

Within the constructs of this essentialized Bengali identity that emerged in the context of the progressive liberation struggle the role of women comes to be framed and legitimized only within the domestic paradigm. In the folds of this paradigm exist middle-class contradictions of morality. Various literary accounts in Bangladesh explore these varied ambiguities of the middle class. It is this double helix of the posturings of modernity of the progressive middle class's resistive politics along with hypocritical value judgements and moral positions that place the raped woman in a place of taboo and transgression. Hence her necessary appropriation is made possible only within their romantic, literary and domestic paradigms.

This chapter draws on research on the public's memories of the sexual violence of *Muktijuddho*. It is based on fourteen months of fieldwork in Bangladesh from 1997 to 1998. In the first section I refer to the historical context of sexual violence during *Muktijuddho*. In the second section I examine the ways in which the imagery of nature is used to idealize the nation both during and after *Muktijuddho*, and also to represent the sexual violence perpetrated during the war. The next section focuses on the ways in which the articulations of gender and nation present and privilege a middle-class notion of gender. This is followed by a discussion of the continued significance of class aesthetics in articulations of gender and nationalism in independent Bangladesh. In the final section I expose some of the ambiguities in the ways in which the body-politic of the raped woman is employed in nation-building, and how middle-class sensibilities again influence this process.

Sexual Violence and the Bangladesh Liberation War of 1971

In 1947, India's independence from British colonial rule resulted in the creation of a new homeland for the Muslims of India. Using Islam as the principle of nationhood, the eastern and north-western corners of the country came together as a single nation. The two parts, East and West Pakistan, were however culturally and linguistically distinct. West Pakistan, the centre of political authority, attempted to transpose that authority to secure cultural dominance on the basis that the East Pakistani practice of Islam was too Bengali (hence too Hinduized/Indianized). Resistance to the imposition of administrative, economic, military, linguistic (Urdu in place of the prevalent Bengali) and political control crystallized in the nine-month-long *Muktijuddho* in 1971. East Pakistan became independent from West Pakistan and Bangladesh was formed on 16 December 1971.

The new nation of Bangladesh was faced with the staggering statistics of three million dead and two hundred thousand women raped in a span of nine months. These crimes were perpetrated both by the Pakistani army and by their local Bengali collaborators. One of the main reasons cited by the middle-class and cultural elites in Bangladesh for the prevalence of rapes during *Muktijuddho* was that since Bengali Muslims were considered as 'Indianized/Hinduized' and only as 'nominal Muslims' by the Pakistani authorities, rape was seen a means to 'improve the genes of the Bengali Muslims' and to populate Bangladesh with a new breed of 'pure' Pakistanis.[4]

Violence in the form of rape has been variedly argued to be 'the depersonalisation of women' (Winkler 1991), 'a conscious process of intimidation by which all men keep all women in a state of fear' (Brownmiller 1975), 'a method of taming a woman who gets out of line' (Ortner and Whitehead 1981), and 'terror warfare' (Nordstorm and Robben 1995). Although these feminist theorizations of rape provide some understanding of the ways in which sexuality may be utilized to inscribe gender inequalities, they fail to recognize the importance of historical, racialized dynamics in understanding the different connotations of sexual violence.

These feminist accounts also cannot address how dramatic episodes of violence against women during collective violence bring to the surface, savagely and explicitly, familiar forms of sexual violence, only now charged with added symbolic meaning. Judith Butler argues that 'gender is an identity tenuously constituted in time, instituted in an exterior space through a stylised repetition of acts' (1990: 140). Thus the gendered performativity of rape during collective violence ensures that the gendering of women's bodies as female constitutes them as political signs, territories on which the political programmes that also affect the nation, community and family get inscribed.[5] Rape thereby becomes an 'explicitly political act, a ritual of victory, the defilement of honour and territory of the enemy community' (Agarwal 1995).[6] It disrupts woman's essentialized role as a medium of producing progeny for the community and a symbol of the honour of the family and community. Rape becomes a means of retribution and pre-emption, as well as a metaphor of sacredness and humiliation.[7]

That the state predominantly wanted to restore the raped women to their essentialized, normative spheres is evident in the Bangladeshi state's eulogizing of the women raped as *birangonas* (war-heroines) in 1971. This policy coincided with a new genre of public persuasive rhetoric that aimed at getting the *birangonas* married, and thus reducing their social ostracism. Rehabilitation Centres were established in different parts of Bangladesh, which aimed at conducting 'marry-off campaigns' or making the women self-sufficient by introducing them to the labour market. Hence the kinship norms of purity and honour were articulated in a public discourse that made them the concerns not merely of the family or the community, but also of the new nation. However, press reports suggest that these women were not easily accepted by their families, so that the campaign to integrate *birangonas* ultimately proved to be unsuccessful. This highlights the unease and ambiguity surrounding the issue of the transgression of 'female virtue' in Bangladesh, an issue I return to later. The *birangonas* eventually disappeared from public discourse and were folded into everyday life, shrouded in zones of silence. An understanding of the process of silencing requires an appreciation of the gendered construction of nationhood and the significance of class aesthetics in these constructions, both of which limit the spaces available for 'rescuing' the *birangonas*.

Gendering of the Nation

My Golden Bengal, I love you.
Eternally your skies and winds play their flute within my heart.
Oh Mother, in the spring, the smell of the mango grove
Makes one beside oneself.
Alas, I die in pleasure.
Oh Mother, in the autumn's harvesting fields,
I have seen your sweet smile.
What a sight, what a shade, what gentle love, what attachment (*maya*)
Unfolds as you spread the ends of your saree,
under the banyan tree, beside the river.
Mother when you speak, your words
ring in my ears like nectar sweet.
Alas I die in pleasure.
Mother when your body is tarnished
Oh mother, my eyes fill to the brim.

The aforementioned popular nationalist song *Amar Sonar Bangla, ami tomai bhalobashi* ('O my golden Bengal, How I do love you!'), written by Rabindranath Tagore (found in *Tagore Swarabitan*, 46), the Bengali poet, in the context of anticolonial struggle during the partition of Bengal in 1905, was adopted as the national anthem of independent Bangladesh in 1971.[8]

Sonar Bangla (Golden Bengal) is a romantic nostalgic depiction of mother Bengal, with her prosperous lands and rivers, inhabited by a peaceful agrarian community living in harmony with its pastoral surroundings, thereby conferring a timelessness and an apparent classlessness on the imagery. This scene of eternal tranquillity, which evokes sorrowful longing and emotion for one's homeland, was utilized politically in order to evoke pathos during the struggle for an independent Bangladesh during *Muktijuddho,* and then passion for the rebuilding of the new nation.

The feminization of the land as mother brings out the 'aestheticizing impulse which lies at the heart of all nation states' (Daniel 1997: 309). The adoption of Tagore's *Sonar Bangla* in 1971 as the national anthem of Bangladesh is an indication of how romanticization of nature was an intrinsic part of the complex sentimentality of the nationalistic feelings of a newly born nation. Here nature has political, ethnic and emotive connotations, and links between the place of domicile/residence and social and political identities are highlighted. Hence the aesthetic contemplation of nature's beauty in post-war Bangladeshi literature is linked to a political and cultural identity, that of being Bengali, in a process that Kaviraj (1994) refers to as the 'selfing of nature'. Abstract space and place are given meaning through the self. The mundane senses, emotions, memory and nostalgia of the smell of the mango grove in spring, autumn's harvesting fields, the banyan tree, the river and finally the tears and pain of seeing the mother's tarnished body seemed to make *Sonar Bangla* an apt national anthem for a war-ravaged Bangladesh.[9]

This gendered embodiment of the nation as mother is explicitly brought out through the figure of the woman adopted in an advertisement for Bata shoes (*Purbodesh*, 26 March 1972). The advertisement utilizes the image of a rural woman (indicated by the lack of a blouse and the way the sari is worn) with a *teep*,[10] collecting *shapla* flowers (the national flower of Bangladesh) from the pond. Its caption is borrowed from the National Anthem ('Oh my Golden Bengal, I love you'). Nationalist emotions are evoked by linking representations of nature, space, earth and mother 'all of which had only existed as separate cultural and aesthetic constructs without any strong internal connection' (Kaviraj 1994). Kaviraj argues that the idea of linking the land with the mother first arose in Bengali nationalism in Bankimchandra Chattopadhyay's novel *Anandamath,* written in the mid-nineteenth century. Chattopadhyay's clarion call of *Bandemataram* ('Hail the Mother') became part of the nationalist struggle against British colonial rule in India, stoking patriotic fervour for the mother nation, and mobilizing people to fight for their nation, to free it from its shackles and to protect this freedom.

In Bangladesh, however, the pathos and pain for a mother who has been wronged both redefines and intensifies these emotions. This pathos is brought out by linking rape with the ravages of nature and of the mother nation. The following poem *Dogdhogra* (Burnt Village), written by Jasimuddin in 1972, compares the ravaging of the pastoral surroundings of Bengal with that inflicted through rape and torture by the Pakistani army.

> Here was the dark village, in the shade of the mango and jackfruit trees,
> It used to bring in a cool breeze and fostered attachment.
> What happened, the human torturers came from the west,
> They set fire to the whole village and roared in laughter,
> The whole village is a burnt crematorium, in the gusty wind
> A deep sigh blows over the sky and earth and over the ashes
> A child was taken away from a mother's lap,
> In front of a father, the daughter was cut up in a bloodbath.

Similar arguments are made by Butalia (1998: 139) when she sketches the ways in which the formation of the Pakistani nation from the territory of *Bharat* (or the body of *Bharatmata*) became a metaphor to the Indian government for the violation of the body of the 'pure' Hindu woman. It was argued that partition violates the body of the mother nation. Hence the 'recovery' operations to rescue 'abducted' women undertaken by the Indian government after 1947 are imaged in parliamentary debates as amounting to the regaining of the pure body of the 'Sita-like' woman. Significantly, it was constantly emphasized that this purity was essential for self-legitimizing the nation and the community (Butalia 1998: 144). The following poem shows the way in which similar processes were at work in Bangladesh too:

> *New Initials*
> In the darkness of my mango groves
> on the dead body of my paddy field,
> on the bloody death of my ravished sister
> New Initials.
> In the death of our doubts
> in the courage of our faith
> on the bayonet point
> of a new flag
> is a new christening.
> (Cited in *Doinik Bangla*, 4 January 1972.)

A caption *Keno go ma tor dhulai aashon, keno go ma tor molin boshon* ('Why mother is your place in the dust, why mother is your demeanour and appearance soiled') (Genocide Special Issue, *Banglar Bani*, December 1972) accompanying an article on the rape of women during the war, however, reveals the double connotation of pathos-revulsion through the use of the term *molin* (soiled or tarnished).

Significantly this rape of nature/nation/woman (sister, wife or daughter) occurs before the male relatives of the women, as is mentioned in the last line of 'Burnt Village.' Men are onlookers unable to stop this rape. The demasculinization of men, through their loss of agency as protectors of the honour of their women, who are conduits for their own honour, can only be corrected by then making them saviours in the nationalist project. This is well expressed in the following extract from Anwar Pasha's[11] (1976) *Rifles, Bread and Women*, concerning his feelings when he came across the body of a raped woman in 1971:

> She was the symbol of helpless Mother Bengal of millions of Bengalis. Tagore had truly observed, our mother was the daughter of gods but she did not have the power of the gods. She loved us but was unable to protect us. But mother your children have grown up – we shall protect you now.

Here we see not only piety and devotion, but also affection and pain for the mother. Instead of the irresistible power that the mother can command, as in Bankim's *Anandamath*, rather than representing her as having an 'avenging power' (Kaviraj 1994), the mother here needs protection. It was this gendered embodiment of nature and nation as mother that I would argue influenced the dominant and valorized construction of women in Bangladesh in the nationalist framework.

Dominant Construction of Women

Although there was no specific women's agenda in the nationalist movement, the mobilization of middle-class women was critical. A small number of women also took up arms and joined the underground resistance in 1971 (though few of them are supposed to have engaged in actual combat). The fact that these images became so dominant within the national pantheon shows that not only were women symbolically equal members of the national collectivity, but that as symbols of national culture and tradition, they were also symbols of modernization, liberation and insurrection.

The bodily practices[12] of middle-class East Pakistani Bengali women became a provocative and visible symbol of resistance. Through their clothing (saris), adornments (flowers in their hair and wearing *teep*) and actions (singing the songs of Tagore, which were banned by the Pakistani government, celebrating Bengali New Year's Day, and sending their daughters to music and dance school and allowing them to perform on stage) they became the icons of Bengali ethnicity, a vehicle for marking cultural (and territorial) boundaries.[13] Women therefore played an important role in forming middle-class nationalist identities in *Muktijuddho,* as they represented all that was simultaneously culturally oppositional to Pakistan and distinctive of Bangladesh.

The metaphorical extension of images of motherhood from the household to the 'imagined community' of the nation is visible in the *Shaheed Minar* (Martyr's Memorial), a statue of a mother and her children. The huge memorial in front of the Arts Faculty of Dhaka University of a female nurse highlights another 'noble' role played by women during *Muktijuddho.* The iconography of the nation in the familial and domestic space was pronounced in Indian nationalist history (Chatterjee 1994). In Bengal particularly, the middle-class, with its aim of furthering the project of modernity whilst also fostering nationalism, tried to resolve the inherent contradictions faced by these projects by presenting women with the responsibility for protecting, preserving and strengthening national culture. It presented woman, as pure and unaffected by the profane activities of the material world, through the paraphernalia intrinsic to middle-class material security (see also Bhatia, this volume, Chapter 6).

It seems that only as a respectable, self-sacrificing mother and wife, and hence as an idealized woman[14] can she be admitted into the dominant nationalist view as a model for society's women. Hence it is only the image of the nurturing and sacrificing woman, as mother, wife or nurse, that is authorized by the discourse of *Muktijuddho.* From the microcosm of the home to the macrocosm of the nation the presence of the impure woman, epitomized in the figure of the *birangona,* seems to be excluded.

Thus in *Muktijuddho* the role of the woman is essentially a designated agency, an agency by invitation only. It makes its appearance not in direct political relation to the liberation, but as a mediated, domestic relation to a man. Women in Bangladesh have been hailed in the national discourse of the war, in various political speeches and personal memoirs, which are given enormous significance in the historical narrative of the war, for allowing their sons and husbands to go to war, thereby subscribing to the image of 'patriotic motherhood' (Ardener and Holden 1987) or 'an ever ready womb' (Cooke 1996). Their trauma is also essentially relational. In the nationalist discourse women are seen as the sorrowful widow, mother and sister,[15] whereas in accounts of sexual violence the pain of a brother/father whose sister/daughter was raped or killed in the war is emphasized as part of the nationalist commemoration of the war.

Recent Gendering of Nature and the Woman's Body

The coming together of nature, mother and nation, a dominant trope against colonial rule, reflected resistance. The fact that it becomes a dominant emotive idiom for the nation in 1971 and again in the 1990s in Bangladesh raises questions about the political and social dynamics in which these images are employed and also the imagination that gives rise to them. However, the image of the tortured, ravaged mother of 1971 who needs to be protected and taken care of has in 1992 given way to a combative mother, at the helm of affairs and providing inspiration and new hopes to the nation (similar to that of Bankim's mother in *Anandamath*). The emergence of Jahanara Imam makes this possible.

An upper-middle-class woman who was known in Dhaka to be the only woman to drive her own car, Jahanara Imam lost her husband and son Rumi (who was a liberation fighter) during the war in 1971. Jahanara Imam became the noble, sacrificing, romantic and yet combative image of the mother-nation in 1992, when she spearheaded a popular movement to demand the trial of Gholam Azum, a collaborator who allegedly was complicit in the acts of rape and genocide of the Pakistani army in 1971. The inspiration that she provided to the younger generation and her subsequent tragic death from cancer has enshrined her in popular memory. To this day she is revered as the embodiment of motherhood in the national discourse. The middle-class narrative and iconification of Jahanara Imam emphasizes the ways in which idealizations of womanhood carry within them notions of respectability, embodied and circumscribed in domesticity. In the 1970s motherhood's emotional and affective intensity was emphasized. In the 1990s, though motherhood is reiterated, it is emptied of its customary emotional and affective load and is vested with a heroic political instrumentality. I would argue that Werbner's 'overt political motherhood' (1999), which constitutes these women as occupying public space and hence challenging their confinement to the domestic sphere, is acceptable precisely because of the connotations of domesticity they bring to public space. Moreover, these notions are also rooted in age and class hierarchies, and the conflation of the imagery of mother and nation is embedded in middle-class aesthetics.

The success of the documentary *Muktir Gaan* (Songs of Freedom) supports this analysis.[16] Made by Tareque and Catherine Masud (1995), this documentary emotively romanticizes Bengal by recreating and revisiting the genre of nation as mother in 1971. The footage follows a group of young Bengali middle- and upper-middle-class men and women from Dhaka who visit various refugee camps, training centres of liberation fighters and Liberated Zones during the war in order to sing songs and provide moral support and inspiration. Its poetic evocation of the Bengali land and nature through images and songs generated/coincided with a wave of romanticism, so that the men and women in the documentary were elevated to the position of celebrities fourteen years after its making. *Muktir Gaan* moved people in urban Dhaka and small towns by arousing an immense nostalgic enthusiasm for being Bengali. As a young woman among the audience responded [as documented by *Muktir Katha* (Words of Freedom) (1999), the sequel to *Muktir Gaan*],[17] 'We were always told that women had been victims. This shows the women did do things during *Muktijuddho*. My legs are shaking. I am absolutely overwhelmed.'

As the cultural troupe sing various songs of Tagore and other Bengali poets the evocation of the beauty and wealth of Bengal in these songs is juxtaposed with the jarring ravages of the war. Hence Bengal is a land of gold as well as blood; it is abundant, green, a land of rivers – the *Podda, Meghna, Jamuna* – rivers on which flow corpses of the people killed. The famous song *Dhono Dhanne Pushpe Bhora* (This earth of ours is filled with wealth, prosperity, grains and flowers) by Tagore is sung at various times along with images of piles of jute fibres, rivers, flowers, nature and common day-to-day activities such as the picking of hyacinths from ponds.

Scenes of young women from the group wading into a pond to pick *shapla* flowers (like the image in the Bata advertisement) and adorning their hair with them, of the sharing of *desher mishti* (country sweets) from an earthen pot – these activities chart out the promises of an emerging nation. *Sonar Bangla* ('Golden Bengal'), the national anthem, is sung when the troupe crosses a river to go to the Liberated Zones, the river representing the liminality between independence and subservience, between which *Sonar Bangla* is the bridge. In the Liberated Zone, songs celebrating the victory of the Bengalis seem to be virtually synonymous with the 'limitless wealth' of Bengal, with its 'rivers filled with fish, trees with fruit, land of gold'.

The documentary charts the group's day-to-day activities: young unmarried men and women of different religion and class backgrounds travelling in a truck through days and nights, huddling around a radio listening to the broadcast of Independent Bengal Radio, singing inspirational songs in refugee camps and among liberation fighters in liberated zones, worrying about their family members who have gone to war. The threat of rape may also be inferred. In the documentary Naila, one of the younger women, reads out an article from the newspaper, *The People*, to Sharmeen,[18] (one of the women in the group) highlighting the demands of the Pakistani army, 'We are tired – we want wine and women.'

Images of young, attractive women walking into the skyline with the flag of Bangladesh fluttering in the breeze to the tunes of *Sonar Bangla* suggest that the beautiful face of a Bengali woman is virtually synonymous with the beauties of the nation. The last scene captures this aptly: as the truck makes its way back to Bangladesh after the war, Sharmeen's hair and the end of her red sari blow in the breeze against the fluttering green and red of Bangladesh's flag to the stirring tunes of *Joi Bangla* ('Victory to Bengal'). Her face, like the nation, is haunting and beautiful. The first flag of independent Bangladesh had the map of the country printed on a red sun.[19] The green background of the flag symbolized the significance of nature.[20] I would also argue that the flag itself represents the metonymic relationship of the nation with nature.

Muktir Gaan can be seen to be a critique of the cocooned, luxurious romanticism and sentimentality of the middle class about the war and the nation. Most of the young men and women came from upper-middle-class backgrounds and spent their time during the war in Calcutta and India, far away from the ravages of the war. However, its immense popularity in the 1990s reinscribes the image of woman within the folds of the mother nation and of middle-class aesthetics.

The Body-Politic of the *Birangona* Within the Nationalist Project

Collapsing the image of female rape with that of the ravages of nature and of mother-nation enables, I would argue, an aestheticization of rape and makes it easier to accept. The emphasis on the role of the nurturing woman in *Muktijuddho,* as mothers or nurses, ennobles suffering. The mothering of the raped woman locates the *birangona* within the realm of respectability. The domesticity intrinsic to motherhood makes her image acceptable and hence available to the political instrumentality of the nation. The imagery of the mother as innocent victim, caring, nurturing, compassionate, desexualized, of whose pure womb sons are born to further the cause of the nation, provides a powerful underpinning for the state to see itself as a caring parent, concerned for the fate and future of its citizens. It is this concern that makes it necessary for the state to rehabilitate and 'normalize' the raped women – to recover the mothers of its future citizens.

Compared to other instances of sexual violence during conflict situations, as in the case of Japanese comfort women, Bosnia and Rwanda, the public discourse on the rehabilitation of the *birangonas* initiated by the Bangladeshi government was significantly different. It has certain parallels with the processes of 'recovery of abducted women' initiated by the Indian government in 1947 after Partition, where the construction of the Pakistani Muslims as the 'other' became the dominant discourse. In Bangladesh, instead of the usual suppression of accounts of sexual violence, the very public discourse of rehabilitation of raped women had two roles. First, through the articulation of this history the government was shown to be progressive. Secondly, the emancipatory image of the rehabilitation programme for the raped women reflected the 'modernity' of the new nation. However, reports of the non-acceptance of women whom the state had attempted to 'marry off', through the rehabilitation programme by their families highlight the inherent 'othering' of the raped women and the prevalent ambivalence towards their acceptance.

It is important to point out that the history of rape during the war is emphasized in government speeches from 1971 till 1975 in terms of the numerical rubric of '200,000 mothers and sisters'. The issue was then ignored, before re-emerging in the 1990s, although literary accounts of rape have abounded throughout the period. In the 1990s many life histories of women who have been raped have been 'unearthed', and this process has once again highlighted the ambiguities towards raped women based on class and sexuality. Anxieties about errant and undomesticated sexuality in the act of rape were brought out in various literary accounts and interviews with liberation fighters, judges, government ministers and social workers involved in the rehabilitation of raped women.

We find that nation-building is enabled through the aestheticized, valorized, respectable and mothered *birangona*, who is permitted to be an image, while the troubled relationship towards her as a raped woman is exempted from this national imagery.[21] Nationalist historiography thus confers freedom by imposing at the same time a whole set of new controls. It defines cultural identity for the nation by excluding the experiences of many from its fold; it grants citizenship to some, while others are confined to eschewed dimensions.

Interestingly, in the 'collective memory' of the nation, the figure of the raped Bengali woman is a powerful symbol of Pakistani lust and barbarism; yet it is a figure riven by anxiety and irresolution. In popular plays on *Muktijuddho*, for instance the violation of individual women is often portrayed as a sacrifice, for the family as well as for the nation.[22] A standard plot revolves around the woman whose husband has been incarcerated by the military, who surrenders her body to the depredations of army personnel in order to secure her partner's freedom. Yet this sacrifice can be redeemed only by the woman's subsequent exit from the plot, for her act signifies betrayal, shame as well as sacrifice. The choice of rejoining family and community in these representations is predominantly unexercised; typically she encounters death through suicide or accident, and is thus written out of the text of community. Once defiled, even if it is for the 'good' of her man and nation, she becomes to the community, the uncomfortable constitutive outside.

This precisely highlights the ambiguity towards the raped women, as it is the very exit of the individual *birangona* that enables her representation as a collective group of nameless raped women. Their accounts are personalized only when their deaths have an element of agency, for example through killing Pakistani soldiers before killing herself. Through such scenarios the action of the woman is transformed to a sacred act, whereby she not only takes revenge against those who violated her, and by that act violated her country, but in the process her actions seem to 'purify' her 'polluted' body, so that her individual name can be placed within the pantheon of martyrs.[23]

Significantly, it is the image of the raped woman and the nation that seems to provide agency to other subjectivities. Hence the husbands, brothers, fathers who have been unable to prevent the rape can retrieve their masculinity by doing something to avenge the act of rape. Similarly, the imagery of rape mobilizes and gives agency to the new nation.

Conclusion

This chapter argues that feminist theorizations of rape that focus solely on the individual woman's body are limited, as they do not take account of the historical and political contexts within which sexual violence takes place.

I have argued that not only does nationalism employ its women instrumentally but that, in Bangladesh, this process is also inherently embedded in middle-class aesthetics. Both middle-class men and women (and not men only) are implicated in the project of gendering the nation, and this is necessary for the masculinist idiom of nationalism. Nationalism enables the recreation of essentialist positions of women through the feminization of land and the selfing of nature. The emphasis on the mother as nation has made motherhood the most significant construct within which the role of the woman has been envisaged in Bangladesh in the context of *Mukti-juddho*. Rape of women is therefore collapsed into the ravaging of nature and of the mother-nation. Class aesthetization, valorization of motherhood and the feminization of the beauty of nature together produce a suitable narrative to contain the history of rape.

I have argued that by locating the history of rape within the idiom of respectability as located in the mother and nation, the nationalist project has domesticated 'errant' sexuality engendered through rape and has aestheticized the gruesome events of rape so that it becomes available for Bangladesh's nation-building project. Subsuming the history of rape within this aestheticizing impulse of nationalist history excludes ambiguities present within the histories of raped women and limits discussions of rape to the collective, the rhetorical, the imaginary. The body of the individual raped woman is only made available by ensuring her exit, through death or suicide. She can therefore only be represented through the select idioms of nationhood. On the other hand, the feminization of the land as mother and raped woman ensures the intervention and masculine agency of the nation and male relatives and motherhood, while not addressing the ambivalences present within these genderings.

Notes

1. This intersection of the symbolic imagery of gender national identity and landscape has been explored in literature on geography/landscape and gender/body (Rose 1993; Monk and Norwood 1987; Nash 1994).
2. Acknowledgements: This chapter develops arguments from my Ph.D. research on 'Sexual Violence, Public Memory and the Bangladesh Liberation War of 1971.' This research was made possible by the Felix Scholarship, Central Research Fund and Emslie Horniman Fieldwork Fund. I am thankful to Dr Christopher Pinney and Dr Caroline Osella, whose feedback and discussions have helped me enormously to hone my thoughts. I thank the editors Nirmal Puwar and Parvati Raghuram for their insightful comments on earlier versions of this chapter. Werbner (1999) uses the terms 'motherhood' or 'woman', and yet does not probe why different issues are prioritized in struggles among different classes of women in the examples she cites (1999: 220). Her

example of the women's movement in Bangladesh also does not take into account the history of the social classes of the women involved in the democratization and anti-Islamization programme, and the discourses of modernity embedded in it.

3. By embodiment I refer to an individual's field defined by perceptual experience and mode of presence and engagement with the world, experiences that are primarily rooted in the body.

4. Similar arguments can also be found in accounts of rape in former Yugoslavia and in Rwanda.

5. For excellent analyses of sexual violence during the partition of India and Pakistan in 1947 and the Indian government's attempts at the 'recovery' of 'abducted women' see Das (1995), Butalia (1998), Menon and Bhasin (1998).

6. Purshottam Agarwal here talks about sexual violence in Surat, in the context of nation-wide riots, following the destruction of the Babri Masjid in Ayodhya in 1992.

7. Agarwal (1995: 39) has shown how the disrobing of Draupadi is an instance of how political discourses constructed by collectivities have consciously contextualized rape exclusively in the problematic of the contest between two nations or communities, thus transforming it into a morally defendable act – in fact into a much needed political strategy. Draupadi, according to the *Mahabharata*, one of the Hindu epics, was the shared wife of five Pandava brothers, and was gambled away in a game of dice with their 'villainous' cousin, Duryodhana. Divine intervention saved her from the ordeal of being disrobed in a public court (which can be read as rape) by Duryodhana. Duryodhana could think of no better way than ordering the public disrobing of Draupadi to emphasize decisively the humiliating and final defeat of the Pandavas in the game of dice, and the Pandavas could not protest for the simple reason that this reprehensible act was justified in terms of the moral paradigm of patriarchy into which they were also bound. Also see Cooke and Rustomji-Kerns (1994: 136–46) for Gayatri Chakravarty Spivak's translation of Mahasweta Devi's short story *Draupadi*, where she uses the metaphor of the mythological Draupadi to narrate the experience of rape of a low-caste woman named Dopdi Mejhen.

8. This song was banned from East Pakistani radio before 1971 by the Pakistani authorities, as it was considered to connote resistance and patriotism.

9. The combination of sacredness with the secular beauty of nature (Chakravarty 1995: 117) means that acts of violation and defilement amount to a breakdown of one's understanding of home. During

interviews with people about their experiences after the war, one of the oft-cited accounts would be that of returning to Dhaka from India. Individuals would talk of the long trek by foot that they had to make from Calcutta to reach Dhaka, seeing the images of their country with a 'lump in their throat'. They would talk at length of their pain when they passed burnt-down villages, empty fields, broken bridges, and the sight of a war-ravaged nation. 'As I cried while sitting on a boat crossing the river, a feeling surged in my heart that I was back in the nature of my country, I could be on the river in a boat again, I could enjoy the winter sunshine. I couldn't see the mustard fields this year, but I thought next year we would again have the mustard fields in winter, the sugarcane harvest in autumn. It was a very peaceful feeling tinged with pain and I had a feeling of enormous love for my country' (Fatema Rumi, head of an NGO, in an interview on 28 October 1997). It is this shared nostalgia of the suburb/urban middle class that places the idyllic village squarely in the middle of the city–country question.

10. *Teep* are decorative spots on the forehead worn traditionally by Hindu women to denote marital status. In Bangladesh the wearing of *teep* is very common. It connotes clothing and stylistic practices, but also political practice, emphasizing a Bengali identity that exists alongside a Muslim identity.

11. Pasha, who wrote this in 1971, was one of 30 intellectuals who were picked up by the Pakistani army and killed in December 1971.

12. Ardener and Holden (1987) talk about the symbolic use of the body by those lacking an effective political voice. Mahashweta Devi's story *Draupadi* (Cooke and Rustomji-Kerns 1994: 136–46) gives a traumatic account of the rape of a low-caste woman who refused to be dressed after being gang-raped. Similarly, when the women of Greenham smeared their naked bodies with ashes on Nagasaki Day 1984, their actions challenged the invisibility of the bodies of the victims of 'the nuclear disaster', but also 'men's stereotypes of naked women' (Jones 1987).

13. My experience of Bengali New Year's Day in Dhaka during my fieldwork surpassed any celebration that I had seen in West Bengal, India, which showed how much this is part of one's identity politics in Bangladesh.

14. In the writings of social reformists in India in the early twentieth century, women were similarly objectified as bodies and divided into the familiar dichotomy of mothers and prostitutes. See Parker, Russo, Sommer and Yaeger (1992: 1–20) for a discussion of competitive

claims of subjectivities of women in nationalism; see Whitehead (1995) for the role of motherhood in the nationalist discourse of India, and Gupta (1991) for that in Nazi Germany.

15. For a discussion of the iconic figure of the sacrificial and revolutionary mother in Afrikaner and African nationalism see McClintock (1995).

16. The film was shot in 1971 by Lear Levin, an American photographer.

17. The documentary film *Muktir Katha,* made by Tareque and Catherine Masud (makers of *Muktir Gaan*), is based on the responses and narratives of people throughout Bangladesh to the screening of *Muktir Gaan*.

18. On returning to their house after the war, Sharmeen had commented 'How come nothing has happened to our house? I thought it would be totally in rubbles. It doesn't feel as if there has been a war' (interview given by Noorjahan Murshid, Sharmeen's mother, who became the Minister for Relief and Rehabilitation under Sheikh Mujib's government, Oxford, October 1998).

19. The map was removed in 1972, as it was felt that it would be difficult for young children to draw the map when drawing the flag. The current flag only retains the red sun against the green background.

20. Parallels to this argument may be found in June Nash's (1994) exploration of the problematic relationship of the map and the body, whereby she highlights the links between the gendered body and the national landscape in Ireland. However, Nash does not adequately explore the class of the gendered body.

21. I refer to the story of Binodini (1863–1941) (Chatterjee 1994: 151) so as to draw comparisons with the *birangonas* in proposing that in this case nationalist emancipation is necessarily a story of betrayal. Binodini was a celebrated actress on the Calcutta stage in the late nineteenth century who became the icon of modernist literati against the backdrop of the Bengal Renaissance. However, being recruited from among the city's prostitutes, in reality she was excluded from respectable social life by the stigma of 'immoral' living and was similarly subject to the contradictions of the new world of middle-class cultural production.

22. This has been a notable theme in plays commemorating Independence and Victory Day written for the state-run Bangladesh Television.

23. Parallels could be found in the act of *jwahar* as practised by Rajput women, who would seem to embrace 'honourable' death instead of 'defilement'. Butalia (1998: 161) also mentions that people talking about Partition violence found it more difficult to mention those who had escaped death than those who had died an 'honourable' death.

References

Agarwal, P. (1995), 'Surat, Savarkar and Draupadi: Legitimising Rape as a Political Weapon', in U. Butalia and T. Sarkar (eds), *Women and Right Wing Movements: Indian experiences*, London: Zed Books.

Anon (1972), New Initials, *Doinik Bangla*, 4 January 1972.

Ardener, S. and Holden, P. (1987), *Images of Women in Peace and War: Cross Cultural and Historical Perspectives*, London: Macmillan.

Bata Advertisement, *Doinik Purbodesh*, 26 March 1972.

Bhatia, N. (2002), 'Romantic Transgressions in the Colonial Zone: Reading Mircea Eliade's *Bengal Nights* and Maitreyi Devi's *It Does Not Die*' in N. Puwar and P. Raghuram (eds), *South Asian Women in the Diaspora*, Oxford: Berg.

Blunt, A. and Rose, G. (eds), (1994), *Writing Women and Space: Colonial and Postcolonial Geographies*, New York, London: The Guildford Press.

Brownmiller, S. (1975), *Against Our Will: Men Women and Rape*, London: Secker & Warburg.

Butalia, U. (1998), *The Other Side of Silence: Voices from the Partition of India*, New Delhi: Viking Penguin, India.

Butler, J. (1990), *Gender Trouble*, New York, London: Routledge.

Chakravarty, D. (1995), 'Remembered Villages: Representations of Hindu-Bengali Memories in the Aftermath of the Partition', *South Asia*, Vol. XVIII, Special issue: 109–29.

Chatterjee, P. (1994), *Nation and its Fragments: Colonial and Postcolonial Histories*, Delhi: Oxford University Press.

Cooke, M. (1996), *Women and the War Story*, Berkeley, CA and Los Angeles: University of California Press Limited.

Cooke M. and Rustomji-Kerns (eds) (1994), *Blood into Ink: South Asian and Middle Eastern Women on War*, Boulder, CO: Westview Press.

Daniel, E. V. (1997), 'Suffering Nation and Alienation', in V. Das, A. Kleinman and M. Lock (eds), *Social Suffering*, London, Berkeley, CA: University of California Press.

Das, V. (1995), *Critical Events: An Anthropological Perspective on Contemporary India*, Delhi: Oxford University Press.

Gupta, C. (1991), 'Politics of Gender: Women in Nazi Germany', *Economic and Political Weekly* XXVI (17): 40–8.

Jasimuddin (1972), *Dogdhogram* ('Burnt Village'), in *Bhoyaboho shei Dingulite* ('Those Terrifying Days'), Dhaka: Naoroj Kitabistan.

Jones, L. (1987), 'Greenham Common', in S. Ardener and P. Holden (eds), *Images of Women in Peace and War: Cross Cultural and Historical Perspectives*, London: Macmillan.

Kandiyoti, D. (ed.) (1991), *Women, Islam and the State*, Basingstoke: Macmillan.

Kaviraj, S. (1994), 'Abstract Affectations: Making of a Language of Patriotism in Modern Bengali', *Commonwealth History Seminar, Oxford* (unpublished paper).

Keno go ma tor dhulai ashon, keno go ma tor molin boshon? ('Why mother is your place in the dust, why mother is your appearance soiled?') Genocide Special Issue, *Banglar Bani*, December 1972.

McClintock, A. (1995), *Imperial Leather: Race, Gender and Sexuality in the Colonial Conquest*, London: Routledge.

Masud, T. and Masud, C. (1995), *Muktir Gaan* (Songs of Freedom). Audiovision.

Masud, T. and Masud, C. (1999), *Muktir Katha* (Words of Freedom). Audiovision.

Menon, R. and Bhasin, K. (1998), *Borders and Boundaries: Women in India's Partition*, New Delhi: Kali for Women.

Monk, J. and Norwood, V. (eds) (1987), *The Desert is No Lady: Southwestern Landscapes in Women's Writing and Art*, New Haven, CT: Yale University Press.

Nandy, A. (1983), *The Intimate Enemy: Loss and Recovery of Self under Colonialism*, Delhi: Oxford University Press.

Nash, J. (1994), 'Remapping the Body/Land: New Cartographies of Identity, Gender and Landscape in Ireland', in A. Blunt and G. Rose (eds), *Writing Women and Space: Colonial and Postcolonial Geographies*, New York, London: The Guildford Press.

Nordstorm, C. and Robben, A. C. G. (ed.), (1995), *Fieldwork under Fire: Studies of Survival and Violence*, Berkeley, CA: California University Press.

Ortner, S. B. and Whitehead, H. (1981), *Sexual Meanings*, Cambridge: Cambridge University Press.

Parker, A., Russo, M., Sommer, D. and Yaeger, P. (ed.) (1992), *Nationalism and Sexualities,* London, New York: Routledge

Pasha, A. (1976) [1973] *Rifle, Roti, Aurat (Rifles, Bread and Women)*, translated by Kabir Chowdhury, June 1976, Dhaka: Bangla Academy.

Rose, G. (1993), *Feminism and Geography: The Limits of Geographical Knowledge*, London: Polity Press.

Sinha, M. (1995), *Colonial Masculinity: The 'Manly Englishman' and the 'Effeminate Bengali' in the Late Nineteenth Century*, Manchester, New York : Manchester University Press.

Tagore, R. (1905), '*Amar Sonar Bangla, ami tomai bhalobashi'*. ('O my golden Bengal, How I do love you'), in *Swarabitan* 46.

Werbner, P. (1999), 'Political Motherhood and Feminisation of Citizenship: Women's Activisms and Transformation of Public Sphere', in N. Yuval-Davis and P. Werbner (eds), *Women, Citizenship and Difference*, London: Zed Books.

Whitehead, J. (1995), 'Modernising the Motherhood Archetype: Public Health Models and the Child Marriage Restraint Act of 1929' in *Contributions to Indian Sociology* (n. s.) 29 (1 & 2), New Delhi: Sage Publications.

Winkler, C. (1991), 'Rape as Social Murder', *Anthropology Today*, 7 (3) (June): 12–14.

Yuval-Davis, N. (1997), *Gender and Nation*, London: Sage Publications.

Yuval-Davis, N. and F. Y. Anthias, (eds) (1989), *Woman–Nation–State*, London: Macmillan.

—— and Werbner, P. (eds) (1999), *Women, Citizenship and Difference*, London: Zed Books.

Part III
Engagements

–10–

A Kiss Is Just A Kiss. . . Or Is It? South Asian Lesbian and Bisexual Women and the Construction of Space
Rani Kawale

Introduction

The relationship between identity and space has taken on interdisciplinary prominence during the last two decades (Carter, Donald and Squires 1995). A number of writers have explored issues surrounding race and space (Sibley 1998), gender and space (McDowell and Sharp 1999) and class and space (Bourdieu 1984). The urban sociologist Manuel Castells (1983) has considered the interaction between sexual identities and space. His work, however, focused on gay men rather than lesbians, as he believed that women (including lesbians) were less in need of territory to express their identity than men (including gay men), as women favoured friendships, relationships and social networks.

Much of the literature on sexuality and space research since Castells' research suggests that urban space offers numerous opportunities and possibilities for dissident sexualities to flourish. For example, a number of researchers have explored the ways in which gay and lesbian people have transformed residential spaces in America. Exemplary in this field have been Lauria and Knopp's investigation of gay men's gentrificaton of New Orleans (1985) and Adler and Brennar's (1992) and Rothenburg's (1995) analysis of lesbian neighbourhoods. With the lack of easily identifiable residential areas associated with dissident sexualities in Britain, much of the work here has concentrated on public places. For example, Hindle (1994), Mort (1996) and Binnie (1995) explore consumption in commercial places and social scenes in cities including Manchester and London; but, like Castells, they concentrate on the experiences of gay men. In Britain social geographers such as Gill Valentine (1993a and 1995a) have however, challenged Castells' findings and substantially developed the field of enquiry in relation to lesbians.

Engagements

It is now firmly established that everyday spaces, such as homes, workplaces, social spaces, service and commercial environments and public open spaces, are all predominantly sexualized on a 'heterosexualized' basis, owing to the heterosexual relations that occur across them (Valentine 1993b). As a result lesbians and gay men have reconstituted a variety of separate spaces in order to avoid having constantly to 'pass' as heterosexual or being subjected to homophobia. Although both lesbians and gay men have constantly to negotiate and manage multiple sexual identities in relation to space, the power of patriarchy means that lesbians and gay men experience space differently (Valentine 1993a, 1993b). Green (1997), for example, highlights the ways in which physical space was utilized as a gendered political space by lesbian feminists in London during the late 1980s. Despite this increasing sensitivity to gender issues, the literature on sexuality and space rarely (if ever) mentions 'race' or ethnicity. Silently, whiteness pervades the character of debates on sexuality and space.

Various anthologies on Black and Asian women, such as *Talking Black: Lesbians of African and Asian Descent Speak Out* (Mason-John 1995), *A Lotus of Another Colour: An Unfolding of the South Asian Gay and Lesbian Experience* (Ratti 1993) and *Plural Desires: Writing Bisexual Women's Realities* (Bisexual Anthology Collective 1995), do exist, but research in this area remains scarce. *Khush: A SHAKTI Report* (Khan 1991) based on SHAKTI, a social and support group for South Asian lesbian, gay men and bisexuals, was funded by Camden Council in London, and is one of the few pieces of research documenting the lives of British South Asian lesbians, gay men and bisexuals. While both sexuality (Brah 1996; Mercer 1994) and space (Puwar 2000; Goldberg 1997; Sibley 1998) have been individually discussed as racialized concepts, the ways in which space, sexuality, gender and race interact together have been underexplored. This chapter attempts to address this gap by considering South Asian women's experiences of public places in London for lesbians, gay men and bisexual women as racialized spaces. It will highlight the whiteness of these spaces and examine how South Asian lesbian and bisexual women are positioned within these spaces. Secondly it will document the importance of alternative spaces that have been brought into existence.

To gather material for this research I spent several weeks formally approaching a number of social and support groups for women that were listed in the lesbian and gay press, including *The Pink Paper*, *Diva* lesbian lifestyle magazine, *Gay Times* and the gay section of *Time Out* magazine. During an initial conversation with the group facilitator(s) I explained that the research would investigate how women experienced lesbian spaces. I also disclosed my sexuality to them before gaining permission to join the meetings and social events as a participant observer. The facilitator(s) of each group advised their members of my presence as a researcher and I also reminded each woman whom I spoke to of my research interests. I also interviewed twenty women between 1999 and 2000, of whom eleven identified with the term 'white' and nine with the term 'South Asian' (this included women who also identified as either Indian, Pakistani or Bangladeshi). When I asked South Asian women how they experienced lesbian spaces, race and difference figured in many of their accounts; and it is these narratives that I draw on specifically in this chapter. While the dialogue generated with these nine women feeds into the issues explored in this chapter, it does not seek to be the mouthpiece of this small group of women or in fact of all South Asian lesbian and bisexual women in Britain in general.

Whiteness of Lesbian, Gay and Bisexual Spaces

The majority of public places in London are constructed as 'white', and this contributes to maintaining its claim to 'naturalness' (Julien and Mercer 1988). As Heidi Mirza (1997) explains, whiteness is a 'powerful place that makes invisible, or re-appropriates things, people and places it does not want to see or hear, and then through misnaming, renaming or not naming at all, invents the truth – what we are told is "normal", neutral, universal, simply becomes the way it is' (1997: 3). This applies to public places for lesbians, gay men and bisexuals too. A group or commercial venue does not need to specify that 'white' people are welcome: this is assumed, because the term 'lesbian' is racialized and usually refers to 'white' lesbians (Creet 1995). Hence lesbian and bisexual women's places that are not overtly racially assigned tend to have little room for 'black' women to be 'black' in them (Hayfield 1995a).[1] White lesbians, gay men and bisexuals are also racialized, but this is exnominated (Williams 1997). The white women I interviewed can ignore their 'whiteness', and hence experience the London lesbian, gay and bisexual 'scene' very differently from the ways that South Asian women experience it. If space is created for 'South Asian' lesbian and bisexual women, this is however usually specified and marked out as such.

During the initial stages of the research I counted a maximum of four black women at any one time in the social and support groups and commercial venues that did not specify the ethnicity or 'race' of the women most welcome. The South Asian women I spoke to also observed the whiteness of the lesbian, gay and bisexual scene in London, noting the lack of non-white women:

> '. . . it's not really common like you walk into a club and you'll see an Asian person there. Especially like at G.A.Y. I went in there and *everyone* was white, just *everybody* was just white, it was just amazing . . .' (Mumtaz).

> 'Due South is a very particular kind of vibe there in terms of, y'know, the lesbians that go there. They don't get many Asian women there, um, a few more black women, but its mainly white' (Bharti).

The whiteness of the spaces, in terms of the numerical presence of South Asian women, can be further accentuated by a 'look' that implies they are out of place:

> 'I actually find the Vespa Lounge intimidating only because its very, very white . . . its intimidating when you walk in and everybody turns to look at you because you're Asian' (Rekha).

Being constantly subjected to 'the Empire of the gaze' (Westwood 1995) by white people, regardless of sexuality, South Asians are already situated by British imperialism as racialized outsiders, as postcolonial subjects, as an inferiorized 'other'. They are both 'invisible' and 'visible'. When white people do see South Asian women, it is usually through limited and reified lenses. Frantz Fanon has stated '(n)ot only must the black man be black; he must be black in relation to the white man' (1986: 110). Lesbian and bisexual women are not immune from instigating this 'look'. There is a tendency to see Asian women as 'passive', 'dependent', 'quiet', 'sensitive' and 'gentle' (Brah 1996). The South Asian women I spoke to felt very visible owing to their brown skin if nothing else, and believed that when they were seen by white people through imperialist eyes they were expected to integrate and abandon or erase their 'Asian-ness' (Khan 1991).

The Struggle For and Against Authenticity

The ways in which white female bodies are perceived as the somatic authentic lesbian norm is illustrated by the processes whereby South Asian women are likely to be seen as (1) heterosexual or bisexual, rather than lesbian, (2) 'inferior' and/or (3) exoticized 'sex objects'. White women in lesbian spaces are more likely to be considered as lesbians than are South Asian women. For example Sujata, one of my interviewees, intended to celebrate a birthday with a group of South Asian lesbian and bisexual women friends at G.A.Y. at the London Astoria, but at the entrance the white (male) bouncer queried their sexuality. He asked them whether they were aware it was a gay night, which other gay venues in London they visited regularly and whether they were indeed lesbians. Sujata interpreted this and other similar experiences with white women as a racism driven by the assumption that 'South Asian women can't be lesbians', especially if they have long hair:

> ... white women ... don't believe that I'm a lesbian because they identify 'lesbian' as being white ... especially if they've got long hair they don't believe they can be lesbian ... or they assume that I'm bisexual because I've got long hair' (Sujata).

Both Valentine (1995a) and Green (1997) have discussed attempts made by lesbians to minimize differences in favour of a shared community, one of which was to share dress codes. While South Asian lesbians may be able to 'dyke spot' white lesbians by these codes they seem less likely to be 'spotted' themselves because the codes tend to ignore or reify ethnic or racial differences. For example Amina described herself as dressing 'like a dyke' when she first began visiting public places for lesbians, gay men and bisexuals. She would wear a tight top, big trousers and big boots and no make-up, just like the majority of the clientele at the particular lesbian bar she visited. She had long hair and this, coupled with her brown skin colour, meant her dyke image was however doubted by the white lesbian bouncer at the bar. Amina spent some time convincing the bouncer of her sexuality so that she could enter the bar, whereas her girlfriend with similar clothing but with short hair and fair-coloured skin had already been allowed entry without any question. I will return to appearance and attire later in the chapter.

White women often stereotype South Asian women according to stereotypical notions of traditional Asian family life, and therefore regard them as being unable to construct lesbian or bisexual identities or lifestyles in the same ways as white lesbians. For example the comments made by white lesbians to Sujata included 'How on earth did you come out to your parents? It must've been so difficult to be growing up in such a strict family' and 'Won't your parents try and marry you?' Pathologized images of South Asian women living in the strict confines of 'traditional' Asian families, circumscribed by the mores of arranged (read forced) marriages do not (Parmar 1982) unfortunately take flight in these seemingly radical circles.

Stuart Hall (1989) explains that racism not only positions blacks as inferior but also as something desired. Fanon (1986) considered the white adoration of the Negro in this specific way to be as 'sick' as whites hating the Negro. Being seen as sex objects and 'exotic' is a subtle form of racism that can make black people feel unwelcome in lesbian, gay and bisexual places (Hayfield 1995b):

'. . . I went to this Waltzing With Hilda and I was doing ballroom dancing and they said "You dance so beautifully, you're so exotic" . . . "You must've done Indian dance, haven't you?" And I'd think "No, I've never done Indian dance, I've grown up exactly the same as you and yet here you are telling me that I dance in a really exotic way" ' (Sujata).

It is clear then that South Asian women are more likely to be seen as heterosexual or bisexual rather than lesbian. However, when they are seen as lesbian this is in very specific ways, usually as inferior and/or as exoticized sex objects, who have the spirit, the rhythm and the long 'traditions' of the Indian subcontinent somehow *a priori* instilled into the pores of their very being.

Constituting South Asian Lesbian, Gay and Bisexual Space

The creation of lesbian, gay and bisexual spaces that are also South Asian is an example of what Hall (1989) would describe as moving from being objects in the margin to subjects in the centre and defining space from the position of the subject rather than the object. Organizing around the term 'South Asian' is similar to political movements organizing around the term 'Black'. The latter term is used to refer to common experiences of racism and marginalization in Britain by groups and communities with different histories, traditions and ethnic identities, to resist being placed on the margins of a white society. In recent years areas in and around the city of London have been the site of space being constituted as both South Asian and lesbian and gay. Arts events in 2000 such as *Sweet Like Burfi* and films like *Chutney Popcorn*, shown at the National Film Theatre as part of the Lesbian and Gay Film festival, were attended by numerous South Asian men and women. In 2001 at the London Lesbian and Gay Pride annual festival a group of South Asian women marched together in *salwaar kameez* and saris. They danced to the beat provided by two South Asian drummers, and occasionally chanted lines from Hindi love songs. These are examples of recent momentary but high-profile South Asian lesbian, gay and bisexual spaces and events. More long-term and low-profile spaces have existed in London for many years.

During the 1980s and early 1990s, a social and support group based in north London offered support to South Asian lesbians, gay men and bisexuals to help them with self-acceptance (Khan 1991). With a name associated with 'creative energy' leading to spiritual liberation in the Hindu religion, the group SHAKTI was a self-funded project, and money was raised from a night club with the same name. After a number of years this set-up was replaced by various organizations and sexual health projects aimed at South Asian gay and bisexual men, such as the Naz project currently based in West London. Some years passed before a social and support group for lesbian and bisexual women was set up with funding by the Naz Project and facilitated by one of their employees, Bharti, within their offices. After a rocky first attempt at running the group for women of South Asian and Middle Eastern descent, the second more successful attempt began in early 1999. Bharti was joined by her friend Sharada to facilitate the group called 'Kiss', and their efforts to run monthly meetings met with great success. Both Bharti and Sharada felt this was largely due to the location of the new venue. Rather than being held in what looked like an old school building in an area of west London that already lacked lesbian and gay venues, it was important that the group met somewhere on the commercial scene in London, but where South Asian and Middle Eastern women in particular would feel comfortable. The Glass Bar in Euston was thought to be the best choice, and not just because it was owned and managed by an out black lesbian. As Sharada explained:

'. . . we have our meetings upstairs normally and, um, its quite a friendly place to walk into because . . . it feels quite cosy, it feels like you're in someone's living-room. So even though as you walk in you're gonna then get all these women looking at you, it doesn't feel too intimidating . . . the venue is crucial I would say . . . Bharti said "I think its really important we access the scene and I think it's really important that we are visible on the scene" and I agree with her . . . the Glass Bar [is] . . . central, it's centrally located and in theory it suits a lot of people in terms of its location because we get such large numbers of women coming . . . we're still sticking with the Glass Bar because of that principle of being visible on the scene, that we are in the *Pink Paper*, that we are in *Time Out*, that we are in *Diva* as a group that exists, so actually yeah, venue and location are really important to us' (Sharada).

Geographically, the Glass Bar is on the margins of the 'London lesbian and gay scene'. Although in central London, it is not in Soho, the site of white lesbian and gay venues, thus paralleling the marginal position of South Asian women on the London lesbian, gay and bisexual scene. However, during Kiss meetings South Asian women are not marginally placed. At such times they occupy the entire top floor, and often out-number white women at the Glass Bar. The music remains on the ground floor, but is switched off on the top floor to create a somewhat formal space for Kiss group discussions. The members form a circle facing inwards and claim all seating space on the top floor. White women have to remain downstairs and are only allowed upstairs to use the bathroom, which is on the top floor. They are clearly visible to the Kiss group as they approach and leave the bathroom, so that it is white women who feel out of place, rather than vice versa. What a rare occasion!

Kiss has over 100 members. Most were born and/or raised in Britain and speak fluent English; some have been or are married and some have children. The age range of members is broad, but the majority who attend the meetings are aged between 20 and 30 years. It has members with different ethnic, religious and linguistic identities and is officially operated under the terms 'South Asian' and 'Middle Eastern', although few women who identify as Middle Eastern have attended meetings on a regular basis.[2] The sexual orientations of its members are broad too, although the group has shied away from identifying as 'queer'. It has opted for 'lesbian, bisexual women or women questioning their sexuality' and more recently this has included 'women who sleep with women'.[3] Each meeting is usually attended by between 15 and 35 women. Those who attend regu-larly do not necessarily attend to 'come out', to come to terms with their sexuality or as a short-term strategy to make friends. For many members, it is an ongoing activity. Some are in long-term relationships and live with their partners, and many have been out to their parents, friends and colleagues for some time and already have a network of white lesbian, gay and/or bisexual friends.

One of the Kiss members is a DJ at Club Kali, a fortnightly club held at the Dome that is described on its flyers as 'an authentic mixing and blending of South Asian spices where bhangra meets house and Hindi meets soul, swing and Arabic flavours'. The club welcomes a mixed-sex crowd described, again on the flyers, as 'attitude-free connoisseurs'. Kiss members can pay a reduced entry fee at Kali, and the club is advertised in the gay press. Like the Glass Bar, the Dome is located on the margins of the London lesbian and gay scene – in Tufnell Park, north London. Several Kiss members expressed surprise when they first visited Kiss or

Kali at the opportunities available for South Asian lesbian and bisexual women in London:

> '[Kiss] created a space for people to come together based on their kind of racial origin and their sexuality and loads of women always say "God, I didn't know there were so many Asian dykes on the scene, I've never seen them on the scene like this"' (Bharti).

> '. . . the girl who came to the group [Kiss] for the first time was saying "I can't believe I'm surrounded by Asian women, can't believe I'm surrounded by Asian gay people, long hair". She was just really over enthusiastic and that's how I felt when I first went to Club Kali. What I instantly felt when I walked in was "Oh my God this is like being at home", which is the most wonderful [feeling] walking into a club and I thought "it's a *club* full of Asian people and they're all gay or bisexual or some sort of', y'know, change from the norm"' (Najma).

Few Kiss members visit the Glass Bar or the Dome outside of Kiss or Kali, when they are predominantly white places. For many of the South Asian women who spoke to me, participating at Kiss and Kali is a spatial expression of their sexuality that is virtually impossible elsewhere. At Kiss, members may eat South Asian food, including samosa and pakora with chilli sauce, and some prefer to consume soft drinks or tea rather than alcohol. Similarly at Kali, South Asian men and women can enjoy each other's company free of sexual tension. Some dress in drag in saris and *kameez*. Same-sex couples are clearly visible, and a mixture of music is played with South Asian influences. Kali also has an overhead screen that projects scenes from Bollywood films. Visual images and music from Hindi films that were popular during the 1970s all stir up childhood and familial memories.

At both Kiss and Kali, language makes an important contribution to the racialization of space. Nirmal Puwar (2001) has discussed the centrality of language, including tones, syntax and grammar, to the occupation of elite white spaces. She refers to both Frantz Fanon's and Pierre Bourdieu's discussions of the symbolic power of language, and explains that language is racialized as well as classed. She argues that '(p)leasant-speaking hybrid post-colonial bodies who, as mentioned by Fanon, speak like a book are much more suited to white spaces. They are after all the acceptable and respectable faces of black bodies' (2001: 667). Kiss meetings are conducted in English, largely because this is the only common language among all the members; but members occasionally slip into other languages including Hindi, Urdu and Punjabi. For example, songs and discussions of Bollywood films are not always translated into English. Puwar (2001) explains that speaking 'legitimate' English in a profession like the civil service is a way of erasing ethnic differences (between employees). Kiss and Kali are spaces of escape from the erasures and pressures of other public spaces in Britain, and there is no particular need for 'legitimate' English to be spoken, because difference is accepted. Kiss does not create a 'formal' space, as in Puwar's discussion; but whether and how one speaks the 'native language' does say something about one's place within a space. The spoken English at Kiss is often broken or with a 'South Asian' accent – whether naturally or in fun. Some words, concepts and meanings do not directly translate from South Asian languages into English either, and so some women use different languages to express themselves. This particular 'illegitimate' form of English in a white space for lesbians and bisexual women would place South Asian women on the margins; but at Kiss, it contributes to the construction of the space as South Asian and locates the members centrally within that space. For the South Asian women in this study, being able to communicate in different languages is an important part of being oneself and not policing oneself, of being able to include family influences and not having to erase them:

> 'I can talk to other Asian people, I can talk in my own language [Punjabi], y'know, its my mother tongue, I can use it. OK, not everyone speaks it but you always find someone there [Kali] that will speak your language and it's just a nice feeling . . .' (Surinder).

It may be argued that South Asian cultures have been diluted at Kiss and Kali and that 'South Asian' space glosses over differences among South Asians, that it ignores differences between Indians, Pakistanis and Bangladeshis and between Hindus, Muslims and Sikhs, as well as other South Asian identities and religions. However, as is shown by Avtar Brah (1996), South Asian women of different (religious) groups have often joined together to challenge racism. Kiss members have also joined together as a group to challenge racial prejudice in the construction of space on the London lesbian, gay and bisexual scene. This has been encouraged and maintained through presentations given at Kiss by representatives of various organizations such as the Newham Asian Women's Project. Information about South Asian and Black events taking place around the country is also regularly circulated during the meetings. The skills directory in the monthly Kiss mail-out enables members to draw on each other's skills for advice and information regarding sexual health, housing, legal rights and reporting homophobic crime. Members can also exchange skills in computing, DIY, therapy, cooking, etc. All of these have contributed to the bonding of the group, despite different identities. So although the women at Kiss differ, there is much that brings them together. These include similar experiences of living in Britain as South Asian, not being heterosexual, feeling excluded in white spaces and experiencing racism and sexism and homophobia or biphobia. They are often confused together by white people as being ethnically the same, and so internal differences are rarely recognized or understood. Similarities in their experience of being non-white and of then being cast as one homogeneous black group has drawn the women at Kiss together spatially. They also want to assert their subjectivity in order (1) to exercise an 'oppositional gaze' (hooks 1992) and (2) to be safe in their visibility. Both Kiss and Kali are spaces where they can exert control over seeing and being seen. While they have in some senses a respite away from racism, the enjoyment apparent in these alternative spaces makes it clear that at the same time their activities are not solely defined in reaction to racism.

Seeing and Being Seen

Seeing other South Asian lesbian and bisexual women and gay men was important for all the South Asian women I talked to, and socializing at Kiss and/or Kali occurred on a regular basis. Many of the white women whom I interviewed suggested a preference for women-only venues to avoid feeling intimidated by men. However, the South Asian women rarely spoke of feeling intimidated by gay men in South Asian venues as against being in venues dominated by white, gay men. They often felt positive about socializing with South Asian gay men. Amina referred to them as 'our boys', indicating the connection she felt with them due to a shared ethnic and religious background. Najma explained this further by interpreting venues such as Kali, with a mixture of men and women, as providing an extended family atmosphere:

'. . . the fact that it's gay and Asian, feel like these are all, kind of, like part of my family and that when I see older people I kind of think 'aunties and uncles', and when I see younger people I kind of think 'brothers and sisters'. I feel . . . I feel affectionate toward people there, which is odd because I may not even know them, but I feel this warmth . . . Um, and it's very, it's a very homey feeling. I always seem to feel like I'm at a wedding (small laugh). I'm at an Asian wedding or I'm at an Asian do, something that I've grown up with but it's the kind of people I wanna be with, so I always get that really nice sensation when I go to Club Kali' (Najma).

Blackman and Perry (1990) acknowledge that attire is important and that some women use dress as a part of their lesbian identity to provide a 'visible connection with their lesbian subcultures' (1990: 67). They offer a very short discussion of how ethnicity figures in lesbian styles of dressing, arguing that some of this 'is a priority to assert their racial and cultural identities in response to invisibility and exclusion' (1990: 73). They also acknowledge that these may be mixed with Western clothing to show identification with British and lesbian subculture without having to deny any one of these. As Amina explained, clothing was one way to manage her multiple identities of being South Asian, British and a lesbian.

'. . . at the beginning, I was still, I looked very much like a stereotypical straight woman and I left home only about 8 months before so I was going through that freedom of knowing that I could wear anything I want and my mum and dad couldn't say anything. So I did wear lots of quite short skirts, but skirts above the knee and I kind of wore, um, those tiny tops and bangles and stuff. And my hair was a lot longer and I still wore quite a lot of make up. Being an Asian woman I did wear quite a lot of make up back then and then after I met [my girlfriend] I kinda went to the opposite extreme and ended up looking really dykey (pause). Dykey with long hair though . . . I thought "I've got to look like a dyke" so for about a year I kinda didn't wear skirts, didn't wear much make up, my hair was still long but I wore kind of like stuff what dykes wear basically. Y'know like dyke clothing, and then . . . I just felt like I'd lost my identity because obviously the way you express yourself is in some ways through your clothes . . . and I said to [my girlfriend] "I just don't feel comfortable dressed like this" and she said "Well, why do you?" and I go "Well, other dykes do" and she said "Yeah, but you're you and you're an individual, you should dress the way you wanna dress" . . . I don't think as Asian or black women our *sexuality* is the be all or end all for what we are, so I don't think we dress a certain, um, I don't think we look a certain way just to fit into what we're supposed to look like as "lesbian"' (Amina).

Najma emphasized the importance of seeing South Asians at both predominantly non-white *and* white venues, and explained that the cultural symbols that she can see on other South Asians, including men, are important to her:

'Most clubs that, y'know, whether they're gay or whether they're straight, they're clubs and they have a club wear. Now with gay clubs you do have this element of where (pause), y'know, girls who feel kind of whatever, this butch/femme thing, people can dress a bit more blokey-casual but, y'know, but then there's the usual club wear, y'know, tight tops and tight trousers and whatever. Yet here [Kali] you *really* can wear anything . . . for example this guy [wears] very traditional, very kind of elaborate gear and you can do that there . . . And it's nice because being Asian you associate elaborate dress with Asian weddings, straight do's, places where you're unaccepted, where no matter how much you're dancing and joking and laughing with everyone you don't really feel yourself. And to be able to wear those clothes and show them off in a gay space is like saying "Yeah, this is *my* wedding, this is *my* do", y'know, and that's what it's about . . .' (Najma).

There is no recognizable form of dress for South Asian lesbian and bisexual women, as indicated by Blackman and Perry (1990). Items such as sari or *salwaar kameez*, jewellery such as earrings and necklaces with symbols of religion or country of 'origin', and having long straight hair may be worn in ways to exert some control over visibility in different spaces. Some enjoyed wearing them to increase their visibility and affirm their South Asianness at Kiss and Kali, but were unlikely to wear them to 'white' venues, where they dressed in more 'appropriate' Western clothing. Spaces provided by Kiss and Kali are very much part of exerting control over being seen, and enjoying it, through dress, style, language, music, clothes and a positive assertion of non-normative sexualities and ethnicities.

As a way of coping with racial prejudice in white society hooks (1992) discusses the observation of white people from a black position. By contesting or confronting the white women's gaze, an 'oppositional' gaze can lead to different interpretations and understandings of what it means to be 'black'. The oppositional gaze of the South Asian women I interviewed was developed to the extent that they were not constrained to seeing themselves or each other as heterosexual, inferior or as sex objects but as South Asian and lesbian and bisexual women in their own right.

(Re)appropriating Ethnicity Using Space

Recent writings on diaspora (Hall 1992; Gilroy 1997; Dwyer 2000; Huang *et al.* 2000) challenge essentialist thinking of ethnicity by considering the construction of 'hybrid' identities (Bhabha 1990; Gilroy 1997) or new ethnicities in new contexts and local conditions (Hall 1989). A term such as 'Hindu', for instance, may have identities and meanings associated with it in Britain that are different to those in Trinidad (Vertovec 1995) and those in India. Flexible identity, fragmentation and cultural hybridity are very much part of the black diasporic experience (Rassool 1997), with different parts of identity overlapping and intersecting (Hall 1989). Being under considerable surveillance from South Asian communities, the managing of multiple identities such as ethnicity *and* sexuality is an essential part of South Asian women's subjectivity, whether they are heterosexual, lesbian or bisexual. This conceptualization of identity helps us to appreciate that some of the women I interviewed initially felt unable to combine their ethnic identity with their sexuality, and felt 'less' South Asian as they began to explore their sexuality. The construction of South Asian lesbian, gay and bisexual spaces enabled them to realize their ethnicity performatively and their sexuality together, through redefinitions rather than forgoing one for the sake of the other. Kiss and Kali are spaces where difference and sexuality have a fruitful and rich relationship. For some, they even offered the possibilities of a sort of 're-homing':

'. . . having ran away from home, there's a large part of me that misses socializing with other Asian people and I miss the culture and the music so much that I go there (Kali) because it gives me all that' (Surinder).

Rekha was raised with her two younger sisters by their South Indian parents in a predominantly 'white' part of South London; she attended a predominantly 'white' school, left home in her early twenties and moved into her own flat in another predominantly 'white' part of South London and was employed in a predominantly 'white' middle-class organization. She found that Kiss and Kali provided space to find a community which she at last felt 'at home' in:

'It [Kiss] is a support group technically for lesbian/bisexual women . . . I actually have found it tremendously useful to share in the Asian perspective . . . it's been fantastic meeting women, reinforcing the identity, that you're not the only one. You're not the only one who doesn't speak an Asian language, doesn't do this, you know, the only one when she was younger was not allowed out . . . [it's] also important in recognizing that (pause) there are lots of women out there who want and demand the support of lots of Asians and feel culturally that they need that . . . and if you think about the struggles most people have gone through to get to Kali to combat their own fears, their own sexual identity, probably hiding from family, hiding from friends . . . it just means there's a load of people who have suddenly released and this release brings this gorgeous atmosphere there (pause), amazing place . . . I feel completely free . . . [at] Kiss, well, I feel completely free in a different respect . . . it depends on who I'm with, so I would go there for security and privacy to talk to my friends openly about things . . .' (Rekha).

When she was a baby Sujata was adopted by a white English couple and she had minimal access to South Asian communities and cultures while growing up in north London. She had been more aware of her sexuality than her ethnicity until she began to visit public places for lesbians and bisexual women:

'. . . I grew up thinking I was white but . . . I identified as black when I came out . . . People often pointed out that I was Asian more in gay pubs than they did outside gay pubs . . . the reason why I went to the Kiss group was because um (pause) I wanted to be around more Asian women . . . I'd been to quite a few women's groups but then there was always the issue of my sexuality and not being out to people . . . so I thought I'd go to the Kiss group and, you know, I can just be myself. It's quite a diverse group anyway, and so I feel, you know, even though I haven't been brought up with Asian parents, I still feel quite comfortable there' (Sujata).

Hennink, Diamond and Cooper's investigation into the sexuality of young Asian women living away from their parents' home in Britain (Hennink *et al.* 1999) uses a fixed binary model. They rely on the identity of the women in the study as being either South Asian *or* British and either traditional *or* modern. Studies such as this tend to support the theory that 'modern' British South Asian women are more independent, while 'traditional' South Asian women are more dependent and passive. This binary was not identified among the Kiss members and women Kali clubbers whom I interviewed. They embraced their South Asianness, but at the same time were far from dependent or passive. They took control of their lives and their sexuality and made decisions to support this such as leaving the parental home without being married; working for organizations that operate in the interest of minority groups, such as Stonewall Housing and the Albert Kennedy Trust, the Naz Project, Galup and the Newham Asian Women's Project; choosing to live with friends rather than relatives; and constructing 'safe' spaces for South Asian lesbians, gay men and bisexuals, such as SHAKTI, Kiss and Kali. While pursuing their independence, none of the South Asian women I interviewed wanted to ignore or abandon their ethnicity, but instead they participated in constructing lesbian and bisexual women's spaces as South Asian.

Conclusion

Space and place are crucial to a sense of identity, because, as Taylor (1997) suggests, identity is not just about *who* you are but *where* you are. Most public spaces in London for lesbians, gay men and bisexuals are constructed as white spaces. Non-whites such as South Asians are marginal consumers of such spaces, and are rarely in a position to reconstruct them as anything other than 'honorary whites' (Fanon 1986). However, this does not mean that they entirely lack power to construct space as South Asian. There is no single way to be South Asian and no single sexuality. Visiting places like Kali and Kiss allows this diversity to flourish, without policing, surveillance and erasure. It provides the opportunity to generate new ways of doing gender and ethnicity with sexuality; another version of 'new ethnicities' (Hall 1989), one that is little recognized in the academic literature in this area. The women have the capacity and energy to construct alternative South Asian spaces, where the joys and pleasures of the familial are re-constituted, outside the 'heterosexual matrix' (Butler 1997) and the in/visibility games of racialized spaces. Here we have experimental styling of an altogether different kind; the fruition of urban dissenting sexualities that are a far cry from those identified by Castells (1983) or Valentine (1993a, 1993b, 1995a, 1995b).

Notes

1. The definition of the term 'Black' used here by Hayfield (1995a) is the broad political term that includes descendants of inhabitants from Asia, Africa, Australasia and the Americas. The women who participated in this research are descendants of those who migrated from South Asia.
2. This may be due to the existence of other groups in London that offer support to lesbian and bisexual women of Middle Eastern origin, such as the Greek and Turkish Cypriot mixed group and Al-Fatiha. It may also be because the space was created and cast primarily as (British) South Asian.
3. It has been argued that as the terms 'lesbian' and 'bisexual' are socially constructed and are not fixed in their meaning. The terms change over time (Hemmings 1993) and across space, although this brings with it problems in constructing 'lesbian' spaces (Taylor 1998).

References

Adler, S. and Brenner, J. (1992) 'Gender and Space: Lesbian and Gay Men in the City' *International Journal of Urban and Regional Research*, 16 (1): 24–34.

Bhabha, H. (1990), *Nation and Narration,* London: Routledge.

Binnie, J. (1995), 'Trading Places: Consumption, Sexuality and the Production of Queer Space', in D. Bell and G. Valentine (eds), *Mapping Desire: Geographies of Sexualities,* pp. 182–99. London: Routledge.

Bisexual Anthology Collective (eds) (1995), *Plural Desires: Writing Bisexual Women's Realities,* Toronto: Sister Vision Black Women and Women of Colour Press.

Blackman, I. and Perry, K. (1990), 'Skirting the Issue: Lesbian Fashion for the 1990s', *Feminist Review,* 34: 67–78.

Bourdieu, P. (1984), *Distinction: A Social Critique of the Judgement of Taste,* London: Routledge & Kegan Paul.

Brah, A. (1996), *Cartographies of Diaspora: Contesting Identities,* London: Routledge.

Butler, J. (1997), 'Performative Acts and Gender Constitution: An Essay in Phenomenology and Feminist Theory', in K. Conboy, N. Medina and S. Stanbury (eds), *Writing on the Body: Female Embodiment and Feminist Theory,* New York: Columbia University Press.

Carter, E., Donald, J. and Squires, J. (eds), (1995), *Space and Place: Theories of Identity and Location,* London: Lawrence and Wishart.

Castells, M. (1983), *The City and the Grassroots,* London: Edward Arnold.

Creet, J. (1995) 'Anxieties of Identity: Coming Out and Coming Undone', in M. Dorenkamp and R. Henke (eds), *Negotiating Lesbian and Gay Subjects.* London: Routledge.

Dwyer, C. (2000), 'Negotiating Diasporic Identities: Young British South Asian Muslim Women', *Women's Studies International Forum,* 23 (4): 475–86.

Fanon, F. (1986), *Black Skin, White Mask,* London: Pluto Press.

Gilroy, P. (1997), *The Black Atlantic: Modernity and Double Conscious-ness,* London: Verso.

Goldberg, D. (1997), *Racial Subjects: Writing on Race in America,* New York: Routledge.

Green, S. F. (1997), *Urban Amazons: Lesbian Feminism and Beyond in the Gender, Sexuality and Identity Battles of London,* London: Macmillan.

Hall, S. (1989), 'New Ethnicities', in D. Morley and K.-H. Chen (eds), *Stuart Hall: Critical Dialogues in Cultural Studies,* pp. 441–9. London: Routledge.

—— (1992), 'What is This 'Black' in Black Popular Culture?', in D. Morley, and K-H. Chen (eds), *Stuart Hall: Critical Dialogues in Cultural Studies,* pp. 465–75. London: Routledge.

Hayfield, A. (1995a), *Black Lesbians and Black Gay Men: The Issues*, London: LAGER.

—— (1995b), *Shot By Both Sides: Black Lesbians and Gay Men Challenging Homophobia in Black Communities and Racism in the White Lesbian and Gay Communities*, London: LAGER.

Hemmings, C. (1993), 'Resituating the Bisexual Body', in J. Bristow and A. R. Wilson (eds), *Activating Theory: Lesbian, Gay and Bisexual Politics*, pp. 118–38 London: Lawrence and Wishart.

Hennink, M., Diamond, I. and Cooper, P. (1999), 'Young Asian Women and Relationships: Traditional or Transitional?', *Ethnic and Racial Studies*, 22 (5): 867–91.

Hindle, P. (1994), 'Gay Communities and Gay Space in the City', in S. Whittle (ed.), *The Margins of the City: Gay Men's Urban Lives*, pp. 7–20 Aldershot: Arena.

hooks, b. (1992), *Black Looks: Race and Representation*, London: Turnaround.

Huang, S., Teo, P. and Yeoh, B. S. A. (2000), 'Diasporic Subjects and Identity Negotiations: Women in and from Asia', *Women's Studies International Forum*, 23 (4): 391–8.

Julien, I. and Mercer, K. (1988), 'De Margin and De Centre', in D. Morley and K-H. Chen (eds), *Stuart Hall: Critical Dialogues in Cultural Studies*, pp. 450–64. London: Routledge.

Khan, S. (1991), *Khush: A SHAKTI Report*, Camden: Camden Council.

Lauria, M. and Knopp, L. (1985), 'Toward an Analysis of the Role of Gay Communities in the Urban Renaissance', *Urban Geography*, 6: 152–69.

Mason-John, V. (ed.) (1995), *Talking Black: Lesbians of African and Asian Descent Speak Out*, London: Cassell.

McDowell and Sharp (1999), *A Concise Glossary of Feminist Geography*, London: Arnold.

Mercer, K. (1994), *Welcome to the Jungle: New Positions in Black and Cultural Studies*, London: Routledge.

Mirza, H. S. (1997), 'Introduction: Mapping a Genealogy of Black British Feminism', H. S. Mirza (ed.), *Black British Feminism: A Reader*, pp. 1–27. London: Routledge.

Mort, F. (1996), *Cultures of Consumption: Masculinities of Social Space in Twentieth Century Britain*, London: Routledge.

Parmar, P. (1982), 'Gender, Race and Class: Asian Women in Resistance', in CCCS (eds), *The Empire Strikes Back: Race and Racism in 70's Britain*, London: Hutchinson.

Puwar, N. (2000), 'Making Space for South Asian Women: What has Changed Since Feminist Review Issue 17?', *Feminist Review*, 66: 131–46.

—— (2001), 'The Racialised Somatic Norm and the Senior Civil Service', *Sociology*, 35 (3): 651–70.

Rassool, N. (1997), 'Fractured or Flexible Identities? Life Histories of 'Black' Diasporic Women in Britain', in H. S. Mirza (ed.), *Black British Feminism: A Reader*, pp. 187–204. London: Routledge.

Ratti, R. (ed.) (1993), *A Lotus of Another Colour: An Unfolding of the South Asian Gay and Lesbian Experience*, Boston: Alyson.

Rothenburg, T. (1995), '"And She Told Two Friends": Lesbians Creating Urban Social Space', in D. Bell and G. Valentine (eds), *Mapping Desire: Geographies of Sexualities*, London: Routledge.

Sibley, D. (1998), 'The Racialisation of Space in British Cities', *Soundings*, 10: 119–27.

Taylor, A. (1997), 'A Queer Geography', in A. Medhurst and S. Munt (ed.), *Lesbian and Gay Studies: A Critical Introduction*, pp. 3–16. London: Cassell.

—— (1998), 'Lesbian Space: More Than One Imagined Territory', in A. Ainley (ed.), *New Frontiers of Space, Bodies and Gender*, pp. 129–41. London: Routledge.

Valentine, G. (1993a), 'Negotiating and Managing Multiple Sexual Identities: Lesbian Time-Space Strategies', *Transactions of the Institute of British Geographers*, 18: 237–48.

—— (1993b), '(Hetero)sexing Space: Lesbian Perceptions and Experiences of Everyday Spaces', *Environment and Planning D: Society and Space*, 11: 395–413.

—— (1995a), 'Out and About: Geographies of Lesbian Landscapes', *International Journal of Urban and Regional Research*, 19 (1): 95–11.

—— (1995b), 'Creating Transgressive Space: The Music of k d lang', *Transactions of the Institute of British Geographers*, 20: 474–85.

Vertovec, S. (1995), 'Hindus in Trinidad and Britain: Ethnic Religion, Reification, and The Politics of Public Space', in P. van der Veer (ed.), *Nation and Migration: The Politics of Space in the South Asian Diaspora*, pp. 132–55. Philadelphia: University of Pennsylvania Press.

Westwood, S. (1995), 'Gendering Diaspora: Space, Politics and South Asian Masculinities in Britain', in P. van der Veer, P. (ed.), *Nation and Migration: The Politics of Space in the South Asian Diaspora*, Philadelphia: University of Pennsylvania Press, 197–21.

Williams, P. (1997), *Seeing a Colour- Blind Future: The Paradox of Race*, London: Virago Press.

'Changing Views': Theory and Practice in a Participatory Community Arts Project

Samina Zahir

Introduction

> . . . if you've come to help me, you're wasting your time. But if you've come because your liberation is bound up with mine, then let us work together (Lila Watson cited in Stringer 1996: 148).

This chapter stresses the value of partnership and community development built on the basis of an ethical relationship from within the principles stated by Lila Watson, an aboriginal social worker. It thus seeks to distance itself from the all too familiar condescending tones that look for a 'solution' or wish to raise the consciousness of marginalized groups. When Birmingham City Council's Arts and Community Team employed me as a 'Cultural Partnerships Officer' I was presented with an opportunity to 'work together'.[1] With a broad range of projects and community groups. This chapter will focus on one specific community arts initiative developed over a year, involving an intensive period of community development work with South Asian women in Birmingham. The project explored ongoing debates around South Asian women and British culture through the thoughts and experiences of the women themselves. A publication and an art exhibition were created through a process of collaboration, exchange and dialogue.[2] The initial funding brief highlighted how the lack of any sense of where people are 'coming from' led communities to "consider their cultural routes/roots as undervalued. The proposal stressed that this made it necessary to consider the 'complex fusions that occur both inter and intra-culturally'.[3]"

The Art of Participation

The categorization of art is intermingled with questions of power with the quality of the product. How art may be expressed or consumed, or indeed, what may be defined as art, always also exposes how power is reproduced through inclusions and exclusions.[4] The relationship between power, representation and imagery, as well as the need for self-representation, is noted by Pratibha Parmar:

> Images play a crucial role in defining and controlling the political and social power to which both individuals and marginalised groups have access. The deeply ideological nature of imagery determines not only how other people think about us but also how we think about ourselves. Because of this under-standing, many migrant and black women photographers are concerned with both representation and self-representation – a process which also guides the formation and construction of identities around gender, race, culture, sexuality and class. It is in representing elements of the 'self', which are considered 'other' by dominant systems of representation that an act of reclamation, empowerment and self-definition occurs (1990: 116).

Thinking about how genuine collaboration can occur in the *process* of representation, Trinh T. Minh-ha (1989) argues that we need to learn to speak *to* and not at and not of. I would like to slightly re-phrase this, and emphasize the importance of speaking *with* each other. I possess a 'hyphenated identity', British-German-Pakistani: European and South Asian. I am visually perceived as 'other' and therefore both object and subject of the research I undertook for this project. Reflexivity about this identity helped me to identify questions that needed to be explored. However, although I shared parts of my identity with those whom I did the research *with*, as an academic and as a council worker, I also occupied positions of institutional power. I sought however to use this position to open up radical possibilities and to problematize positionality (Spivak 1990).

Gayatri Spivak argues that 'what we are asking for is that the hegemonic discourses, and the holders of hegemonic discourse, should dehegemonize their position and themselves learn how to occupy the subject position of the other' (Spivak cited in hooks 1992: 177). I attempted to engage in the contradictory and extremely difficult labour of dehegemonizing hegemonic discourses from a position of being within them. Hence the research process continued to be one of self-discovery –

including self-conflict – as much as one of learning about others (Reinharz 1992). I also actively sought to move away from the view of 'human nature as passive, always acted *upon* by outside forces beyond the individual's control' (Fonow and Cook 1991: 8). Throughout the project this reflexivity along with a commitment to dialogue over the research themes and the project as a whole led to the emergence of a 'trusting relationship'.

All too often academic fieldwork only focuses on the academic context, on the production of academic text, and contributes only to debates within the academy. Consequently, early on, in the planning of the project, with the participants, we identified collective aims and objectives. I sought to *let* the women I worked with set the agenda. Academic research practice often focuses on the analytical rather than the critical, i.e. the possibility for facilitating change. I opted for a critical approach, for research methods stemming from epistemological traditions that have the potential to 'assist research subjects in improving their quality of life, as opposed to the impersonal, exploitative conventions of logical positivism' (Stanfield and Rutledge 1993: 35). As Maria Mies comments, 'one has to change something before it can be understood' (1983: 125). I therefore aimed to produce not only an ethnographic text and a council report, but also a cultural product that would offer the views of those whom I was researching, as a sort of 'living archive' (Hall 1997). This product was to be set within the local context, whereby the production would have meaning for the participants as well as for their intended audiences.

The Participation of Art

The project began when the members of over seventeen groups[5] were invited to participate in workshops. Although several groups were interested in the project, only five groups were able to commit themselves to participate in workshops for the three-month duration of the project. In order to encourage creative participation from as wide a range of people as possible, smaller, bespoke projects were designed for some of the groups who could not make the longer-term commitment.

Working with three artists the five groups developed a diverse range of pieces. Two groups created *tohran* (door hangings), some of which were influenced by established designs in this area and others by contemporary designs. Two groups used ceramics as a form of creative expression, with some focusing on decorative skills and others on technical skills such as sculpture and firing. The fifth group used 2D skills to produce miniature paintings.

The workshops were held in a range of venues, all of which were selected on the basis of their geographical proximity to the participants, and their acceptability as 'safe' spaces. These spaces ranged from schools to community centres to individuals' homes. Interviews were held in the same venues as the workshops. The interviews, along with life stories and oral narratives, became the basis for a publication. All of the interviews involved general debate and thoughts on identity, alongside more specific questions regarding cultural production and representation, particularly as they pertain to 'being here' in B??.[6]

At the end of the workshop and interviews, an exhibition highlighting the backgrounds and experiences of South Asian women in Birmingham and their methods of cultural production was curated. The exhibition reflected mixed backgrounds, and represented a cross-section of the wider community, albeit a cross-section who were clearly motivated and had the time to participate in the project. The final exhibition was displayed in the gallery of Soho House Museum, a community museum in Handsworth, an area of Birmingham with a large South Asian and African-Caribbean population. The museum was also close to locations where some of the workshops had taken place.

Since the exhibition was initially only to be on display for a short period of time, we organized a number of half-day workshops to encourage an audience. The workshops were extremely popular, so the exhibition was seen by a large number of, particularly South Asian, women. However, other events at the community museum drew a varied audience. The exhibition was in place when Soho Museum's Education Room was formally opened, with funders and other dignitaries attending the opening ceremony viewing the exhibition. For the period that the exhibition was on display, the gallery recorded some of their highest viewing figures for a community exhibition.

Throughout the project it was made clear to all of the participants that they would be able to 'censor' any quotes they provided and that they would be presented anonymously. There was a considerable amount of censoring done during and after the interviews, particularly as the book was likely to be seen by parents, relatives and friends. The following poem, for instance, had to be printed anonymously, as the author didn't want to come out as a smoker:

Shalvar Kameez
Kick box – ouch!
Jungle dancing
Cigarette smoking
Roti eating
Mis behaving
Punjabi speaking
English chatting . . .

. . . Believe in God
Lost my faith, found it again
Mum told me stuff
Dad told me stuff
I know stuff
Boom Boom beats
Bhangra beats

My life's a contradiction but it's not fiction.

Once all the participants had seen the final copy, the publication was produced and sent out to both academic circles and the arts sector, offering an insight into the lived experiences of the women who participated. The audience also went beyond these circles and offered something towards curing 'the ultimate evil [of] stupidity' (Du Bois 1999: 58) as well as influencing the direction of arts policy and equalities strategy.

The art forms utilized during the course of the project were identified through consistent dialogue with the artists and the women participants. As a result, the group who wanted to use textiles to create *tohran* worked with both historical and contemporary designs, thus re-working and transforming the look of tohran. The artist working on the project commented on how they began by looking at 'designs and patterns, the ladies developed their own patterns from ideas that they had such as mango leaves, floral designs, paisley.[7] Then we expanded on that, initially working on basic stitches. We mainly used stitches from Bangladesh, *Kantha* stitch . . . we also did mirror, block printing and appliqué work' (1999: 3).

One group worked with a miniatures painter from Pakistan and used age-old techniques alongside more recent designs. The artists initially explored classical techniques associated with miniature painting and then adapted these techniques – which involved making the paper, brushes and the paint themselves – to suit the participants and the time-frame of the project; watercolour paints, inks and acrylics were introduced. They also used techniques of painting such as 'spray painting and marbling, both techniques which wouldn't traditionally be used in miniature paintings but are suitable for this context' (2D artist 1999: 4). A key element was the manner in which the method was adjusted to acknowledge and internalize British influences and their importance in defining the artistic aesthetics of the group.

Another group worked alongside ceramic artists, developing designs on clay pots or *gharas*. These pots are often used in the Indian subcontinent for carrying food and water. The participants decorated these pots in such a way that:

> The decorations on the pot reflect the influences upon each person, their backgrounds, family and history. The group tried to capture feelings, ideas and thoughts they have about living in a mixed society. It's important therefore for us, as individuals, to grow feeling balanced in order to gain the best of both worlds and respect each other (ceramic artist, 1999: 5).

The exhibited final pieces were accompanied by texts compiled by the participants. Jacques Derrida comments that there is a need to find new ways of writing a variety of texts, 'so that the power of people in positions of authority, the cultural producers, to impose their perceptions and interpretations is minimised' (cited in Stringer 1996: 154). Edward Said (1994) has highlighted the ways in which authors write their ideology, either explicitly or implicitly, directly into their material. The participants of this project were no exception. One participant painted a theatrical image through which the viewer could see a face representing her. With this she sought to highlight the need for people to see past superficial façades and look beyond stereotypes and prejudices. While established artistic methods were drawn upon within the majority of workshops, innovation generated new fusions.

It was unfortunate that when the project was completed there was no further funding to continue the workshops, and attendance at the centre fell. A core group did however work to establish themselves as a community-based enterprise. They developed their existing textile skills throughout the project, to the point where they created a stunning piece of embroidery without professional assistance, encouraging them to establish themselves as a small business.

By designing a project that aimed to achieve more than just an academic output, the project encouraged individuals to take the project in their own directions. Paul Routledge (1996: 406) has commented that this method of working 'reworks earlier positions of engagement articulated by people such as Fanon (1963) and Freire (1970), in that it is explicitly concerned with engagement as a process of continual becoming, flux and transformation, that entangles academic and political space'. Academic spaces certainly have the potential to offer 'research subjects' a route for themselves that re-routes metropolitan metropolitan living in the West (Birmingham), but only if the researcher is prepared to act as a catalyst within the process, rather than appearing as the source.

Some Representations of South Asian Women

This project offered space for South Asian women to use artistic representation in order to challenge stereotypes. One of the artists working on the project commented how for the participants, 'art was a different way of expressing themselves; what they wanted to say through this visual language. They were not so much conscious of expressing their *identity* as of expressing *themselves*' (2D artist 1999: 4). Hence art opened up the possibility for creative expression and allowed 'people to know about your identity and what you are – it just helps'. Many of the participants stated that they wanted to 'tell white people about us and our lives in order to get to know them and for them to know more about us', to 'tell it like it is'. The use of art was an important way of 'letting other people know what you think'. It is only through allowing voices to speak that one can ensure the self-production and self-representation of diverse cultural identities.[8] But as the speech act entails both speaking and listening, speaking does not necessarily mean that voices are heard (Spivak 1988a). The relationship between self and society thus needs to be dynamic, an integrated process that ensures individuals contribute towards, as well as work within, defined social realms of association (Said 1994). Understanding the relationships between the participants, the arts institutions and the wider social context became a fundamental element of this research.

Art also helped the participants to question any 'simple notions of identity which overlap neatly with language or location' and 'to become deeply suspicious of any determinist or positivist definition of identity' Spivak (1990: 8). Thus one group of participants wondered how they 'were going to do a modern Punjabi woman, . . . what is a modern woman. What represented her?' The multiple routes of identity and the 'unrootedness' of identity were crucial to both the community I researched and to me. It was important for those producing work that they and the work they produced were not predetermined. Clifford and Marcus (1986: 10) argue that '"Cultures" do not hold still for their portraits.' The art project worked against narrow forms of representation and notions of the 'other' by seeking to place the 'other' in the same room (Bright and Bakewell 1995: 14). The pieces of art produced expressed the complexity involved in the process 'of continual becoming, flux and transformation' (Routledge 1996: 406), since for many of the participants the complexity of their own cultural identification was an ongoing issue; a challenging subject that they frequently debated. For some participants their placement within a diversity of cultures was an advantage that they drew upon: 'I feel that I am mixing cultures together because you can wear a mixture of clothes, we have mixtures of foods and we have a mixture of "races" that we mix with, so we are mixing cultures together and we mix our ideas together too.' Yet there was also a cautionary note, as one participant commented: 'I don't think it will ever be seen as the same [British culture and South Asian culture], because that's the difference between the two cultures, but I do think, this generation that are mixing cultures, there will be a new culture, but it will never be a complete mix.' There is an asymmetrical relationship between the two, with one marked as ethnic and the other as truly British.

Hence, while Birmingham sells itself on its diversity, and is known for its 'Balti Belt', *mehndi* and *bindi* have become the latest fashion trends, and Chicken Tikka Masala is the new national dish, people of South Asian origin continue to experience racism. The consumption of 'Asian' products does not preclude racism, as consumption may be simply based on reified static notions of South Asian culture and sites of consumption may themselves become sites for racist practices. The unsettling nature of the complexities of location, of the vulnerabilities that ensue, were expressed by one participant: 'the British themselves don't allow us to be British, if there is a clash or friction, immediately the white people turn and go "go back to Bangladesh"'.

To Educate the Viewer

Reina Lewis (1996: 2–3) has highlighted the value of being aware that 'representations do not have intrinsic meanings in themselves. Rather meaning is constructed in the interaction between the reader/viewer and the text (simultaneously constructing meanings and identities for both the viewer and the text).' The participants were very aware that the viewer might not fully understand their thoughts and the experiences that contributed towards the processes of cultural production behind the pieces. They consequently sought to encourage an appropriate understanding through the accompanying text. The participants were also keen to educate the viewers about the dynamics of cultural change and fusion that ran throughout the project, the cultural or religious backgrounds, and, crucially, the shifts in approach and style of artistic work as their art ultimately (re)presented the ideological frame of reference through which they were coming to understand their own experiences.

Some of these changes were a result of 'being here', a process that has influenced different generations to varying degrees and in different ways, while also organically changing the very nature of being British. As Brah (1996: 18) argues, 'cultures are never static: they evolve through history, that is why the process of cultural reproduction is, in part, a process of cultural transformation'. Participants who were older, first-generation migrants highlighted the view that: 'ours is not the host generation's culture, but it is that of the younger generation, just living here doesn't mean that you are living without cultural identity – we have an identity here'. Hence, for many of the participants, cultural production was also done with a need to educate the viewer about the necessity for a productive 'transaction between speaker and listener' (Spivak 1988b) to encourage those in positions of power to consider their own cultural identity. As one participant commented, 'the project made me think, I'm watching life and what I've done or do in life, I hope that others do too'. This opportunity was extended to all those who viewed the exhibition or read the publication.

Developing the project towards an exhibition did not prove to be an easy process. We experienced untold obstacles, most frequently with larger, institutional arts organizations. A request for gallery space in Birmingham Museum and Art Gallery was rejected. The exhibition was not considered to be of 'good enough quality' and this verdict was handed out without seeing the work. The lack of South Asian presence in the larger museums and galleries in the region was recognized by many of the participants. They frequently commented that: 'I've been to the museum before but I haven't really noticed any Asian stuff there. There's nothing Asian about it, so I think it would be good to put what we're doing in such places.' We eventually found space in a community museum, but I brockered this opportunity. I wondered at the treatment the groups would have experienced alone. As an 'insider' who worked within the arts system, I was able to advocate and lobby, frequently acting as a go-between. In overcoming the obstacles and seeking to represent ourselves we realized why such projects rarely took shape and the rarity of the opportunities available for some communities.

Conclusion

Cultural representation is shown never to be free, but always laden with the subtexts and politics of marginal/minority relations. Yet, as Parmar's quote highlighted at the beginning of this chapter, a key benefit of a participatory approach is that an act of 'reclamation, empowerment and self-definition can occur' through the representation of elements of the 'self' that, in turn, combat representations that are 'othered' by the existing dominant systems. Who heard them and how they were heard remains open to the black hole of power and representation. Let this not, however, stop us from partaking in the labour of representation; the troubled search to listen through the undoing of our own privileges continues.

Acknowledgements

To all the participants and artists on Changing Views, who gave up time, ideas and creative energy; also to Parvati and Nirmal, who have been enormously helpful editors.

Notes

1. I am grateful to Judy Stubley, my line manager at Birmingham City Council, without whose support the approach outlined in this chapter would not have been so well received.
2. Birmingham City Council, 'Changing Views' Publication, 1999, Exhibition at Soho House Museum, Birmingham April to July 1999.
3. The project was funded by West Midlands Arts, the regional arts board; this quotation is taken from an internal, free text, application for funding to WMA, made in 1998 by Birmingham City Council's Arts Team.
4. The seemingly ongoing conflict between 'culture' as 'high art' and culture as a set of customs, beliefs and practices incorporated into one's daily lived experience was not specifically researched within this project. This is primarily because the boundary lines that exist are as much (if not more) concerned with issues of access, representation and

power. Subsequently, when the groups visited the museum, experiencing certain types of art in such a space was, in some ways 'odd', since art forms that might be considered 'high art' in Western society were part of one's daily lived experience in many other countries. An example of this was the manner in which the women who were participating in the embroidery project (*tohran*) interacted with the famous Burne Jones tapestries. They wanted to view them in close detail, examine and feel them as pieces of craft, none of which was permitted in the museum. Indeed, the Arts Council and funding bodies are becoming increasingly interested in art that interacts without proclaiming itself as distinct from daily life. Accordingly, while practices such as Rangoli are becoming increasingly popular in museums and galleries, they are still seen in Asian culture as part of one's daily experience, rather than a distinct item of spectacle.

5. Contact was made with a wide range of groups, including community centres, artists' groups, sheltered women's hostels, neighbourhood fora, cultural centres, primary schools, women's groups, secondary schools, youth clubs, projects and girls' groups, mental health fora and family centres.

6. The publication, named 'Changing Views' after the exhibition, was printed by Birmingham City Council in 1998. Copies are available from Birmingham City Council's Arts Team, and cost £5.

7. Paisley was chosen since it is a design that originated in India, rather than in Scotland, as is often presumed.

8. Yet the problem for many South Asian artists has been the manner in which they are not permitted to freely use any artistic or culturally led expression to represent themselves. I came across many examples of artists who felt pushed into producing 'acceptable' work that is understood by power-holders such as the Arts Council and training bodies, amongst others. Many artists reject the label 'ethnic' places such as the Drum in Birmingham and the Chinese Arts Centre in Manchester highlight how many artists feel a need to enter what are considered 'safe spaces' (in a manner similar to the workshop participants) before they can move into more 'mainstream' spaces.

References

Brah, A. (1996), *Cartographies of Diaspora*, London: Routledge.
Bright, B. J. and Bakewell, L. (1995), *Looking High and Low: Art and Cultural Identity*, Tucson, AZ: University of Arizona Press.

Clifford, J. and Marcus, G. E. (eds) (1986), *Writing Culture, The Poetics and Politics of Ethnography*, Berkeley, CA: University of California Press.

Du Bois, W. E. B. (1999), *The Souls of Black Folk*, London: W.W. Norton & Company.

Fanon, F. (1963), *The Wretched of the Earth,* New York: Grove Press.

Fonow, M. and Cook, J. A. (1991), *Beyond Methodology: Feminist Scholarship as Lived Research*, Bloomington, IN: Indiana University Press.

Freire, P. (1970), *Pedagogy of the Oppressed*, New York: Herder & Herder.

Hall, S. (1997), *Representation: Cultural Representations and Signifying Practices*, London: Sage.

hooks, b. (1992), *Black Looks: Race and Representation,* London: Turnaround.

Lewis, R. (1996), *Gendering Orientalism: Race, Femininity and Representation*, London: Routledge.

'Living Archive', African and Asian Artists' Archive (AAVAA) and the journal *Third Text* organized a conference at Tate Britain, London, March 1997.

Mies, M. (1983), in Gloria Bowles and Renate Duelli Klein (eds), *Theories of Women's Studies*, London: Routledge.

Minh-Ha, T. T. (1989), *Woman, Native, Other: Writing Postcoloniality and Feminism*, Bloomington, IN: Indiana University Press.

Parmar, P. (1990), 'Black Feminism: The Politics of Articulation', in J. Rutherford (ed.), *Identity: Community, Culture, Difference*, London: Lawrence & Wishart.

Reinharz, S, (1992), *Feminist Methods in Social Research*, New York: Oxford University Press.

Routledge, P. (1996), 'The Third Space in Critical Engagement', *Antipode*, 28 (4): 399–19.

Rutherford, J. (ed), (1990), *Identity: Community, Culture, Difference*, London: Lawrence & Wishart.

Said, E. (1994), *Culture and Imperialism*, London: Vintage.

Spivak, G. C. (1988a), *In Other Worlds: Essays in Cultural Politics*, London: Routledge.

—— (1988b) 'Can the Subaltern Speak?' in C. Nelson and L. Grossberg (eds), *Marxism and the Interpretation of Culture*, London: Macmillan.

—— (1990), *The Post-Colonial Critic: Interviews, Strategies, Dialogues*, London: Routledge.

Stanfield, J. H. and Rutledge, D. M. (1993), *Race and Ethnicity in Research Methods*, London: Sage.

Stringer, E. T. (1996), *Action Research: A Handbook for Practitioners*, London: Sage.

–12–

South Asian Women and the Question of Political Organization
Shaminder Takhar

Introduction

The colonial image of South Asian women as being unable to resist the power exerted by patriarchal relations (Mani 1990, Spivak 1993) in the face of *dharma* and *karma* (Trivedi 1984) has been transported (over time) to the postcolonial British context as a racialized discourse (Brah 1992; Parmar 1982; Rattansi 1994). Despite this negative portrayal, historical accounts highlight the involvement of South Asian women in nationalist and feminist movements (Thapar 1993; Kumar 1989). Such protests have been borrowed and reworked by high-profile organizations such as Southall Black Sisters in Britain (Siddiqui 2000). Moreover, this political agency has not been limited to left-wing 'freedom' movements. Rather, South Asian women demonstrate agency in movements across the political spectrum, with the nature of the ideologies having an impact upon the character of the agency. This chapter contributes to explorations of women's political agency by focusing on the political organization of South Asian women within the context of contemporary British society. Questions of identity, political categorization, and power as well as empowerment are considered through an engagement with a range of organizations. In this chapter I am not seeking to represent all South Asian women; rather, the focus is on a self-selected group of activists.

Understanding the South Asian Experience

I explore questions of subjectivity, identity and political agency through an analysis of in-depth interviews conducted with twenty-four women working in London-based voluntary or statutory bodies with South Asian women. The term 'South Asian woman' carries within it boundaries based on religious interpretations, caste and class, so that South Asian feminist political coalitions too are riven by these differences (Bhachu 1988; Westwood and Bhachu 1988; Brah 1994; Bhopal 1997; Puar 1996; Sudbury 1998). Some of the women I interviewed were born in England; others migrated with their parents, and others entered the country as spouses. All of them, including those whose parents had migrated to East Africa and Mauritius, stated that their origins were from the Indian subcontinent – India, Pakistan or Bangladesh. The interviewees were from three religious groups: Hindu (8), Muslim (9) and Sikh (7), and their ages ranged from 25 to 57 years. The women were mainly approached through Asian women's projects, and to facilitate access to these projects I became a member of the management committee of one project for a period of three years. Of the women-based projects I consulted, three were originally set up for Muslim women and one for Pakistani women. The women I interviewed were employed in a variety of organizations, including refuges, resource centres, women's centres, anti-racist organizations, youth projects and employment and educational projects that work with South Asian women, as well as religious organizations for women. They were engaged in these organizations in a range of capacities, as refuge workers, caseworkers, debt counsellors, counsellors, campaign co-ordinators and trainers.

The chapter will now consider these women's narratives in order to see how the women located themselves with regard to issues of racism, sexism, feminism and religion.

Racism and Sexism

South Asian women's projects have become visible for challenging racist and sexist stereotypes, structures and expectations, found both in South Asian 'communities' and in British organizations. The importance of notions of shame (*sharam*)[1] and honour (*izzat*),[2] often used to explain the limits to women's participation in social and political arenas, has been challenged. Thus Asian women's projects have entered the psyche of 'Asian communities' and policy-makers. Despite being accused of 'washing their dirty linen in public', Asian women's organizations have pursued the struggle against both patriarchy and racism. By placing questions of gender on the public and political agenda they have attempted to change patriarchal attitudes within their communities. However, as was noted by one of my interviewees, this is by no means a comfortable position *vis-à-vis* 'the community':

> I think that the Asian community in general does not like organizations such
> as ours because they do feel threatened by it and we are sort of labelled as
> homewreckers, anything that tears the fabric of the Asian community (Inter-
> view with a worker in an Asian Women's Project 1997).

Tearing the fabric of the community is tantamount to being sacrilegious:
it is an offence, particularly in the face of a hostile white society that
regards Asian practices as 'strange' or 'inferior'. Far from 'containing'
controversial issues within the community, Asian women, by setting up
organizations, have challenged so-called male 'community leaders'.

South Asian women have also baffled anti-racists and multiculturalists
alike in their efforts to 'defend' black communities against racism. They
have questioned the role and actions of white feminists, who have made
political efforts to 'rescue' Asian women from their terrible fate. It must
thus be stressed that questions of 'race' remain central to Asian women's
organizations, and indeed important to the way in which their feminism(s)
is/are forged.

Participation in projects provides a space for self-expression outside
confining frameworks, and a place to communicate with other women
with whom they can foster a collective identity. As one project worker
remarked:

> When I joined [. . . . . .], I was eighteen at the time, oh that just gave me a new
> lease of life. I was with women who were political, who were aware of Asian
> women's needs and they talked in a language that I wanted to talk in, you know.
> You could really relate to what they were saying, they wanted to change
> attitudes in the community. They wanted to make services accessible to Asian
> women and where there weren't services, then we would create those services
> (Interview with a worker in an Asian Women's Project 1996).

The projects offer an alternative to the dominant discourses of Asian
femininity and challenge ideas of honour and shame, particularly with
reference to domestic violence. Although there are some studies of 'black'
women's organizations in Britain (Mama 1995; Sudbury 1998), academic
work relating specifically to Asian women's activism is scarce. The
exception has been the input of those involved in high-profile organizations such as Southall Black Sisters (Siddiqui 2000; P. Patel 1997). Both
Hannah Siddiqui and D Pragna Patel have commented on the need to place
the needs of Asian women before the needs of Asian males, the community, religion or culture. It is this dynamic force that has led to women's
projects being set up, offering a sense of empowerment against disem-

powering practices within communities. This is evident in the following statement made by a project worker:

> It's not just having another Asian worker, it's about having the right Asian worker. It's really important to have that because we get judged all the time outside, we get judged in society and we get judged everywhere really. I think for the women that come to see us, they value the non-judgemental aspect and the confidential aspect of it . . . very often a lot of our work is actually challenging some of the attitudes of other Asian workers, other professionals as well, like social workers and doctors (Interview with a worker in an Asian Women's Project 1996).

It is important to note that being a South Asian woman is not enough in itself to qualify a person as having an 'appropriate' or 'right' attitude. Reminding ourselves of how experience is mediated and articulated by political discourses, we need to note that there are South Asian women who work as professionals with Asian women, but do this in a patronizing manner or with a corrective gaze. The above quotation clearly indicates the importance of being vigilant to certain ideas with the notion of the 'right' Asian worker, complicated further by different conceptions of feminist principles of freedom and equality. The 'right' cultural exposure in terms of educational and political training (through networks and organizations like Amnesty International) can also be important to the acquisition and performance of the 'right' attributes. These may also be linked to attire, dress, style of speech and accent. Selection is no doubt important to the effective functioning of organizations, especially if the organization is constantly struggling to survive both ideologically and financially. Nonetheless, selection can also be peculiarly elitist in highly invisible ways, which poses the danger of a closed type of social cloning that is self-perpetuating and reluctant to change or to accept 'new blood'.

'Asianness' and 'Blackness'

Attachment or a distancing from the collective political identity 'black' also contributes to who is or is not the 'right worker'. The political identities 'Asian' and 'black' are important in locating the basis for political agency (Sudbury 2001: 30). Sudbury (2001) analyses the ways in which the political identity 'black' can be retrieved for collective action. The fluidity of 'black' identity is reflected in her use of the term 'multi-racial blackness', in which a number of groups can strategically adopt this identity and avoid homogeneity or essentialism. 'Black' is an identity that can be used effectively as one of many identities oppositional to hegemonic forces. In this respect it offers the possibility of building alliances between different groups of women, as exemplified by Southall Black Sisters and in the past, by the Organisation of Women of African and Asian Descent (OWAAD) (Parmar 1990).

By specifically setting up Asian women's projects, South Asian women are drawing on certain aspects of an ethnic identity or fixing it temporarily. While the term 'black' is important in recognizing similarities of experience as postcolonial subjects within a racist society, at the same time it does not necessarily have to deny or compromise an 'Asian' identity or culture (Hazareesingh 1986; Modood 1988). 'Black' as an organizing political concept has represented and still can represent a political consciousness that resists erasure of other differences (Housee and Dar 1997). The particular relationship between 'black' and other ethnic identities cannot be predicted prior to any formation, but is something that entails a continuous process of struggle and negotiation, as illustrated by one interviewee:

> I mean I use black in certain contexts but I perceive myself as British Asian, black Asian even but you know if you expect me not to acknowledge that I'm Asian, I don't think that is very good (Interview with a worker in an Anti-Racist Organisation 1996).

Where *Asianness* is used by women to mark their difference, South Asian women are drawing on certain aspects of an ethnic identity. Moreover, in many cases there is a re-definition of Asian femininity occurring alongside the actualization of a 'black' identity. The claiming of both 'black' and Asian can be one way of positioning oneself as 'Asian' in contradistinction to stereotypical images and expectations of Asian women both within and outside South Asian communities:

> I just didn't want to end up as an Asian female stereotype . . . sort of you know wearing a *salwaar kameez*, going to community functions, being the perfect daughter, being able to make tea in the right way (Interview with a worker in an Anti-Racist Organisation 1996).

The interviewee above wanted to distance herself from dominant stereotypical representations of South Asian women, from acceptable markers of their femininity that include behaviour (passive, docile, obedient) and dress. She views the wearing of certain forms of dress, because of what it is stereotypically associated with, as a form of compliance. Asian women have however also used Asian dress to subvert these stereotypes. Refusal to wear 'respectable' Asian gear can be a statement of resistance against the control of women as the bearers of community traditions; but the wearing of Asian clothing in Western metropoles can also be a statement of contestation in the face of racist preconceptions of aesthetics. For example 'Radical Sista' (Ranjit Kaur), a successful DJ who wears Asian dress styles in new and different contexts, comments:

> '. . . I know it's a political thing – the very fact that as an Asian woman I am actually out there for a start, and the fact that I'm wearing Asian gear makes the point in itself in a way. Because people look and go "What's she doing there?" You know, if I was wearing ragga shorts and a little bra top, they would hardly bat an eyelid. Asian guys would, they'd look "phwaar, hey", but other people wouldn't really give a damn. But, seeing someone in full 'traditional dress' doing something that's like a Western concept doesn't correlate with the expected images of Asian women (Radical Sista cited in Sharma, Hutnyk and Sharma 1996: 98).

By wearing what is marked out as Asian dress in a public arena DJ Radical Sista subverts *expected* ideas of Asian women. She utilizes clothes to present an identity that at once supports the perceptions of outsiders and confuses them with a public and 'out there' posture – a return of the gaze, perhaps?

Perceptions of Asian women as conforming individuals often result in people asking the question 'It must be so hard leading a double life?', i.e. doing what white people do and being Asian. This is of course based on the perception that Asian people suppress one aspect of their lives in order to live comfortably with another, resulting in unbelonging and alienation (Narayan 1989, cited in Mama 1995: 13). I would argue that although Asian women may feel a sense of dislocation and displacement, recognizing multiplicity of experience and the ability of women to occupy several contexts simultaneously helps us to move away from the notion of a fragmented self to a multi-layered self, a self that temporarily and strategically fixes certain forms of identity, outside the traditional/modern dichotomy.

The Blurred Boundaries of 'Asian'

The boundaries of belonging to the category 'Asian' appeared to be blurred in some organizations, especially in refuges, where the topic is an ongoing source of deliberation. In one refuge the category 'Asian' had been widened to include Chinese, Vietnamese, Iraqi and Iranian women because:

> Although it's supposed to be an Asian women's refuge, we do take other women but we don't take white women, to tell you the truth we don't have the space, because then the whole political argument is lost, because the whole reason for coming into being is that we wanted a refuge specifically for Asian women, we didn't want Asian women to go into women's aid refuges where they couldn't identify culturally or linguistically (Interview with a worker in an Asian Women's Project 1996).

Being a category with no fixed origins, it is subject to the elasticity of changing political and social tides. Religion and faith can also be used as a basis for widening the term 'Asian'. In one refuge, for instance, women from Morocco and the Yemen were included. The project co-ordinator stated:

> If they can identify either with one of the faiths or with the culture of this group then we will accept them (Interview with a worker in an Asian Women's Project 1996).

The process of self-identification with a culture or religion is regarded as satisfactory for acceptance into a project. The rise of religious identities has witnessed the demise of the term 'South Asian women' as a political organizing entity. The creation of Muslim women's refuges as opposed to Asian women's refuges from the late 1980s onwards is a clear indication of how this trend is etched in women's political organizations.

The Question of Feminism

The question of feminism raised suspicions amongst some of the women interviewed, even though they adhered to principles commonly associated with the 'rights of women'. The women preferred to say that they were not outright feminists or that they were 'womanist'. This is captured in the following statement made by a counsellor in an advisory organization:

> I think there's some element of influence because I've worked with women for sixteen, eighteen years. I've worked with very strong feminist organizations. We were known for our campaigning work for promoting women's rights but I personally don't define myself as a feminist. I would define myself as a womanist. Being a woman I have mixed feelings about defining myself as a

feminist. I agree with sixty or seventy per cent of the issues but a lot of the things I don't agree with. Feminism is often labelled within the Asian community as something negative and I feel that being a woman doesn't mean being a womanist or a feminist, it doesn't mean putting down men. It's about making our rights known, being assertive and looking for equality (Interview with a worker in an Asian Women's Advisory Service 1997).

Although women's organizations have developed autonomously, and are significant sites for the operation of agency, some have developed solely into service providers. When faced with questions of feminism or political activity, most of the women were apprehensive about their answers and stressed that they provided a service. Siddiqui (2000), in her comparison of organizations, also suggests that not all Asian women's organizations use a feminist or a political approach. In fact the underlying principles of some Asian women's organizations are, from her perspective, non-feminist.

Siddiqui notes that political activity amongst women's groups has declined owing to the focus on service provision, and yet that political activity is crucial, particularly in challenging the criminal justice system, and in cases where Asian women have displayed behaviour contrary to that which is expected, i.e. the stereotypical 'squeaky clean' image (Siddiqui 2000: 89). Thus some South Asian women's organizations such as Southall Black Sisters have an overtly political agenda and involve black feminist activists, white feminists and anti-racists in their movements (with a gradual movement towards the anti-racist movement). Others regard their work as apolitical, but interestingly enough direct their activities towards gaining equality and rights. This is particularly evident in organizations that base themselves on religion. Could this form of organizing be regarded as subversion, a type of 'conform to transform' strategy (Mirza 1997)?

Religion

The importance of religion, most notably Islam, in some South Asian women's struggle for equality and freedom is noticeable; a religious framework can be used to overcome oppression and to gain rights (Bano 1999). Thus some Muslim women use their religious loyalties to argue for equality within the religion, to contest religious orthodoxies (Kandiyoti 1988). For instance, for one organization the key to equality lies in encouraging women to read and utilise the Koran:

The Koran teaches that women are equal. Our culture tells us that women are not equal. The Islamic way is for women to learn and gain knowledge (Interview with a worker in an Muslim Women's Organisation, 1997).

Bringing about change within orthodoxies and communities while still belonging to them can be a fraught process. This is particularly so, when those who want to bring about change are seen as repositories of 'tradition'. Many writers have stressed that women are often used as markers of tradition and culture, highlighting the preoccupation with the position of women and their role in the family community and religion (P. Patel 1997; Anthias and Yuval-Davis 1992; Saghal and Yuval-Davis 1992).

Within the South Asian diaspora, religious identity or cultural identification with being Hindu, Muslim or Sikh is politicized at the international level, with the reverberations of events occurring on the Indian subcontinent being felt in Britain. Examples include the Hindutva[3] movement in India, which is anti-Muslim and anti-Christian (Sarkar and Butalia 1995), the Sikh movement for an independent state (Puar 1996) and Islamism, the placing of Islam politically at the centre of one's identity (Sayyid 1997: 17). These movements have reconfigured feminism in the South Asian diaspora.

Feminists have shown great apprehension about the consequences of religious revivalism for women's rights, noting the re-assertion of patriarchy and the policing of women's sexuality (Sudbury 1998; V. Patel 1994). Pragna Patel (1997) states: 'Women's bodies and minds are the battleground for the preservation of the "purity" of religious and communal identities. So the role of women as signifiers and transmitters of identity within the family becomes crucial' (Pragna Patel 1997: 26). In Britain, although secular women's organizations have openly challenged certain versions of religion and maintained an active struggle against oppression, they do not grapple with the ways in which some women view their liberation within or alongside religious affiliations.

Conclusion

Patricia Hill-Collins (1990) suggests that empowerment is the power of self-definition and affirmation, which effectively means the rejection of disempowering discourses, the setting up of alternative forms of engagement and political activism. Through their ability to organize in autonomous spaces[4] based on a collective but not necessarily a homogeneous 'Asian' identity, South Asian women reject dominant discourses and negative portrayals. Some women may conform to transform, so that their agency is not an overt manifestation of resistance but is subversive and transformative in more covert ways.

Notes

1. The concept *Sharam* refers to the concept of shame and shyness, and is usually used in conjunction with *Izzat.* It implies the safeguarding of one's reputation, and is frequently applied to South Asian girls' and women's behaviour (Wilson 1978).
2. *Izzat* refers to family, group or personal honour, respect or standing. It can be specifically applied to women's behaviour with reference to bringing family honour into disrepute.
3. Hindutva demonstrates the intimate connection between the State and religion in India. Hindu fundamentalist parties consist of the Bharatiya Janata party (BJP), the Rashtriya Swayamsevak Sangh (RSS), and the Vishwa Hindu Parishad (VHP). There are other militant organizations, such as the Shiv Sen, which have mobilized Indian women through a symbolic usage of the goddess Durga, who is the consort of Shiva, one of the most important Hindu female deities.
4. These organizations can be regarded as 'autonomous' because they are explicitly run *by* South Asian women *for* South Asian women. They are usually registered as charities. Most of the funding is through local government, housing associations and the London Grants Unit. Some organizations also use fundraising events.

References

Anthias, F. and Yuval-Davis, N. (1992), *Racialized Boundaries: Race, Nation, Gender, Colour and Class and the Anti-Racist Struggle,* London: Routledge.

Bano, S. (1999), 'Muslim and South Asian Women: Customary Law and Citizenship in Britain', in N. Yuval-Davis and P. Werbner (eds), *Women, Citizenship and Difference,* London: Zed Books.

Bhachu, P. (1988), '*Apni Marzi Kardhi:* Home and Work: Sikh Women in Britain', in S. Westwood and P. Bhachu (eds), *Enterprising Women: Ethnicity, Economy and Gender Relations,* London: Routledge.

Bhopal, K. (1997), *Gender, 'Race' and Patriarchy: A Study of South Asian Women,* Aldershot: Ashgate.

Brah, A. (1992), 'Difference, Diversity and Differentiation', in J. Donald and A. Rattansi (eds), *'Race'. Culture and Difference,* pp. 126–45. Milton Keynes: Open University Press, 126–45.

—— (1994), '"Race" and "Culture" in the Gendering of Labour Markets', in M. Afshar and M. Maynard (eds), *The Dynamics of 'Race' and Gender: Some Feminist Interventions,* London: Taylor & Francis.

Hazareesingh, S. (1986), 'Racism and Cultural Identity: An Indian Perspective', *Dragon's Teeth,* 24.

Hill-Collins, P. (1990), *Black Feminist Thought: Knowledge, Consciousness and the Politics of Empowerment,* New York: Routledge.

Housee, S. and Dar, M. (1996), 'Re-mixing Identities: "Off the Turntable"', in S. Sharma, J. Hutnyk and A. Sharma (eds), *Dis-Orienting Rhythms: The Politics of the New Asian Dance Music,* London: Zed Books.

Kandiyoti, D. (1988), 'Bargaining with Patriarchy', *Gender and Society* 2: 274–90.

Kumar, R. (1989), 'Contemporary Indian Feminism', *Feminist Review,* 33.

Mama, A. (1995), *Beyond the Masks: Race, Gender and Subjectivity,* London: Routledge.

Mani, L. (1990), 'Multiple Mediations: Feminist Scholarship in the Age of Multinational Reception', in H. Crowley and S. Himmelweit (eds), *Knowing Women,* Cambridge: Polity Press.

Mirza, H. S. (ed.) (1997), *Black British Feminism: A Reader,* London: Routledge.

Modood, T. (1988), '"Black", Racial Equality and Asian Identity', *New Community,* XIV: 3.

Parmar, P. (1982), 'Gender, Race and Class: Asian Women in Resistence', in CCCS (eds), *The Empire Strikes Back: Race and Racism in 70's Britain,* London: Hutchinson.

—— (1990), 'Black Feminism: The Politics of Articulation', in J. Rutherford (ed.), *Identity, Community, Culture, Difference,* London: Lawrence and Wishart.

Patel, P. (1997), 'Third Wave Feminism and Black Women's Activism', in H. Mirza (ed.), *Black British Feminism: A Reader,* London: Routledge.

Patel, V. (1994), 'Impressions of Asian Life in Britain', *Women Against Fundamentalism,* 1 (5): 46–50.

Puar, J. K. (1996), 'Resituating Discourses of "Whiteness" and "Asianness" in Northern England: Second-generation Sikh Women and Constructions of Identity', in M. Maynard and J. Purvis (eds), *New Frontiers in Women's Studies: Knowledge, Identity and Nationalism*, London: Taylor and Francis Ltd.

Rattansi, A. (1994), '"Western" Racisms, Ethnicities and Identities in a "Postmodern" Frame', in A. Rattansi and S. Westwood (eds), *Racism, Modernity and Identity on the Western Front*, Cambridge: Polity Press.

Saghal, G. and Yuval-Davis, N. (1992), *Refusing Holy Orders: Women and Fundamentalism in Britain*, London: Virago Press.

Sarkar, T. and Butalia, U. (eds) (1995), *Women and Right Wing Movements*, London: Zed Books.

Sayyid, B. (1997), *A Fundamental Fear: Eurocentrism and the Emergence of Islamism*, London: Zed Books.

Sharma, S., Hutnyk, J. and Sharma, A. (eds) (1996), *Dis-Orienting Rhythms: The Politics of the New Asian Dance Music*, London: Zed Books.

Siddiqui, H. (2000), 'Black Women's Activism: Coming of Age?, *Feminist Review*, 64.

Spivak, G. (1993) 'Can the Subaltern Speak?', in P. Williams and L. Chrisman (eds), *Colonial Discourse and Post-Colonial Theory: A Reader*, Hemel Hempstead: Harvester Wheatsheaf.

Sudbury, J. (1998), *'Other Kinds of Dreams': Black Women's Organisations and the Politics of Transformation*, London: Routledge.

—— (2001), '(Re)constructing Multiracial Blackness: Women's Activism, Difference and Collective Identity in Britain', *Ethnic and Racial Studies*, 24 (1): 29–49.

Thapar, S. (1993), 'Women as Activists; Women as Symbols: A Study of the Indian Nationalist Movement', *Feminist Review*, 44.

Trivedi, P. (1984), 'To Deny Our Fullness: Asian Women in the Making of History', *Feminist Review*, 17: 37–50.

Westwood, S. and Bhachu, P. (eds) (1988), *Enterprising Women: Ethnicity, Economy and Gender Relations*, London: Routledge.

Wilson, A. (1978), *Finding a Voice*, London: Virago.

–13–

Engendering Diasporic Identities
Hasmita Ramji

Introduction

Diasporic populations present an analytical preoccupation for contemporary academics concerned with cultural identity and its maintenance in the post-modern/colonial global metropolis. This chapter contributes to this literature by highlighting the active role played by South Asian women in identity formation in migrant communities. I focus on the specific experiences of professionally employed London-based Kutchi Hindu Gujarati[1] women in order to challenge dominant conceptions in academic literature on women, work, education and families (Bhopal 1997; Saifullah-Khan 1979). Here I particularly focus on the ways in which occupational achievements are being utilized by these women to negotiate a more powerful position for themselves within social practices such as marriage.

The Research

This chapter draws on twenty in-depth interviews carried out with professionally employed, married women (referred to in the research as the daughters' cohort; comments from members of this group are identified by the label 'DS' below) from Northwest London's Kutchi Hindu community and twenty interviews conducted with their mothers (referred to as the mothers' cohort; comments from members of this group are identified by the label 'MS' below). The ages of the daughters ranged from 25 to 35 years, and all were born and educated in the UK. Their mothers were interviewed primarily to examine any generational trends that might be evident. The mothers were aged between 60 and 65 years. None of them had any formal education beyond primary school.[2] All the mothers had histories of full-time employment in manual labour, and although most of them had now retired, some still continued to work part-time. The research focused specifically on the ways in which British Hindu Gujarati women from two generations discussed their experiences of education, work and family. This discussion suggests that women are using their educational and employment achievements continuously to renegotiate their gender, ethnic and class locations.

Analysing Professional Asian Women

Much academic work on South Asian women and work views them as being 'consigned' either to low-status employment or to their reproductive roles. This literature perpetuates their status as victims, concentrating on the negative experiences of low-status employment and 'homework'. There is little recognition that Asian women may also occupy professional spaces.

Feminist analysis on the impact of education and employment on gender relations within 'white' populations has on the other hand argued that women's increasing occupational achievements are challenging patriarchal family formations (Crompton 1999). As women have gradually established and secured their rights as individuals within the post-industrial occupational sphere, the nuclear family, at least in its traditional form, is waning (Beck and Beck-Gernsheim 1995: 1–2; Crompton 1999).

This competing and incompatible relationship between traditional and modern social forms is an analytical framework often applied to British Asian women without revision (Walby 1990). A focus on white populations as the regular norm means that the specificities of the Asian experience are not fully discussed (for further illustration of this point see Caplan 1985; Westwood and Bhachu 1988; Mani 1992; Rayaprol 1997). A universal model of the family ignores the complex and changing relationship between residential and kinship units, as well as the ways in which both the family and the household play different roles in the lives of women of colour in a racially divided society (see Carby 1982; Saradamoni 1992). Although race is not the sole indicator of a common experience – there are other layers of identity and location – the importance of the family in resisting racism has altered the meaning of family among black populations.

A second interrelated body of literature, which attempts to account for Asian women's successful encounter with Western education, is the 'clash of culture' thesis (Taylor 1976).[3] This suggests that women who do well and achieve professional careers abandon their traditional cultures and opt instead to assimilate British cultural norms. A great deal of politically charged discourse exists on women as mothers of the nation, who nourish and reproduce the traditions of nations and communities (Yuval-Davis 1997; also see Mookherjee, this volume, Chapter 9). These notions take on racialized forms, whereby South Asian women are seen to carry the responsibility of being the bearers of what are seen to be the good family values of their 'culture' (Rattansi 1992, 1994). By framing questions of culture as dichotomous and oppositional, traditional or Western, the clash of culture thesis fails to come to grips with the complex realities of South Asian women's everyday lives. These discourses tell us far more about the Eurocentric framing of research agendas than about the subjectivities they are trying to account for. Using Eurocentric norms as the yardstick by which to measure other cultures preserves and legitimates their dominance (Mani 1992). Bhopal's research (1997) on the relationship between marriage, education and employment in the lives of South Asian women has been significant for noting how education can act as a lever of agency for women, especially for gaining autonomy in matters pertaining to marriage. Unfortunately, however, what she fails to appreciate is how this agency can then be utilized to re-negotiate gendered relations within the domestic realm, *with* rather than *apart from* families and relatives. Thus her study concludes:

'Traditional' South Asian women want to retain the custom of arranged marriages and the partaking of dowries, they want to hold on to these traditions as part of their South Asian identity. 'Independent' South Asian women become highly educated and enter the labour market, they no longer want to have arranged marriages, instead they want to co-habit with their partners (Bhopal 1997: 153).

This analysis overlooks differences within South Asian communities. The category 'South Asian woman'[4] is heterogeneous, and, like the concept of the 'South Asian diaspora', needs to be deconstructed. For instance, there are at least three major axes of differentiation[5] amongst the South Asian population of Britain. The first centres on origin (region, language and religion); the second is structural (wealth, caste occupation and education) and the third is what might be called contingent geography (current residence, network clusters, economic enclaves). The clash of culture thesis requires the adoption (and then the clash) of singular identities and the erasure of other forms of difference.

Neither of these theses offers us a way of reading the more complex processes whereby women's 'agency' interacts with and is at the same time limited by the structures and ideologies based on ethnicity, gender

and class. There is a real dearth of material on women as cultural reproducers, who actively manufacture their identities, who do not merely
perpetuate but *modify* their cultural systems by engaging with them
positively. There is little perception of Asian women as *active* negotiators
of the cultural values they accept, the lifestyles to which they subscribe,
or of their role as innovators and originators of new cultural forms, which
are influenced by their ethnicities and are continuously reformulated in the
context of their class and local cultures. Their role as cultural entrepreneurs who are actively engaging with cultural frameworks, whilst continuously transforming them, is one that is largely absent both from the
majority of the literature and from common-sense understanding.

In this research I aim to outline the complex agency of professional
Asian women and the active roles they are playing in the (trans)formation
of British Asian identities. By using the example of marriage trajectories,
and particularly the ways in which they challenge, collude and collaborate,
I suggest that current theoretical frameworks need to be reworked, to
accommodate a more reflexive approach.[6] Using interview data from two
generations an attempt will be made to introduce a new discourse that
challenges both the classic feminist and the 'clash of culture' analyses.

Work and Marriage: Contours of Gender, Class and Ethnicity

So much discussion of South Asian *families* is articulated with reference
to the practice of 'arranged marriage'. A large amount of media attention
has been given to the stereotypes of arranged marriages as being forced
and performed against the wishes of the young (Anwar 1979; Kalra
1980).[7] Ideological constructions of Asian marriage norms, which in fact
vary significantly across different categories of South Asian society, are
viewed as an alien 'problem for British society'. This view has been
critical in legitimating post-war immigration control and post-war racism
(see Brah 1996 for a discussion on British assumptions about South Asian
female sexuality and how these legitimated virginity-testing as part their
immigration experience). There has been some attention given to processes of individualization whereby the younger generation is having
more say within the marriage process amongst 'Asian' communities; but
not enough emphasis has been given to the gendered nature in which
transformation is occurring, nor on the impact the British context has on
these reformulations (see Bhachu 1991).

Engendering Diasporic Identities

Professionalism provides opportunities for social manoeuvring by reconfiguring women's entitlements in the public sphere – one of the greatest limitations of Asian women generally – and therefore to choice. Indeed, professional work was certainly perceived by the women who spoke to me as a way of being able to gain freedom away from sedimented gendered expectations. Women cited employment as an essential means to preserve a sense of identity away from how they were defined elsewhere.

A high income has had a tremendous effect on the power relations that exist between a husband and wife in the Kutchi Hindu community. As the first generation really to attain this financial capacity in significantly large numbers the women interviewed were in a more powerful position to define their roles and responsibilities than their mother's generation – a development of which they were acutely aware. Premila, a 31-year-old accountant, poignantly comments: 'My mum never used to have a wage high enough for her to get real independence; I mean the ability to set up her own financial security.'

Contrary to both the feminist and the 'clash of culture' prognoses, the women did not find their professional work incompatible with their home lives. Their role as income providers allowed them to set up nuclear family units on re-negotiated (relatively egalitarian) terms. The nuclear family is not breaking down, but rather the terms are being re-constituted. Kavita (DS: 13) comments:

> My parents have a very traditional division of labour. My mum is in charge of running the household . . . Her income was always the secondary one . . . for me it's different because I have a job on the same level as my husband and we get paid very similar amounts so both of our incomes are depended on to pay the mortgage! So I have a more equal relationship.

Meena (DS: 9) similarly compares her own home to her mother's:

> I have different time commitments and different sights for my future. I think it's different because of the roles my husband and I have, I mean he does a lot more around the house, than my dad . . . he helps me with the cooking, cleaning and the children. It never occurred to him that this was not what it was going to be like marrying me. He knew exactly what married life would be for him and he knew it would be something very different from his own home. I just think things are more shared in my house. There is no 'your role' and 'my role', and these roles are not determined by gender either. I do whatever I can and so does he. It has to be a team effort to really work; you can't stick to the old ways of doing things when they no longer feel relevant to you.

Educated and professional achievers continued to participate in their so-called 'traditional' cultural groups and showed a real reluctance to abandon their family cultures upon gaining success in the public sphere. Significantly, instead of abandoning these connections aspects of their family kinship life were also being re-negotiated in order to respond to their new positioning.

Marriage and Agency

On the question of marriage, the daughters' cohort was clearly not forced in any way into finding a spouse within the Kutchi community. The range of initial meetings between the women and their future spouses indicates the level of active participation amongst these women. To say that these women did not take a proactive role in the selection of their spouses would be a huge underestimation of their agency. This also points to the necessity for differentiating between arranged marriages and forced marriages, as is illustrated through the case study of Deepika and her mother. The latter, a double migrant from Africa with only primary-level education, had a part-time manual position, and the former was a university-educated Finance Analyst.

Deepika (DS: 3) met her husband when she started working. After the initial introduction by her friends, she notes:

> I had already told my parents when I got back from going out with my friends that I had met him and was going to meet him again. They were very cool about it, my mum always said if I found someone I liked at University or at work I shouldn't worry about bringing him home. So then about three weeks after that his mum rang my mum . . . we carried on seeing each other for about a year . . . before we decided whether we wanted it to go any further.

For her part Deepika's mother, Mrs Vekaria (MS: 4) did not mind the active role her daughter played in securing a spouse: 'I didn't mind how she met him, whether it was in University or whether she wanted us to introduce her, as long as she made a good choice.'

Members of the younger generation wanted to marry a person 'who they could develop an identity with' (DS: 1). Although the prospective spouse's caste identity and community standing and the economic wealth of his family were utilized to identify possible partners, it was the daughters on an individual level who would ultimately decide the right spouse for themselves. The significance these women attached to the cultural background of their prospective spouses would classify them as traditionalist in some writers' analysis. Bhopal (1997), for example, argues that class has become a more important identity signifier as women have attained greater education and occupational experience, leading to the relegation of ethnic cultural identity as an unwanted source of constraint. However, my interviewees seem to suggest that choosing a partner was more complex. '. . . he had a modern outlook to everything, which is what I really liked . . . He was just the right balance between old and new. I can't stand people who are ashamed to be Indian . . .' (DS: 1).

The vast majority of the younger community members studied continued to marry within 'conventional' circles. The importance wealth, class and caste considerations have in spouse selection needs to be understood not just in terms of qualities internal to this group (caste, economic status, etc.), but also of external influences (racist ideological and structural forces) arising from experiencing Britain as a member of a racialized minority. The reasons for wanting such a tightly organized community and exclusive marriage market, while accepting the obvious limitations their sustainability entails for individual 'choice' regarding spouse selection, are not intrinsic to the culture or 'tradition' of these women, but part of their identity formation developed in the context of Britain. The 'choices' available in marriage are not only limited by caste or religious affiliation but also by the circumstances this particular community finds itself in a postcolonial set up. Thus the conceptualization of South Asian women demands an analysis that goes beyond the traditional–modern dichotomy and on to a more complex understanding altogether (see Rayaprol 1997; Bhelande and Pandurang 2000).

Working Lives

The women in the research worked in fields such as accountancy and law, where women and black men are visibly present, but black women are less so (see Bhavnani 1994).

The interviewees were acutely conscious of the impact of racialized identities upon workplace relations. They recognized that they needed to secure qualifications in order to achieve occupational momentum and 'get a good job'. Participant observation and my subsequent field notes reveal the extent to which these women encountered racist stereotypes at work and how they dealt with them. However, there was a palpable strain in the interview when I tried to broach the subject of racism experienced in the workplace. These women understandably saw their chosen professions as a positive in their lives, and were reluctant to critique the structures through which they themselves had benefited.

They were also reluctant to project themselves as different within work contexts. It appeared that there was a consensus amongst this generation of Kutchi women around what type of 'identity' they needed to project at work. This was an 'ethnically neutral' identity, one that would 'fit in' with those around them. Having obtained a job in spite of their differences, they quickly learned to hide these differences in order to stay within the profession. Thus they had to not only face and in many cases ignore the discrimination in the recruitment process, but they also had to erase their difference from the cultural norm once they had achieved positions. For example, one woman was reluctant to tell her boss that she wanted to take a holiday to celebrate Diwali and the Hindu New Year, because she did not want to stand out from her colleagues.

Attempts were made to minimize visible signs of difference when at work. None of the women would wear South Asian clothing to work or speak Gujarati on the phone to personal friends. When I rang them at work I deliberately spoke in Gujarati to try and engage them in conversation, but they always replied in English. There was a clear sense in which these women were leaving their cultural differences at 'home' when they came to work, because this made their lives easier within the public sphere, where appropriate and inappropriate attire and behaviour are based on a white, male, middle-class consensus. They are also thus attending to the equal opportunities policy of being equal to be the same. Many felt that the best way of getting rid of racism was to overturn myths about their inferiority, by being better than the 'white' majority. Thus, although the workplace was a site of both racist and sexist discrimination, it also presented a site for challenging these assumptions in non-confrontational terms.

The relationship between the Kutchi women I interviewed and the workplace raises very interesting questions about whether the occupational success of these women marks a decline in racism or not. One could argue that it is these women who are changing to fit into the occupational structure, not the structure accommodating them.

While the South Asian women I interviewed both reinforced and questioned racism at work, the benefits of work also helped them to challenge their gender roles at home. A visible impact of the professional occupation of these women is their increasing ability to obtain a wage sufficient to build up savings that would allow them to move out into a home of their own soon after marriage. They utilized their professional wages within 'traditional' marriages to secure a reformulated nuclear family, and contrary to both the feminist and the clash of culture theses, this did not necessitate their leaving their ethnic cultural traditions and practices behind. Many women saw this as an essential move for empowerment and governance in their own lives, reducing the dominance of their husbands as key decision-makers and controllers of economic resources. Mrs Pindoria 2 (MS: 15) comments:

> Because people are more affluent you can afford to move out into your home quicker as a young couple. This is very important because it makes the couple stronger than the extended family, and as women it takes a lot of pressure off you. Also of course a lot of the traditional obligations on you are lifted because they're just not practical, so you have a lot more you can do as you like.

Vasanti (DS: 4) a 34-year-old financial strategist and mother of one, explains the balance of work, home and wider family commitments: 'There's little conflict but I do have to make it clear to everyone in my family that I have a full-time job and child and do not have time to do things mid-week.' Like many in this cohort, she was quite open about the need for her family to adapt to accommodate her own changing lifestyle. The link between having a well-paid job and independence from traditional patriarchal constraints is also illustrated by Jaya (DS: 8), a financial analyst and mother of one:

> Since I've got married and had a child, I have progressed sharply at work so as both responsibilities increased . . . with more pressures at work I am still supposed to do as much as I did before. Impossible really, so something needs to give, and usually unless it's really close family I put my work first . . . there's always something going on and so I just avoid going. Since I've moved out I find it much easier to say I can't go. I think that everyone sees how well we're doing and assume that we must work very hard and this buys us a lot more space. So if I say I have got too much on at work to come and do this or that, people think it's acceptable . . .

Professional occupations and adherence to marriage structures do produce some contradictory pressures (as suggested by feminists), but my research shows that these pressures are not resolved through a dissolution of family structures, but through a re-articulation of the household in the form of a nuclear family and by limiting and redefining responsibilities at the extended family and community level. These professional women utilize their financially successful work identities to avoid engagement in activities they no longer see as relevant to their lives or as somehow their natural responsibility. There is a growing acceptance within the contemporary British Kutchi community that women with full-time professions may indeed be too busy to attend some functions. Excuses of 'long hours' and hard work' were previously the exclusive preserve of men.

Contradictory Challenges

While using identities created through occupational success to challenge the predominant gender and racial discourses, these women are also contributing to the creation of new classed hierarchies. As education and employment become crucial markers of identity, a distancing between the professional cohort and 'low achievers' within the community is heightening class divisions. A clear hierarchy is present between the women who do well in these spheres and those who do not, with the former emerging as the more desirable marriage partners and social acquaintances.[8] There is an inability to appreciate 'why they ['low achievers'] would settle for no career' (DS: 3). Vandana, a 30-year-old Financial Analyst, highlights the importance that educational achievement now has for women's status within the Kutchi community: 'I'm sure that I wouldn't command the same position within both my family and work environments was it not known that I was in fact degree qualified.' By differentiating themselves from 'low achievers' within their own community, the women were gaining and preserving status as well as power within the caste based community.

Marriage was being utilized by these women to situate themselves not just in racial or caste culture but also within a class culture (for a similar analysis focusing on professional Indian women see Raghuram 2000). Deepika (DS: 3), a 34-year-old Financial Analyst, also highlights the links with marriage prospects:

> Nowadays if you want to find a suitable person then you have to match them in so many ways. If you want an educated husband then you yourself have to be well educated. Boys' families are now looking for exactly the same thing as girls' families traditionally used to . . . you can demand a lot more in your relationships with your parents, husband, or parents-in-law if you are educated.

Education is being utilized to gain more 'independence', a space for re-articulation of identity aside from both patriarchal and racist structures. It therefore played a vital role in the marriage prospects of these women.

I know that my parents were a lot more liberal with us because we had all studied than if we had not. And again it was the perception of my parents' friends of me; it was [more] OK with them for my parents to give me lots of leeway, particularly around marriage, than if I had not been educated (DS: 7).

All the women wanted to marry someone of a similar class background to themselves. This was achieved by marrying men in similar fields to their own. But caste too remained important in the choice of marriage partner. The women I interviewed were aware of their high caste position and of their 'heritage', and differentiated themselves from 'Others' outside their community. This desire to maintain group identity was manifest in the selection of marriage partners. Caste remained an important variable influencing how the women organized their lives, the temples they went to, the women's groups they attended, the organizations and charities they ran or supported. What is interesting is how racial and cultural boundaries are only minimally renegotiated, and may even be solidifying. The older generation of interviewees were more open to the notion of 'marrying-out' than the younger.

Conclusions

It is frustrating, though not unsurprising, that the post-modern 'reflexivity' so freely available to Western subjects is not bequeathed to minorities, especially to minority women in the heart of their own metropolis. A true appreciation of the agency and reflexivity of Kutchi Hindu Gujarati women would acknowledge that these women might often stress the importance of 'traditional' structures, but that, by doing so, they do not necessarily accept as legitimate the hierarchical organization of the household, or the unchecked exercise of male power within it. It also suggests the need to rethink the concept of the implied incompatibility of 'traditional' and 'modern' social forms so often applied to British ethnic minorities without revision (see Crompton 1999 for a conventional discussion).

Young British-born Gujarati women in Britain seem to be constructing diasporic identities that simultaneously both assert a sense of belonging to the locality in which they have grown up and yet also proclaim a 'difference' that marks the specificity of the experience of being an 'Other'. Their direct relationship with the labour market as wage-earners has led to an increase in their powers of negotiation, an ability to make choices and to increase their influence in the domestic domain. Their newly empowered class status is permitting and facilitating a re-negotiation of old gender divisions. However, contrary to the clash of culture thesis, this is not leading to friction between the mothers and the daughters or to an abandonment of cultural traditions, but to a re-definition of these traditions. But stressing the contradictory nature of Kutchi Hindu Gujarati identities in contemporary Britain requires avoiding the temptation of creating idealized images of South Asian women (see Gandhi 1998), and recognizing growing class divisions.

Acknowledgements

The preliminary thoughts behind this chapter were presented at the second *Theoretical Considerations on Gender and the South Asian Diaspora Workshop* organized by Nusrat Shaheen at the Department of Sociology, University of Manchester, January 2000. I would like to thank Nirmal Puwar for creating the space in which these themes were first aired. I owe a big thanks to the editors of this work for their patience and perseverance, especially Parvati Raghuram.

Notes

1. The article draws on Ph.D. research carried out in the London-based Kutchi Hindu Gujarati community between 1998 and 2001. The Indian State of Gujarat lies to the north-west of Mumbai and is a centre for trade and emigration. The women studied belong to the Levi Patidar caste. Caste is understood here to be a social hierarchy determined by the Hindu belief in pre-destined birth. Kutchi Patidars are a regionally concentrated caste of well-to-do, high-caste Hindu farmers. The vast majority of them are adherents of the Swaminarayyan movement, which originated in Gujarat and enjoys much economic and political leverage in the region, as well as a presence throughout North India.
2. It could be argued that although this generation of women interviewed did not receive formal education, they imbibed the value of education as a result of their settlement in East Africa and their membership of

the middle strata of East Africa's tripartite society (see Bhachu 1991). It is prudent then not to ascribe *all* education experience to the British context. Rather, immigration to Britain may have accelerated this aspirational tendency.

3. The clash of culture thesis holds that the British-born and -raised generation of 'Asians' are caught between two incompatible cultures: their home culture and the culture of the mainstream society in which they live. As this generation exposes itself to higher levels of education and employment they will move to the more dominant cultural model. Succinctly, the cohort should be exhibiting signs of disenchantment with their own cultural heritage and attraction to British mainstream culture.

4. Similarly Britishness is also increasingly being questioned (Mirza 1997) as Britain faces decentralization within its boundaries and pan-Europeanism without. For discussion in the light of David Blunkett's Nationality White Papers see M. Riddell: 'Teach Us All to be British', *The Guardian*, 10 February 2002; and J. O'Farrell: 'How to Pass for British', *The Guardian*, 9 February 2002.

5. As it becomes increasingly apparent (see Anwar 1985; Modood *et al.* 1997) that settlers of different backgrounds are following varied and often sharply contrasting social trajectories, so it is becoming steadily more difficult and indeed increasingly inappropriate to make generalizations that are valid for all 'Asians' in Britain. For recent findings see 'Ethnic Minorities in the Labour Market: Interim Analytical Report', published by the Cabinet Office, 2002.

6. The Home Secretary Mr David Blunkett's Nationality White Paper called on ethnic communities to accept 'norms of acceptability', including learning to speak English. Taking up the Cantle report recommendations, it called for citizenship classes and for new nationals to make a formal statement of allegiance to Britain.

7. The discussions of arranged marriage in the Labour Government's White Paper 'Secure Borders, Safe Havens' (2002) highlights the urgent need to address these issues.

8. Raghuram (2001) has argued that professionalism has become a part of middle-class femininity in India and has redefined both class culture and feminine culture. I am grateful to her for highlighting the idea that the same phenomena may be occurring in the British context and may merit further analysis.

References

Anwar, M. (1979), *The Myth of Return,* London: Heinemann.

—— (1985), *Pakistanis in Britain: A Sociological Study,* London: New Century Publishers.

Beck, U. and Beck Gernsheim, E. (1995), *The Normal Chaos of Love,* Cambridge: Polity Press.

Bhachu, P. (1991), 'Culture, Ethnicity and Class among Punjabi Sikh women in 1990s Britain', *New Community* 17 (3): 401–12.

Bhavnani, R. (1994), *Black Women in the Labour Market,* Manchester: Equal Opportunities Commission.

Bhelande, A. and Pandurang, M. (2000), *Articulating Gender,* New Delhi: Pencraft International.

Bhopal, K. (1997), *Gender, 'Race' and Patriarchy: A Study of South Asian Women,* Aldershot: Ashgate Publishing Limited.

Brah, A. (1996), *Cartographies of Diaspora: Contesting Identities,* London: Routledge.

Caplan, P. (1985), *Gender and Class in Indian Women and their Organisation in a South Indian City,* London: Tavistock.

Carby, H. (1982), 'White Women Listen! Black Feminism and the Boundaries of Sisterhood', in Centre for Contemporary Cultural Studies, University of Birmingham, *The Empire Strikes Back: Race and Racism in 70s Britain,* pp. 18–35. London: Hutchinson.

Crompton, R. (ed.) (1999), *Restructuring Gender Relations and Employment: The Decline of the Male Breadwinner,* Oxford: Oxford University Press.

Gandhi, L. (1998), *Postcolonial Theory: A Critical Introduction,* Edinburgh: Edinburgh University Press.

Kalra, S. (1980), *Daughters of Tradition,* Birmingham: Third World Publications.

Mani, L. (1992), 'Multiple Mediations: Feminist Scholarship in the Age of Multinational Reception' in H. Crowley and S. Himmelweit (eds), *Knowing Women: Feminism and Knowledge*, pp. 306–22. Milton Keynes: Open University.

Mirza, H. S. (ed.) (1997), *Black British Feminism*, London: Routledge.

Modood, T., Berthoud, R., Lakey, J., Nazroo, J., Smith, P., Virdee, S. and S. Beishom, (1997), *Ethnic Minorities in Britain: Diversity and Disadvantage,* London: Policy Studies Institute.

Mookherjee, N. (2002), 'Gendered Embodiments: Mapping the Body-politic of the Raped Woman and the Nation in Bangladesh', in N.

Puwar and P. Raghuram (eds), *South Asian Women in the Diaspora*, Oxford: Berg.

Phizacklea, A. (1983), *One Way Ticket: Migration and Female Labour*, London: Routledge.

Raghuram, P. (2000), 'Gendering Skilled Migratory Streams: Implications for Conceptualising Migration', *Asian and Pacific Migration Journal*, 9 (4): 429–57.

—— (2001), 'Placing Skilled Migration within Household Formations – The Case of Tied Migrants', presented at European Science Foundation-funded Exploratory Workshop on *Family Migration and the Life Course*, Leeds, 7–9 September 2001.

Rattansi, A. (1992), 'Changing the Subject? Racism, Culture and Education', in J. Donald and A. Rattansi (eds), *'Race', Culture and Difference*, pp. 18–39. London: Sage.

—— (1994), 'Western Racisms, Ethnicities and Identities in a Postmodern Frame', in A. Rattansi and S. Westwood (eds), *Racism, Ethnicity and Identity*, pp. 15–86. Cambridge: Polity Press.

Rayaprol, A. (1997), *Negotiating Identities: Women in the Indian Diaspora*, New Delhi: Oxford University Press.

Saifullah-Khan, V. (1979), *Minority Families in Britain: Support and Stress*, London: Macmillan.

Saradamoni, K. (ed.), (1992), *Finding the Household: Conceptual and Methodological Issues*, Delhi: Sage.

Taylor, J. (1976), *The Half Way Generation*, Windsor: NFER Nelson.

Walby, S. (1990), *Theorising Patriarchy*, Oxford: Basil Blackwell.

Westwood, S. and Bhachu, P. (eds) (1988), *Enterprising Women: Ethnicity, Economy and Gender Relations*, London: Routledge.

Yuval-Davis, N. (1997), *Gender and Nation*, London: Sage.

Index

Index

Index

Index

globalization, 2, 67, 90, 117
  gender issues, 8
  debates, 31
  studies of, 29
global multiculturalism, 5
Goldsmiths College, 7
green cards, 89
Gujarati, 74, 76, 92, 234
  British Hindu, 228
    Kutchi Hindu, 227, 231–2, 234,
      236–8

Hall, Stuart, 24, 36, 60, 196
Harlem, 33
health practitioners, 137
heteronormativity, 126
heterosexual, 186
  gaze, 126
Hills-Collins, Patricia, 223
Hindi, 189
Hindu, 190, 193, 216, 223
  ancient civilization, 105
  BNP, 46
  codes of womanhood, 103
  culture, 26, 91
  female subjectivity, 91
  golden age of, 104
  mythology, 104
  upper-caste, 139
  upper-class,
    orthodoxy, 108
    women, 108–9
Hindutva, 223
hijab, 45, 47, 52, 54, 59
home country, 79, 87, 90
  culture, 91
home critic, 88
Home Office, 49
homophobia, 182, 191
hooks, Bell, 1, 33, 191
host nation, 89
hybrid identities, 31, 193
hybridity, 32, 37, 45
  cultural, 193
  discourses of, 32
hypothetico-deductive model, 10–11

international division of labor, 29
imagined community, 165

imagined homeland, 119
Imam, Jahanara, 166
immigration, 87
  post-war control of, 230
    South Asian, 118
imperialism, 13, 184
Independent Bengal Radio, 167
India, 10, 105–6, 110, 129 190, 216
  colonial rule, 120, 162
  economic liberalization, 89
  government, 90, 163, 169
  history of clothes, 127
  independence, 159
  middle class, 70, 89–90
  migration, 75
  nation state, 87, 90
  national history, 165
  nationalism, 121
  partition, 163, 169
  scholars, 10, 92
  women,
    autobiographical writings, 100
    colonial constructions of, 99
    emigrant, 88
    exotic, 101–4
    lower-class, 100
    native, 102
    orientalist construction, 105, 111
    upper-class, 99
    see also Hindu
Indian subcontinent, 87, 118, 128
Indianness, 70
indigenous scholars, 5
Indo-chic, 78
insider knowledge, 56, 87, 209
Institute of Contemporary Arts, 31
inter-racial relationships, 102, 106
Islam,
  feminism, 55
  gender relations, 51
  militant, 47
  movement, 52
  perceived attitudes, 53
  'terrorist,' 46
  women, 222
  see also Muslim
Islamism, 52, 223
Islamophobhia, 48, 52, 55
izzat, 44, 216

Index

Index

Index

melodramatic construction, 36
Sweet Like Burfi, 186
Syal, Meera, 35

Tagore, Rabindranath, 100, 104–5,
  107–8, 161–62, 164–5, 167
Taliban, 46–8, 53
Tanzania, 74, 91
Tarlo, Emma, 76, 121, 127
texts, 4, 29, 36
  and meaning creation, 208
  misinformed, 53
  political position of, 4
  women of colour, 26, 33
textual production, 4
Third World, 2, 8, 10, 26, 29–30, 128
  feminism, 145
    feminist studies, 26
  nationalism, 121
  postcolonial intellectuals, 88
  reproductive health, 141
  seminars, 10
  students, 2
  women 8, 29–30, 57, 112
The Far Pavilions, 107
The Glass Bar, 187, 188–89
The Home and the World, 107
The Pink Paper, 182
Time Out, 208
tohran, 203, 205
Toronto, 148
Toynbee, Polly, 48
tradition-modernity dichotomy, 15, 37,
  59, 69, 90, 198, 220, 228, 233
'*Transmission*,' 93
transnational corporations, 67
Trinh, T. Minh-ha, 202
Trinidad, 193
Turner Prize, 7

Uganda, 74, 91, 124
ultrasound scan, 143
University of Chicago, 100, 105
University of Mumbai, 93
Urdu, 189
USA, 77, 89, 117, 123, 129
US foreign policy, 118

US racial economy, 124, 129
Uttar Pradesh, 139–40

Valentine, Gill, 181–2, 186, 196
Vancouver, 148
Vssanji, M.G., 92
veil, 44, 109
  western assessment of, 52

Walby, Sylvia, 57, 228
Washington State, 148
Watson, Lila, 201
Whitman, Walt, 105
Widow Remarriage Act of 1856, 139
West Pakistan, 14, 159, 161
western women, 25
  agency, 25
  as enlightened agents, 25
  self representation, 112
white intellectuals, 4
whiteness, 7, 14, 182, 183
  of gay and lesbian scene in London,
    184
  power of, 14
  state sponsored, 125
Williams, Patricia, 33
Wilson, Amrit, 27
women,
  and rape, 158
  as cultural entrepreneurs, 230
  as cultural reproducers, 230
  as markers of tradition, 223
  body politic, 159
  Chistian, 55
  Jewish, 55
women of colour, 13, 33, 35
  affects of scholarship, 13
  family, 228
    objectification, 35
    postcolonial movements of, 93
  see also texts
Woolf, Virginia, 36

Yemen, women from, 221
Yuval-Davis, N., 142, 157, 223, 229

Zambia, 74, 91